The Encyclopedia of
CROSS STITCH
Techniques

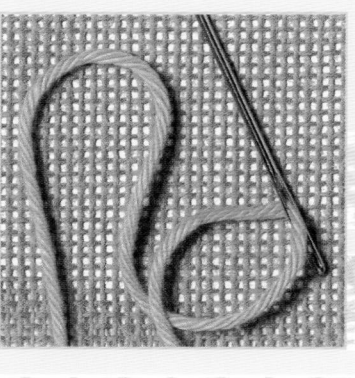

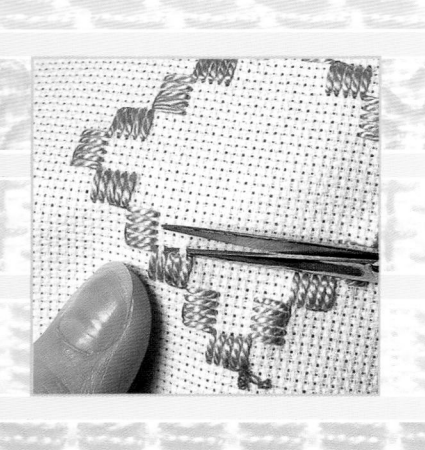

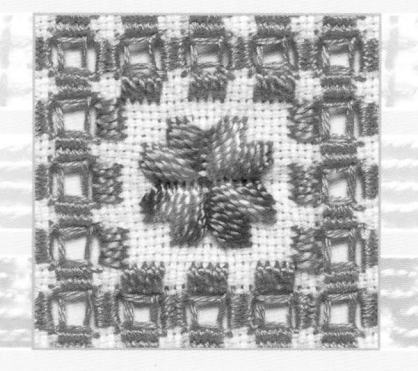

The Encyclopedia of
CROSS STITCH
Techniques

A step-by-step visual directory, with an inspirational gallery of finished works

BETTY BARNDEN

RUNNING PRESS
PHILADELPHIA · LONDON

A QUARTO BOOK

9 8 7 6 5 4 3 2 1

Digit on the right indicates the number of this printing.

Library of Congress Cataloging-in-Publication Number 2003100659

ISBN 0-7624-1664-5

Conceived, designed, and produced by
Quarto Publishing plc
The Old Brewery
6 Blundell Street
London N7 9BH

QUAR.ECST

Project editor Kate Tuckett
Senior art editor Sally Bond
Designer Heather Blagden
Copy editor Gillian Kemp
Photographers Paul Forrester, Colin Bowling
Illustrators Coral Mula, Jennie Dooge
Proofreader Sue Viccars
Picture researcher Sandra Assersohn
Indexer Diana Le Core

Art director Moira Clinch
Publisher Piers Spence

Manufactured by Universal Graphics Ltd, Singapore
Printed by Leefung-Asco Printers Ltd, China

This book may be ordered by mail from the publisher.
Please include $2.50 for postage and handling. But try your bookstore first!

Running Press Book Publishers
125 South Twenty-second Street
Philadelphia, Pennsylvania 19103-4399

Visit us on the web!
www.runningpress.com

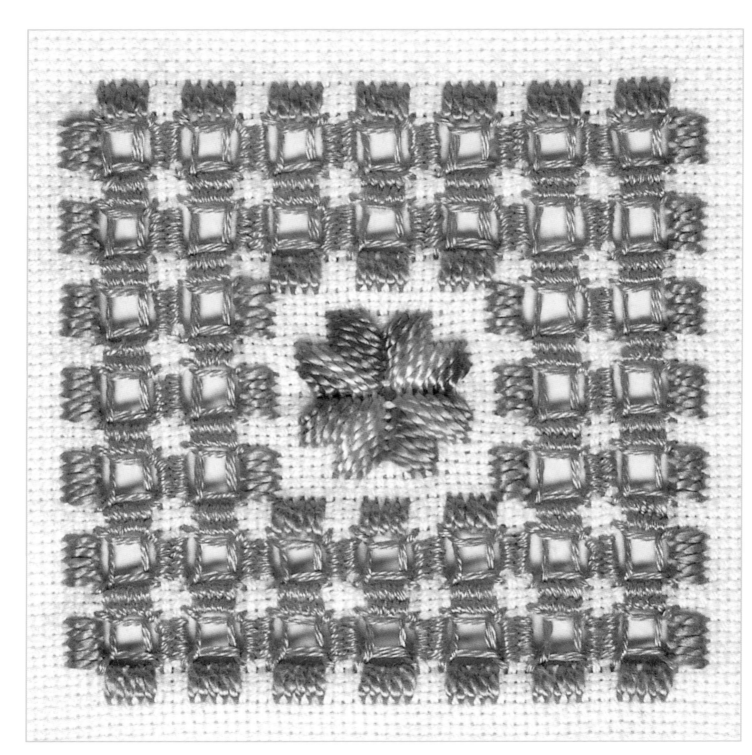

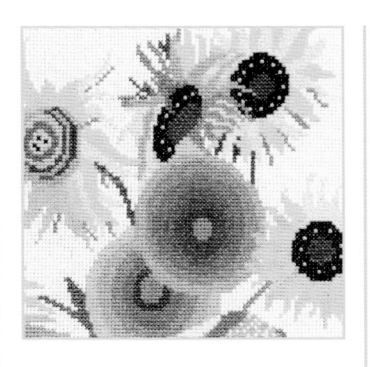

Contents

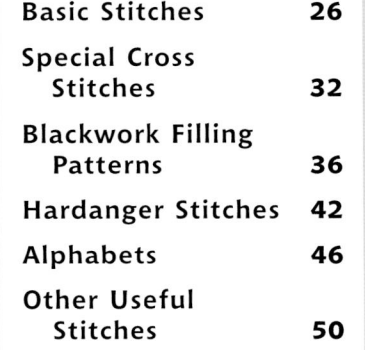

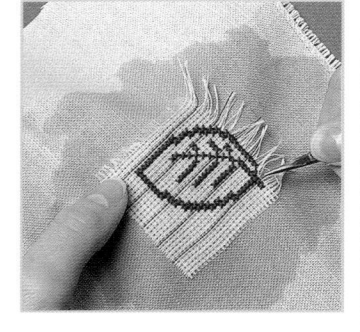

CHAPTER 3

CHAPTER 4

CHAPTER 5

CHAPTER 6

INTRODUCTION

Cross stitch is one of the many stitches used in counted thread embroidery. A counted thread stitch is an embroidery stitch worked evenly by counting the fabric weave, placing the needle between the fabric threads to make stitches of identical size. Besides cross stitch and its variations, counted thread stitches include half cross stitch and tent stitch. Many other embroidery stitches such as satin stitch, stem stitch, chain stitch, and herringbone stitch may be evenly worked by the same method. This versatile collection of stitches and techniques can be used to produce widely different effects. The materials and equipment required are simple and readily available. For the stitches to be accurate, the fabric must be evenly woven, preferably with the same number of threads to the inch in each direction, and the threads of such a size as to be easily counted. The embroidery thread should be smooth and strong, and a blunt-tipped needle will slip easily between the woven threads without splitting them.

Designs may be abstract geometric figures, or stylized, natural forms, including fantastic, or realistic representations of any subject. In past times, counted thread embroidery was adapted to many forms and purposes—clothing, upholstery, furnishings for public buildings and for the home, commemorative or instructive pieces. Today we can make our own adaptations to practice this versatile craft in any way we choose.

▲ *Indian and Thai cross stitch pieces, showing geometric figures. Once such a motif is created, it is easily repeated in other colors and different directions.*

THE ORIGINS OF CROSS STITCH

Fabrics and threads are perishable, so the earliest examples of embroidery remaining to us today are no more than 1,000 or 2,000 years old. Early historical accounts tell of Indian, Greek, and Chinese work, 2,000 years ago and more, but no examples survive to show us exactly which stitches, fabrics, and threads were used. However, we can imagine that any society producing, say, jewelry or decorated pottery would probably have also produced clothing decorated with woven or embroidered patterns. The act of sewing cloth (or fur, or leather) with a series of stitches makes a pattern in itself, from which it is a short step to invent simple decorative patterns— crosses, zigzags, and stepped lines.

Once devised, a simple counted thread motif is easily copied by example. Repeating designs are easy to produce, depending for their decorative effect on careful spacing and contrasting colors. To repeat a motif satisfactorily, a fairly evenly woven fabric is required—homespun linen, cotton, or wool, woven on a simple loom, would be ideal, together with dyes from plant or mineral sources to color the embroidery threads, and needles of bone or iron. Ancient historical accounts and archeological evidence (loom weights, needles, and traces of dye plants and pigments) tell us that these basic materials and equipment have been in use for several thousands of years, even though the perishable fabrics produced have disappeared completely.

◀ *Early Peruvian and Mexican designs demonstrate the worldwide appeal of decorating woven fabric with cross stitch and other counted thread stitches.*

► *Early Chinese designs were worked with silk threads and fabrics. Ancient trade routes allowed such exotic materials into Western Europe.*

Fragments of traditional folk embroidery from areas such as Egypt, Eastern Europe, and the Greek islands have been preserved from the sixteenth and seventeenth centuries. The motifs are derived from many sources, some of them possibly handed down for centuries. These illustrate the methods of working with simple equipment and materials and copying by example.

TRADE AND CULTURAL EXPANSION

Ancient trade routes across Europe and Asia made the Mediterranean a meeting place of different cultures for thousands of years. Silks, cottons, linens, wools, and dyestuffs were traded by land and sea across the known world from China, Persia, and India to Northern Europe. Silk fabric was known in Greece by 400 B.C.E; it must have originated in China, where at that time the production method was a closely-guarded secret. Along with the raw materials went finished articles of trade— not just fabrics and carpets, but metalwork, ceramics, and examples of other crafts. Embroiderers, together with other artists and craftsmen, have always drawn inspiration not just

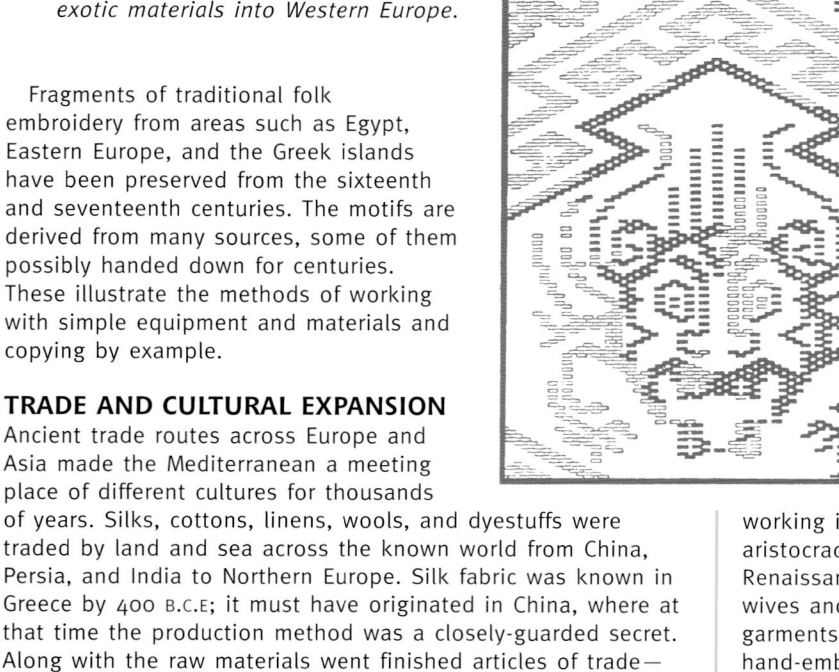

◄ *Traditional motifs were often worked in a simple repeat, using a single bright color.*

▲ *Cross stitch and Holbein stitch decorate the border of this linen bib, surrounding a bird motif in Assisi work.*

from their own familiar world but from the exotic products of other cultures, copying, interpreting, and redesigning to suit their own beliefs or purposes.

In Medieval Europe and Asia, splendid robes, hangings, and other decorations for royal courts and religious ceremonies were produced by professional craftsmen working in specialized studios, patronized by the wealthy aristocracy. With the growth of trade and leisure during the Renaissance, the art of embroidery became a pastime for the wives and daughters of the rich and powerful. Fashions in garments and furnishings changed through the centuries, but hand-embroidered fabrics always indicated high status. These might be ordered from skilled embroiderers, or produced at home, and would be imitated by the less wealthy in more affordable materials.

SOCIAL AND TECHNOLOGICAL DEVELOPMENTS

Technological advances in metalwork, introduced into Spain by the occupying Moors in about the tenth century, made possible the production of tempered steel. Besides weapons and tools, this was also used to make strong, slim needles and razor-sharp scissors. In turn, this new equipment made possible the intricate effects of Renaissance blackwork and cutwork. The fashion for blackwork spread across Europe from Spain during the fifteenth and sixteenth centuries, developing from the stylized geometry of Moorish-inspired designs into the elaborate scrolls, flowers, and foliage favored in Elizabethan England. In Italy, elaborate openwork embroidery developed, alongside the combination of cross stitch and blackwork known as Assisi work.

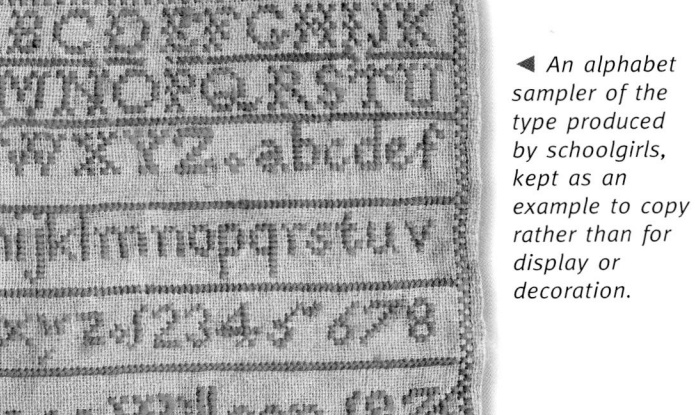

◄ An alphabet sampler of the type produced by schoolgirls, kept as an example to copy rather than for display or decoration.

► Intricate, stylized lettering was often used to embellish household linen, as on this glass-cloth from Sweden.

▲ *For centuries, learning the art of embroidery by making samplers was an important element of a girl's education.*

Canvases, silks, linens, and other requirements could be obtained from specialist shops in large cities, while smaller items such as threads, thimbles, pins, needles, scissors (and eyeglasses!) might be purchased from traveling pedlars. Pattern books became available in the late sixteenth century, along with herbals and bestiaries, providing illustrations of plants and animals both familiar and exotic for the embroiderer to trace or copy.

Even so, books were still rare, so the stitch sampler was an important item. This was a length of cloth (often linen), stitched with examples of motifs and patterns; such samplers were not for display, but kept rolled in the workbox for

reference and often passed down from mother to daughter. Girls in the schoolroom were required to produce their own samplers as proof of their skill, often incorporating alphabets. In large establishments, household linen was usually marked with embroidered initials or symbols, and this was considered an important skill for any girl to learn.

GLOBAL INFLUENCES

From the sixteenth century onward, the growth of worldwide trade and the discovery of unknown continents brought a huge influx of exotic influences. India, China, Japan, Africa, and the Americas provided examples of embroideries, printed fabrics, sculptures, pottery, jewelry, metalwork, and other crafts featuring unfamiliar animals, birds, and flowers, outlandish

◄ *A simple, repeated Hardanger motif is combined with satin stitch on this lace-edged tray cloth.*

alongside a range of colored wools, together with suitable canvases, and "Berlin wool work" became all the rage: elaborate multicolored pictures, often worked in cross stitch. Designs became more realistic, incorporating shading. The development of various synthetic dyes throughout the nineteenth century made possible a much wider range of bright colors.

▼ *Charts and printed patterns were produced from the nineteenth century onward to promote sales of threads, fabrics, and canvas.*

buildings, costumes, and native artefacts. Illustrated books and exhibitions provoked fashions across Europe and America for embroidery of various kinds, both in dress and in interior design.

Settlers of the Americas took their traditions with them, applying techniques such as cross stitch, needlepoint, and patchwork to the materials they found available or were able to import. They left behind the formal mannerisms of the Old World and created their own vigorous folk art. At the same time, European embroidery techniques were absorbed by native Americans, who adapted them to work with their own traditional materials, such as moosehair and porcupine quills.

In 1835, hand-colored charts were first produced in Berlin, soon followed by color-printed versions. These charts were sold

◀ **SUNFLOWERS**
Bothy Threads
12½ x 13 in (312 x 325mm)
Cross stitch stranded cottons on 14-count Aida fabric
The bold, bright colors of the painting by Vincent van Gogh translate easily into cross stitch.

▼ *Before the advent of tumble dryers, many sets of bed-linen were required to last through a Swedish winter; the housewife would bundle each set together, with an embroidered linen band.*

▲ **A NEW LEAF**
Charlotte's Web Needlework
8⅞ x 11⅞ in (220 x 298mm)
Cross stitch and backstitch using stranded cottons on 16/32-count linen
Simple cross stitch and outline stitches, used with a restricted palette of colors express the variety and wonder of the natural world.

Toward the end of the nineteenth century, there was a renewed interest in the traditional folk embroideries still extant in Europe and the Mediterranean. Examples were collected and cataloged for museums; their stylized forms and bright colors were admired for their simplicity and boldness.

At about the same time, artists and designers were also influenced by Japanese and other oriental cultures, promoting a return to flatter, less realistic designs in more muted colors. The values of craft production were also highly influential,

► **THE TILSTOCK PARISH MAP PROJECT**
113 x 79 in (2860 x 2000mm)
Communities all over the world produced commemorative embroideries to mark the recent millennium; this example from England combines cross stitch and tent stitch panels with other embroidery and needlecraft techniques.

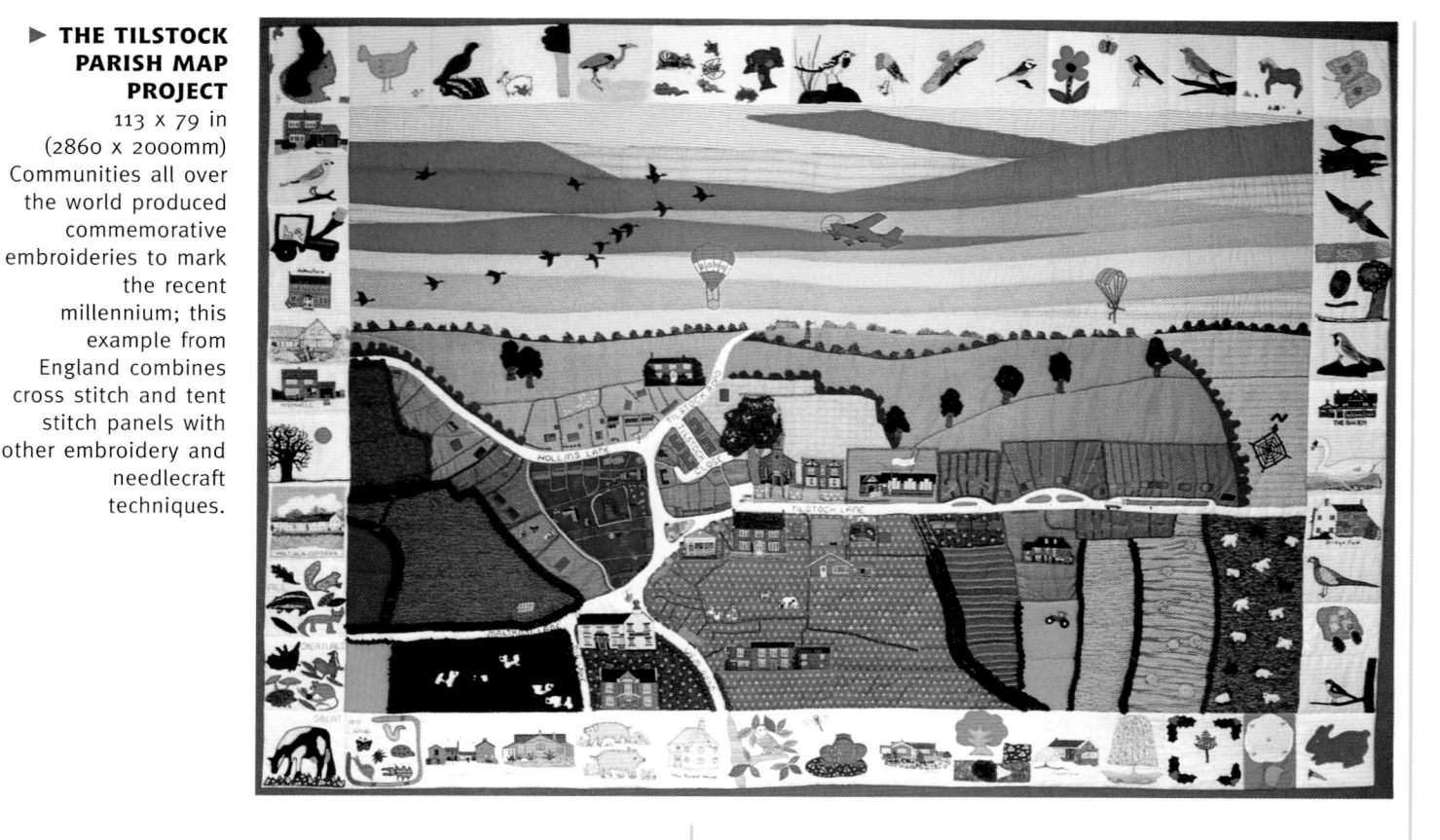

and acted as a backlash against the increasing mechanization of industrialization.

CROSS STITCH TODAY

During the twentieth century, rapid advances in the manufacturing processes of weaving, dyeing, and color printing made possible the types of cross stitch designs and kits we know today. Intricate, multicolored pictorial designs have become popular, and these often imitate the realism of photography.

From the Battle of Hastings, as shown in the Bayeux Tapestry, to the turn of the last millennium, embroidery has been used to commemorate important dates and events. In the year 2000, imaginative community projects such as Parish Maps were produced. These were often designed to incorporate the very simplest counted thread techniques (such as cross stitch), so enabling as many people as possible to take part in the project.

Throughout recorded history (and probably before it) the embroiderer like any other artist has responded not only to the world around her, but also to advances in technology and to influences from other lands and cultures. Such influences are always absorbed and changed by the personality of the maker. Unfamiliar subjects, materials, and equipment have always provoked interest and experimentation; we love to play with new toys!

With the advent of computer technology, sophisticated color printing and photocopying, and new products on the market, there is more for us to explore than ever before. Without any particular drawing skills we can invent our own designs; we can choose man-made or traditional threads and fabrics, available in a vast range of colors that stitchers of previous times could only dream about. I hope this book will inspire you to explore this endlessly fascinating craft in a new and exciting way.

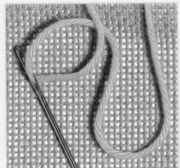

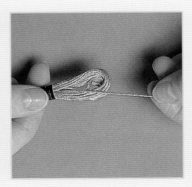

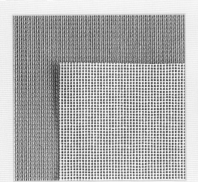

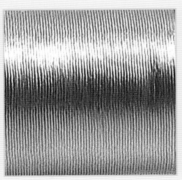

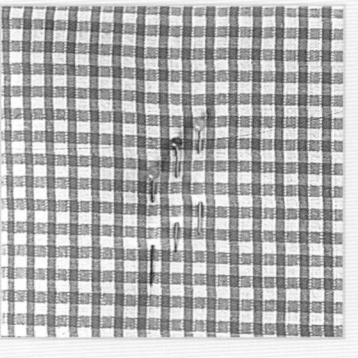
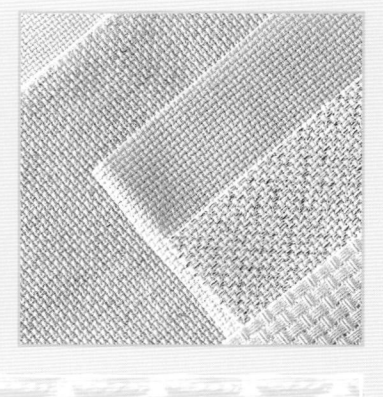

CHAPTER 1

Materials & Equipment

A guide to the basic threads, fabrics, and tools used for all types of counted thread embroidery. So many different materials and accessories are available today, you might think embroidery was an expensive hobby—but the opposite is true. With the help of the information in this chapter, you will be able to purchase the correct materials and the accessories required for each project, so avoiding expensive mistakes. In time you will build up a store of favorite materials and discover the tools that suit you best.

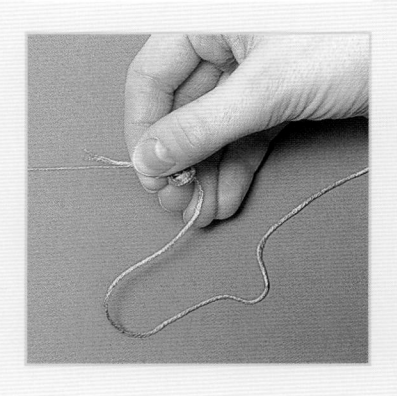

Threads

A bewildering variety of threads for embroidery is available today, in a wide range of plain and random-dyed colors and special effects. Some are versatile and suitable for most types of embroidery. Others are designed for a particular use.

Stranded cotton

Six fine strands are usually loosely wound together into a small skein. Any number of strands may be combined, so this is a very versatile thread, suitable for most counted thread work.

Pearl cotton

A firm, twisted thread with a glossy finish suitable for most types of embroidery, unless the stitches are required to blend together—the formation of most stitches in this thread will remain distinct. It is available in four different weights: no. 3 (the heaviest), no. 5, no. 8, and no. 12. Pearl cotton may not be split into strands.

Coton à broder

This is a fine, twisted thread with a matte finish. It makes distinct stitches and may not be separated into strands. It is often used for blackwork.

Soft embroidery cotton

A heavy, twisted matte thread with a soft finish and a muted appearance, but making distinct stitches. Strands may not be split. It is suitable for work on coarse fabrics and on canvas.

Stranded cotton

TIP Most thread colors are identified by a shade number (or name) on a skein band or spool label. If you need to remove this label, make a note of the shade number. You can keep a notebook, taping the label (or writing the details) next to an inch of each thread used.

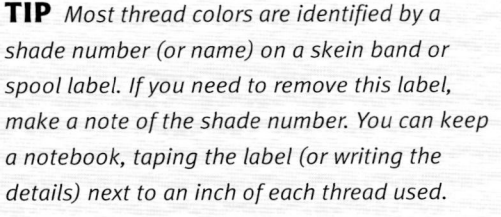

Pearl cotton no. 8

Coton à broder

Soft cotton

Pearl cotton no. 5

Stranded silk

Often called silk floss, this usually consists of four to six strands, similar to those of stranded cotton. It is used in the same way as stranded cotton, but has a more luxurious feel, with the depth of color and subtle sheen associated with silk.

Viscose threads

These have a high sheen and may be used alone, or combined with stranded cottons. Some are supplied as a single strand on a spool, while others come in skeins of four or more strands wound together. They are not suitable for stitching on rough canvas (or any rough fabric) as the thread tends to catch, making the stitches uneven.

Persian wool

This is supplied as three two-ply strands, loosely wound together into a small skein. One strand may be used alone for embroidery on fabric. Any suitable number of strands may be combined together for work on canvas.

Tapestry wool

This is a heavier wool, similar in weight to double knitting, but with an extremely smooth finish. Strands may not be separated, so it is normally used only on canvas or Binca fabric (pages 19–20).

Metallic and other special threads

These are available in a range of weights; fine (no. 4), medium (no. 8), and heavy (no. 12) are shown here. The finish may be metallic, pearlized, or fluorescent: use these threads to add accents to a design in another thread.

Metallic ⅛ inch (3mm) ribbon

This is a heavier metallic thread in the form of a flat strip or ribbon, for bold accents and details.

Blending filaments

These are very fine single strands, designed to be combined in the needle with another thread. They may be metallic, pearlized, or fluorescent.

Metallic thread

Persian wool

Tapestry wool

⅛ inch (3mm) ribbon

Viscose threads

Stranded silks

Fine blending filament

HANDLING THREADS

As a rule you should work with a thread length of no more than 18 inches (460mm). A longer length is more liable to tangle, and softer threads may fray as you stitch, making the stitches appear uneven.

1 Many threads have a "smooth" and a "rough" direction. Run a single thread between your fingertips (or across your lips) in one direction, then the other, to feel the difference. To make stitching easier, always thread your needle with the smooth end first.

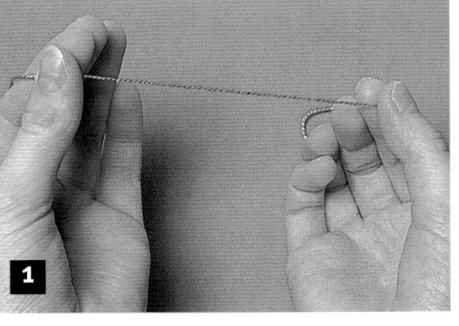

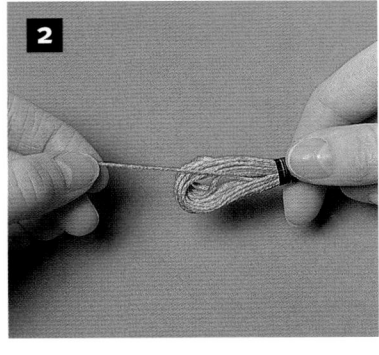

2 The smooth end is often the end that is inside a flat skein, so if you can, pull out the thread from the middle. The skein will not tangle and the labels will remain in place.

3 Twisted hanks (such as Pearl cotton) must be opened and untwisted. They are often wound to such a size that if you cut straight across the loops, you will obtain a bunch of threads of a suitable length for stitching.

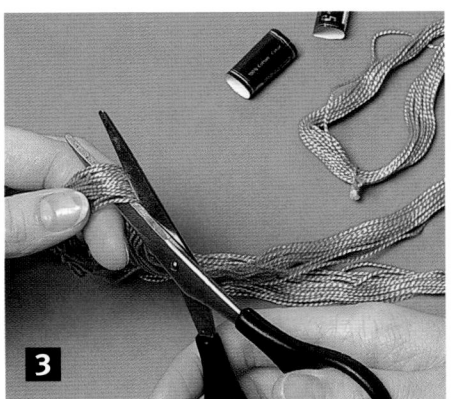

DIVIDING THREADS

Skeins of stranded cottons, silks, and wools consist of several strands wound together, but not twisted around each other. The strands may be easily separated and used singly. To make a heavier thread, two or more strands may be combined as required.

1 Cut off an 18-inch length (460mm), then separate the strands at the beginning and pull out the strands one by one. Lay the strands on your table with all the smooth ends at the same side.

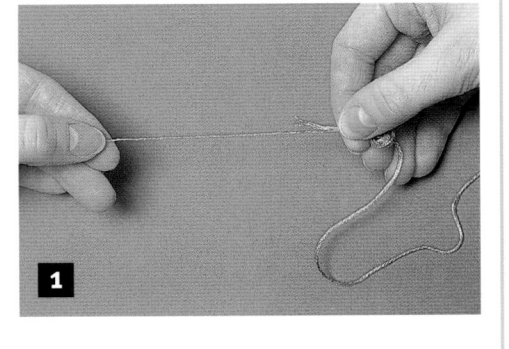

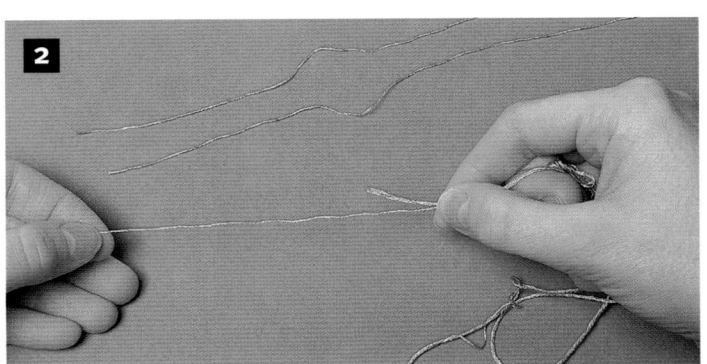

2 If you want to work with two or more strands together, always separate them, then recombine the number you require. The strands will then lie flat side by side, covering better and stitching more smoothly.

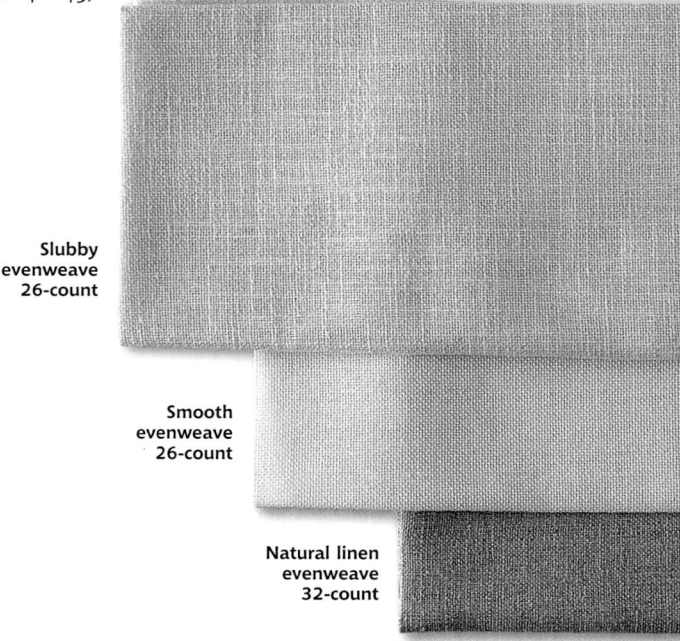

Fabrics

Several types of fabric and canvas are suitable for counted thread embroidery. Aida and evenweave fabrics are not usually completely covered with stitches, so they are available in a wide range of colors, and the fabric is sufficiently solid to form a pleasing background to any design. Canvas is an open mesh, normally completely covered by stitching, so the color range is limited.

Binca fabric (6-count)
This is woven in the same way as Aida fabric. The large grid size makes it suitable for children's or beginner's projects.

Hardanger fabric
(22-count and 24-count)
This is also constructed in the same way. The smaller squares make a firm fabric, suitable for the cutting and withdrawing of threads that is a feature of Hardanger work (pages 42–45).

Evenweave fabrics
These are woven with an accurate number of threads (or holes) per inch in each direction, also called the "count." 8-count is a coarse weave, 36-count is very fine. Unlike Aida fabric, there is no pattern of squares, so the stitches are counted over the individual threads of the weave. These fabrics may be either cotton, linen, or blended fibers.

Aida fabrics
These are evenly woven with equal groups of intersecting threads, forming a pattern of squares and tiny holes, over which cross stitch and other counted thread stitches may be evenly worked. They are normally made of cotton, although other fiber blends are available for a softer "handle," or to obtain a special finish. The size of the grid is indicated by the "count," which is the number of squares (or holes) to the inch. Counts of 10 to 18 are commonly available; 12-count and 14-count are the most popular sizes for cross stitch.

Slubby evenweave 26-count

Smooth evenweave 26-count

Natural linen evenweave 32-count

Aida 18-count cream

Aida 14-count beige

Aida 14-count pink

Aida 14-count with lurex

Binca 6-count beige

Hardanger 22-count white

CANVASES

These are also woven with an accurate number of threads, or pairs of threads, to the inch in each direction, making a square mesh pattern. The number of threads (or holes) to the inch is called the "gauge." Canvas is normally made of cotton or linen, and available in white or natural, as stitches usually cover the surface completely. Several different types are available. Single interlock canvas is suitable for both cross stitch and tent stitch designs. Double canvas is woven with pairs of threads between the holes (the gauge being counted over the holes), so the holes are relatively small, keeping the stitching regular. Gauges of 10 to 22 are commonly available.

Plastic canvas

This is not woven, but molded in sheets. It is perfectly stable, and may be used to make three-dimensional items such as boxes. It is manufactured in a range of different colors and gauges.

Waste canvas

This is a loosely woven canvas, stiffened with a water-soluble glue, designed to fall apart when wet. It is used to work counted thread designs onto plain fabric, then removed after stitching (pages 76–77).

CUTTING FABRIC AND CANVAS

Work on a smooth, flat surface. Always cut along a straight row of holes, using large scissors such as dressmaker's shears.

Plastic canvas 7-gauge

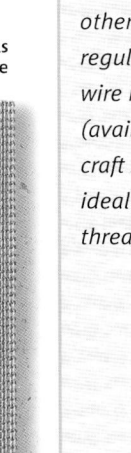

Waste canvas 14-gauge

Single canvas 14-gauge

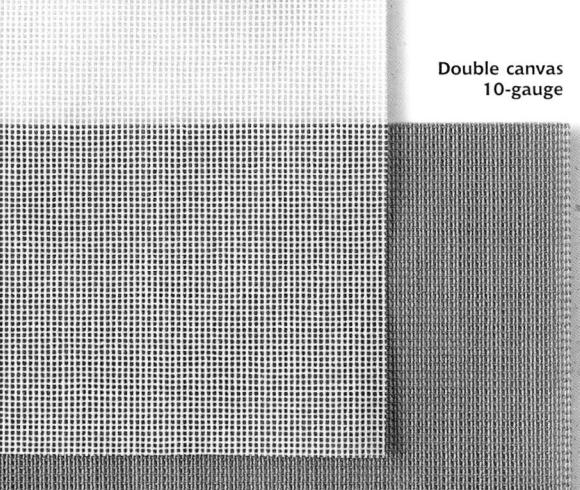

Double canvas 10-gauge

TIP *Keep a lookout for other materials with a regular pattern of squares: wire meshes like these (available from any craft supplier) are ideal for counted thread work.*

Equipment

Choosing the correct equipment

for each project will help you to

produce a well-finished piece.

NEEDLES

The eye of a needle should be large enough to easily take the thread you are using. The needle will then carry the thread through the fabric without fraying it.

A needle with too small an eye will be difficult to thread and to push through the fabric, making the thread liable to break.

Too large a needle will make uneven stitches, and may permanently enlarge the holes in the fabric.

embroidery, as the blunt tip slips between the fabric threads without splitting them. Use them on Aida fabric, evenweave fabric, or canvas, choosing the smallest size that will easily take the thread you are using.

Tapestry needles

These are blunt-tipped needles with long, slim eyes. They are the most common type of needle used for counted thread

Sharp needles

Occasionally you may need a sharp needle for a particular purpose: choose needles with fairly large eyes, so they are easy to thread.

OTHER EQUIPMENT

Needle threader

This is a useful accessory when dealing with very fine threads and blending filaments. It is NOT used to thread a small-eyed needle with too thick a thread!

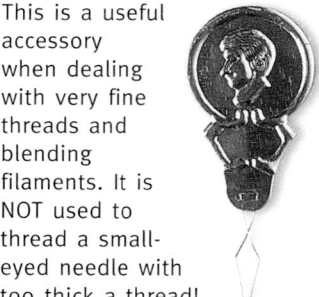

Simple embroidery hoops

These consist of two plastic or wooden rings. Plastic hoops have an outer ring which is flexible and slightly stretchy, to be pushed over the inner ring with the fabric in place (page 60), so

plastic hoops are not suitable for heavy fabrics. The outer ring of a wooden hoop is usually adjusted by means of a screw, allowing for different weights of fabric.

Hoops are available in several sizes. To avoid damaging stitches, choose a hoop that is large enough to enable you to complete the work without repositioning the hoop over completed stitching. Hoops may be held by hand, or else clamped to a stand, leaving both hands free.

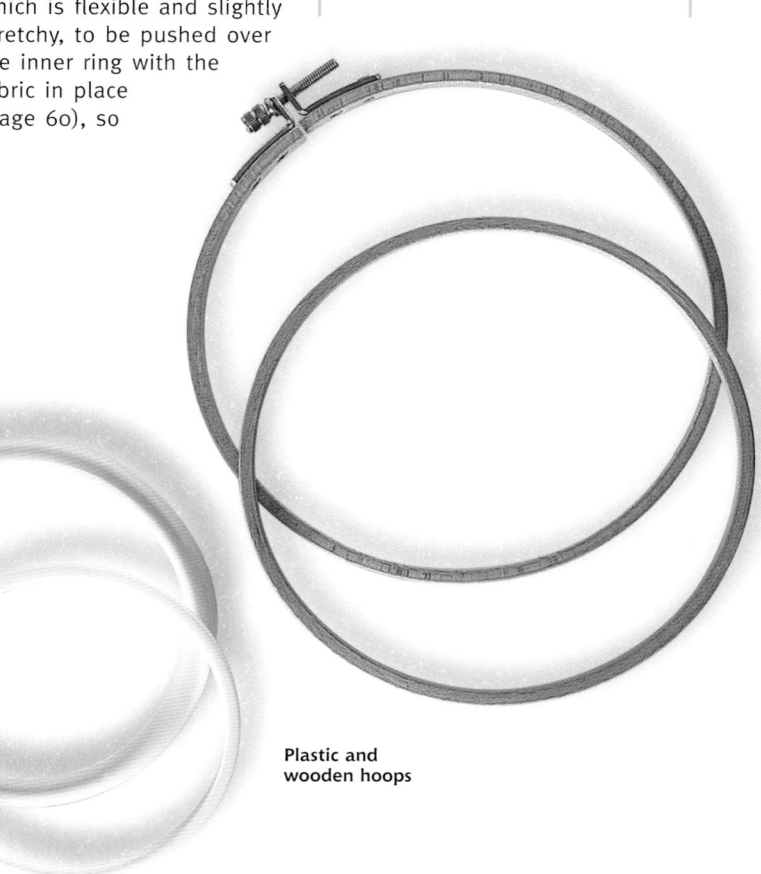

Plastic and wooden hoops

Slate frame (or square frame)

These are available in several sizes, from small handheld frames to very large frames on stands. The fabric is stretched between two rollers at the top and bottom by stitching it to webbing attached to the rollers, which are then tightened to take up extra length. The side edges of the fabric may then be laced to the sides of the frame (page 61).

Scissors

A small pair of sharp, fine-pointed scissors is essential. Keep a larger pair for cutting fabric, and never use good scissors to cut paper!

Tweezers

After snipping through unwanted stitches at the back of the work, use tweezers to pull out all the thread ends (page 66). Special tweezers are available with a magnifying glass attached.

Thimble

A thimble is not always necessary for counted thread work, but you should keep one in your sewing box for difficult moments! Choose the correct size to fit your middle (second finger), with deep indentations to catch the needle end without slipping.

Magnifiers

Various types of magnifying glass are available, and many people find them extremely helpful.

Pins

Choose steel dressmaker's pins to prevent damage to fabrics. For blocking (page 67) you will need either thumbtacks, map pins, T-pins, or pins with large heads.

Light source

It is most important to work in a good light, both for accuracy and to avoid eyestrain. Daylight is best, but a daylight light bulb in a desk lamp is a good substitute.

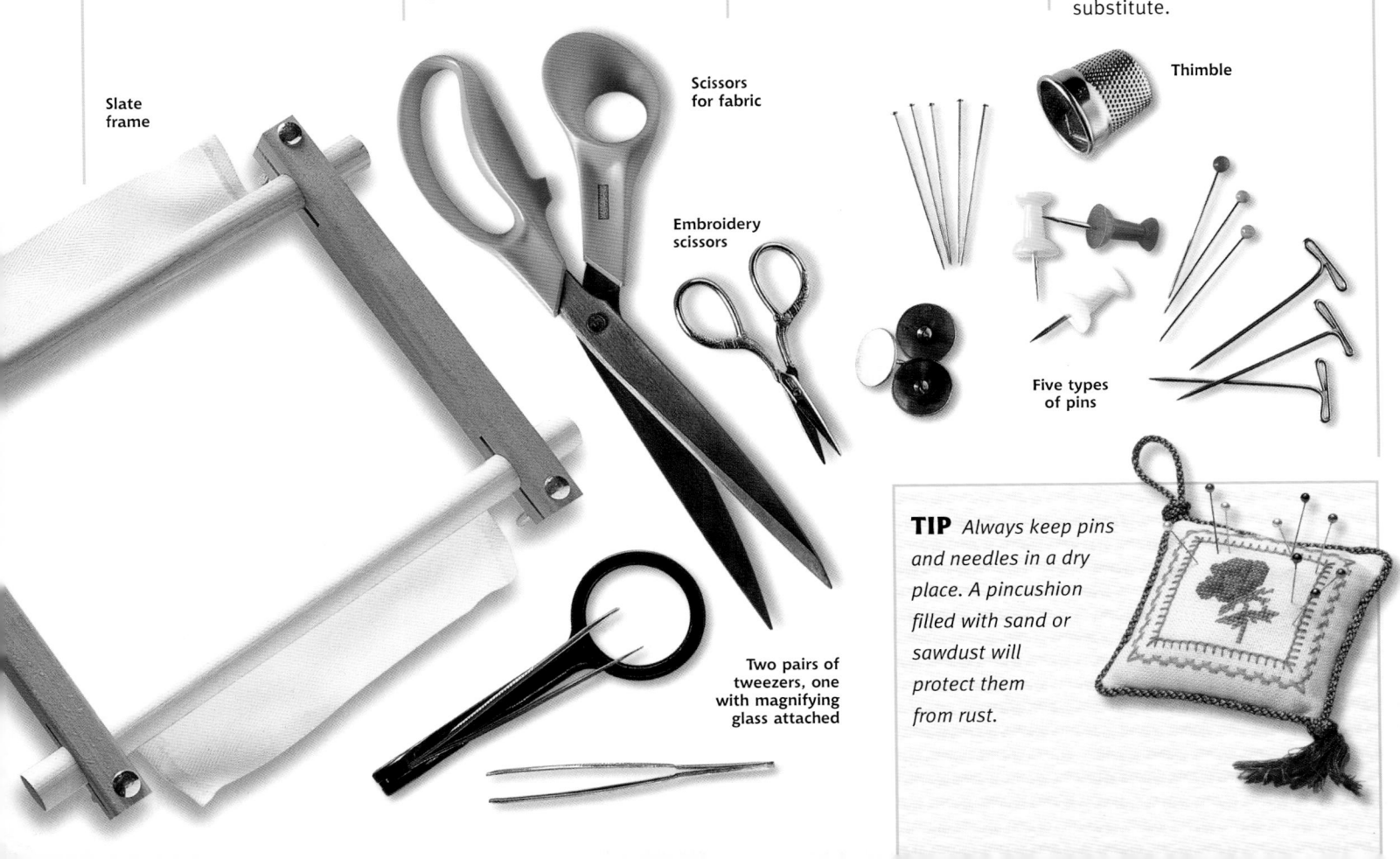

Slate frame

Scissors for fabric

Embroidery scissors

Thimble

Five types of pins

Two pairs of tweezers, one with magnifying glass attached

TIP *Always keep pins and needles in a dry place. A pincushion filled with sand or sawdust will protect them from rust.*

Specialist fabric markers

Use these to mark fabric temporarily. A quilter's or dressmaker's chalk pencil makes marks that may be brushed away. The ink in special pens may be water-soluble or vanishing (the marks vanishing after about 48 hours). Always test on a scrap of fabric before use. Water may permanently stain some fabrics, such as silks.

Ruler and tape measure

Use a ruler or tape measure for checking the count of fabric, and for measuring and marking fabric accurately. Old tape measures stretch with use: replace them!

Masking tape

This may be used to bind the edges of fabric or canvas to prevent fraying (page 59). It is also useful when tracing and drawing up designs (page 99).

Blocking board

Some types of embroidery require blocking rather than pressing (pages 66–67). You can use your ironing board for small pieces, but a separate blocking board is a useful accessory. Make any size you require: cover a piece of smooth board with a layer of batting, folded neatly over to the back and secured with glue or staples. Cover this with a top layer of white or colorfast cotton fabric, secured in the same way. Woven gingham fabric is ideal, as it provides a ready-made grid for blocking your work square.

Fabric-marking
pen and pencil

Masking tape

Daylight
light bulb

Blocking
board

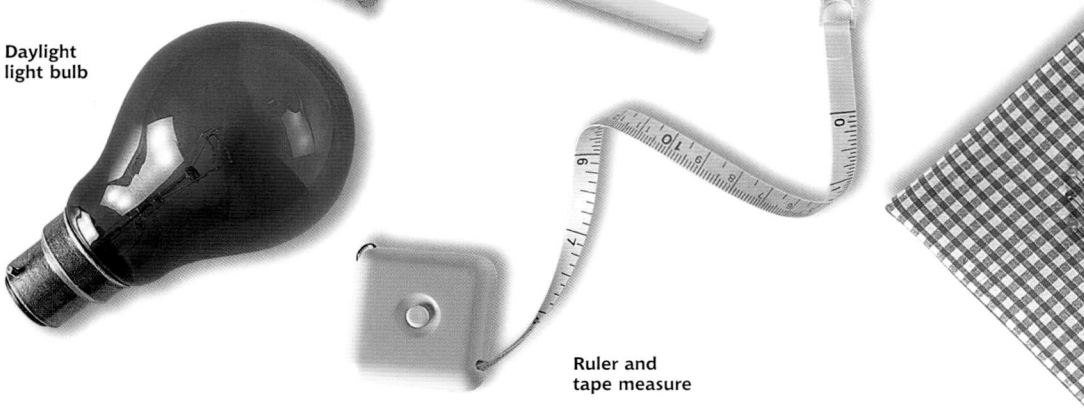

Ruler and
tape measure

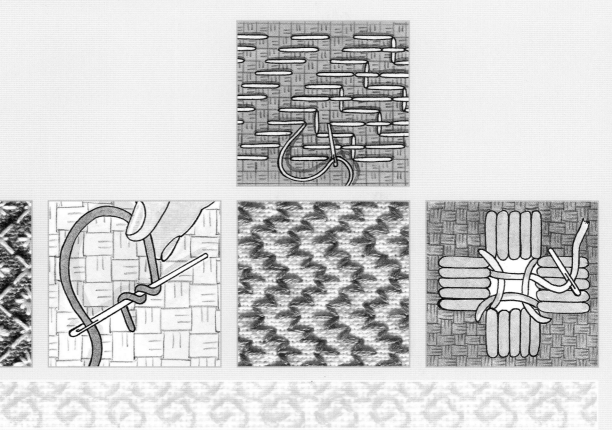

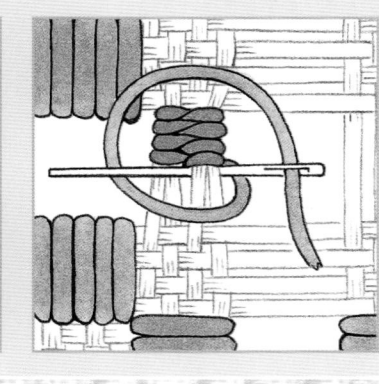

CHAPTER 2

Stitch Library

In this section you will find detailed instructions for counted thread stitches used for various kinds of cross stitch, blackwork, and Hardanger work. Other useful stitches that may be worked by counting threads are also included, together with charts for alphabets and numbers.

Try out any stitches unfamiliar to you, following the instructions and numbered diagrams, to add to your repertoire and discover new effects to use in your stitching.

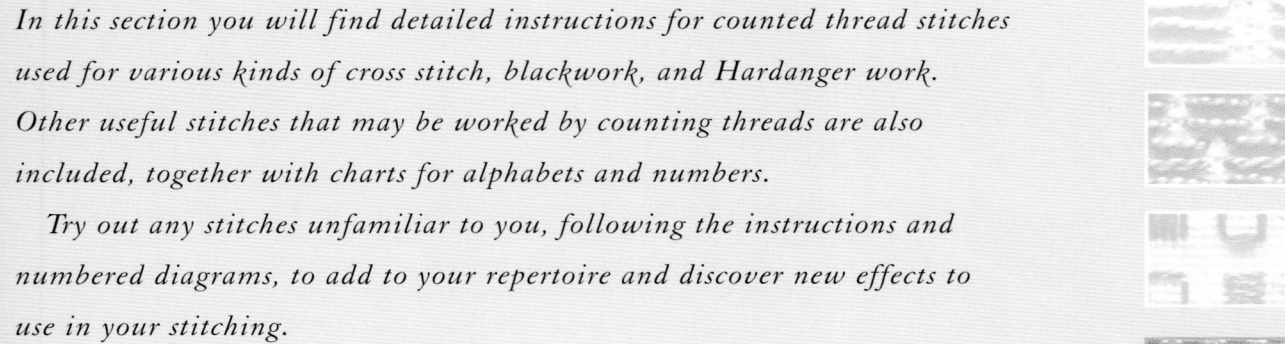

Basic Stitches

This section covers the basic stitches needed for cross stitch, blackwork, and Assisi work. They are all shown in the photographs on either Aida fabric or evenweave fabric, and in the diagrams on Aida fabric.

Normally, one stitch is worked over one square of Aida fabric, or two threads of evenweave in each direction. However, three quarter and quarter cross stitch involve inserting the needle at the center of an Aida square, or over just one intersection of evenweave; and the outline stitches (backstitch and Holbein stitch) are sometimes worked at a slope across two Aida squares to make an angled line, or as part of a curve.

◄ **HEART OF MY HEART**
Charlotte's Web Needlework
5⅞ x 5⅞ in (150 x 150mm)
Cross stitch using stranded cottons on 14-count Aida fabric
Simple heart motifs repeat to form a "patchwork quilt" design.

CROSS STITCH

Known in the past as sampler stitch, this is one of the most versatile embroidery stitches, used to build up simple motifs in silhouette, decorative repeating borders, or pictures in many colors. It is also often used in blackwork.

It may be worked singly, completing each stitch before beginning the next; this method gives the neatest appearance. It may also be worked in horizontal or vertical lines, used to fill large areas more quickly, working all the diagonals in one direction and then all those in the other direction. However, if you mix the two directions within a single area of color, the slight difference may be visible.

For an even appearance it is very important to make sure all the top threads of the crosses in the whole design lie in the same direction: from bottom left to top right is usual, as shown in the diagram below.

Worked on Aida fabric, each cross stitch normally covers one fabric square. On evenweave fabric, two threads in each direction is the usual size.

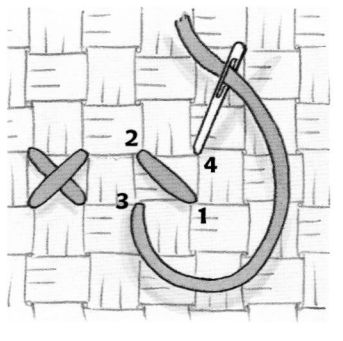

Single cross stitch
Bring the needle up at 1 and insert it at 2, making a diagonal stitch from bottom right to top left.

Bring the needle up at 3 and insert it at 4, making a second diagonal stitch crossing the first, from bottom left to top right.

The single cross stitch may be repeated in lines to fill an area: work the first row of crosses from right to left, and the second row from left to right, then repeat these two rows.

Horizontal lines of cross stitch

Each line is made in two journeys, beginning at the right end of the line:

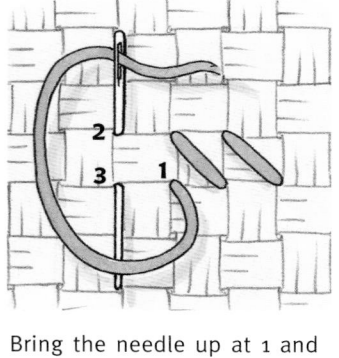

Bring the needle up at 1 and insert it at 2, making a diagonal stitch.

Bring the needle up at 3, directly below 2, to begin the next repeat to the left. Repeat as required.

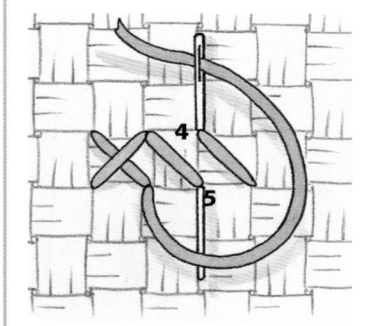

At the end of the line, reverse direction and work a stitch to cross each diagonal stitch made on the first journey, inserting the needle at 4 and then bringing it up again at 5.

A solid area may be filled by working lines of stitches in this way, beginning with the line at the top.

Vertical lines of cross stitch

Each line is made in two journeys, beginning at the top:

Bring the needle up at 1 and insert it at 2, making a diagonal stitch.

Bring the needle up at 3, directly below 1, to begin the next repeat downward. Repeat as required.

At the bottom of the line, reverse direction and work upward, crossing each diagonal stitch made on the first journey, inserting the needle at 4 and bringing it up again at 5.

A solid area may be filled by working lines of stitches in this way, beginning with the line at the right.

▼ **FUCHSIAS BOOKMARK AND LAVENDER SACHET**
Textile Heritage Collection
7 x 2 in (180 x 50mm) and 3½ x 2 in (90 x 50mm)
Cross stitch using stranded cottons on 15-count Aida fabric
The outlines are added in backstitch, with single straight stitches for the flower stamens.

THREE QUARTER AND QUARTER CROSS STITCH

On Aida fabric, these stitches require the needle to be inserted at the center of a square, where there is no obvious hole. Use the needle tip to open a hole between the threads, then check to see if it is central before making the stitch.

Working on evenweave fabric over two threads in each direction, there is, of course, a hole at the center.

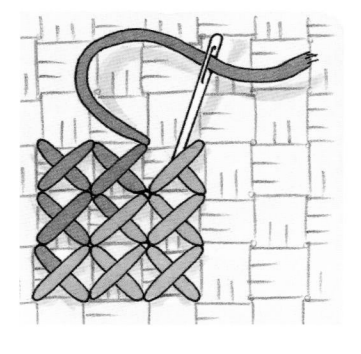

Quarter cross stitch

Sometimes it is necessary to fill the remaining quarter of a square (next to a three quarter cross stitch) with another color.

Bring the second color up at the empty corner and insert the needle at the center of the square.

HALF CROSS STITCH

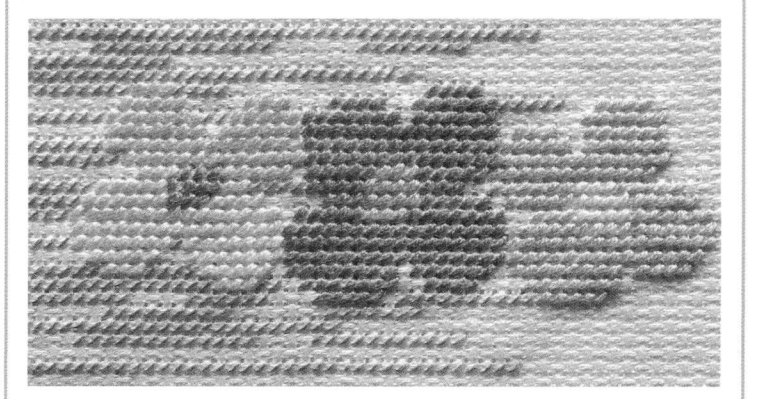

Three quarter cross stitch

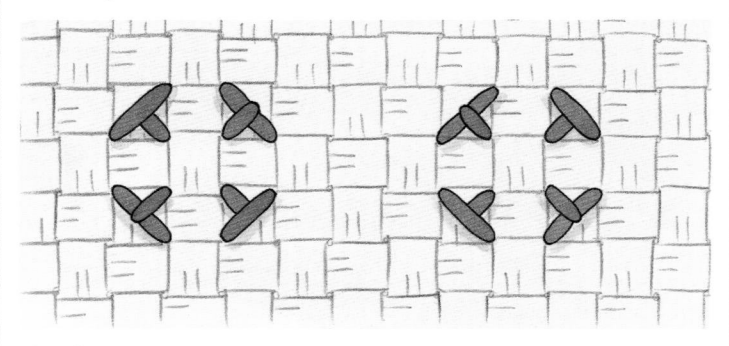

The three quarter cross is normally only used at the edge of a shape, to avoid steps in a curved or slanted outline.

The stitch may be worked in any one of four directions, as the design requires, and with the top thread slanting in either direction to match the whole cross stitches.

First work the complete diagonal stitch (half cross stitch) slanting in the direction required to fit the design outline.

Then work the half diagonal stitch (quarter cross stitch), bringing the needle up at the required corner and inserting it at the center, either under or over the diagonal stitch, to match the top threads of the other cross stitches.

This stitch is useful for filling in large areas, especially backgrounds, with a muted effect. It uses thread very economically. It does not cover the fabric so completely as cross stitch, so the thread color blends with the fabric color.

It may be worked in horizontal or vertical rows; avoid combining the two within the same area as the difference will be visible.

The fabric should be stretched in a hoop or frame to avoid distortion; this stitch will probably need careful blocking (page 67).

Horizontal rows

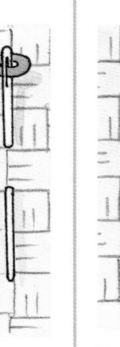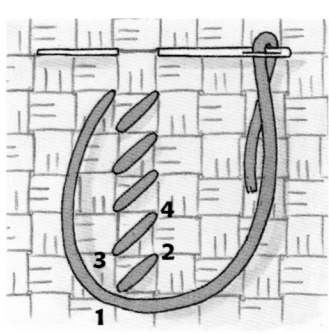

Work from left to right:
Bring needle up at 1 and
insert it at 2. Bring needle
up again at 3 and insert it at
4. Repeat along the row.
At the end of the row, turn
the work and stitch the next
row in the same way from
left to right, so that all the
half cross stitches slope in
the same direction.

Wrong side

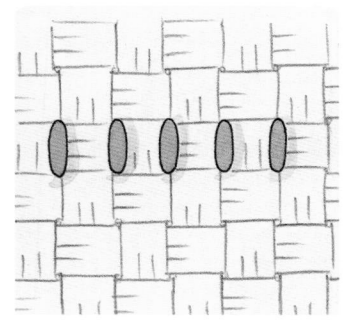

Small vertical stitches will
form on the wrong side of
the work.

Vertical rows

Work from bottom to top:
Bring needle up at 1 and
insert it at 2. Bring needle
up again at 3 and insert it at
4. Repeat to top of row.

Turn the work and stitch
the next row from bottom to
top in the same way.

Small horizontal stitches
form on the wrong side of
the work.

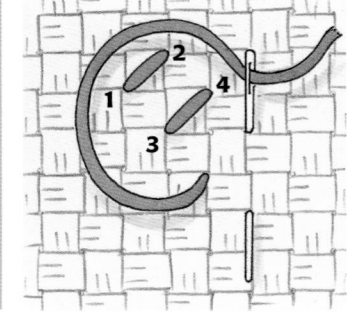

TENT STITCH

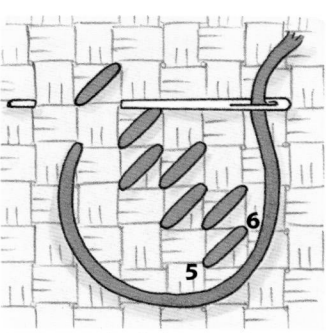

This stitch is very similar in
appearance to half cross
stitch, but the different
method of working makes it
less likely to distort the
fabric. This stitch uses more
thread than half cross stitch.

It may be worked
diagonally, horizontally, or
vertically, to suit the design.
Avoid combining different
working directions within the
same area as the difference
will be visible.

◄ Diagonal rows
Work from top left to bottom
right, as shown in the
diagram left.

Bring the needle up at 1 and
insert it at 2. Work the next
stitch diagonally down and

to the right, leaving one hole
empty: bring the needle up
at 3 and insert it at 4.

Repeat stitching down to
the bottom right.

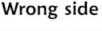

At the end of the row, bring
the needle up at the lower
point of the first stitch of the
next row at 5 and insert it at
6, then work back up to the
top left. Stitches will end in
the empty holes of the
previous row.

Repeat these two rows
working up and down the
required area.

Wrong side

The wrong side of diagonal
rows shows a basketweave
pattern, demonstrating why
tent stitch worked in this
way is less likely to distort
the fabric.

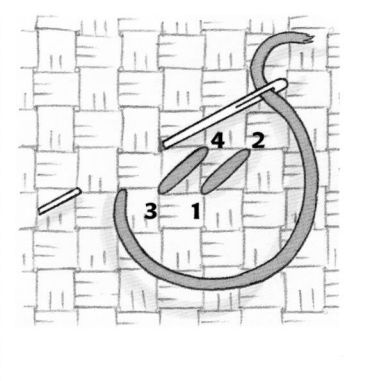

Horizontal rows

Work from right to left. Bring the needle up at 1 and insert it at 2 across one square. Bring the needle up again at 3 and insert it at 4. Repeat to the end of the row.

Vertical rows

Work from top to bottom:

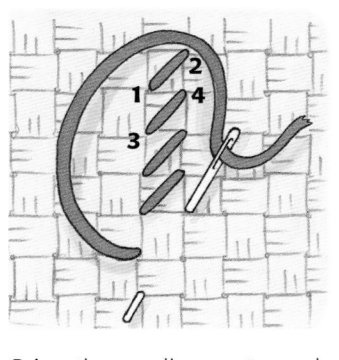

Bring the needle up at 1 and insert it at 2 across one square. Bring the needle up again at 3 and insert it at 4. Repeat to the bottom of the row.

BACKSTITCH

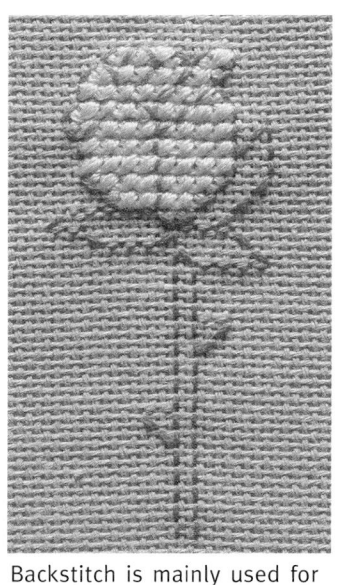

Right side

Wrong side

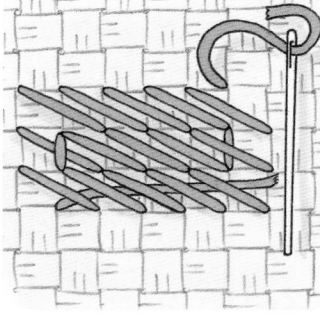

Work the next row in the opposite direction: if it is difficult to turn the piece, work as shown here, bringing the needle up at 1 and inserting it at 2. Otherwise, turn the work, and stitch the next row from right to left as before.

The wrong side of the work shows long stitches all slanting in the same direction.

Work the next row in the reverse direction: if it is difficult to turn the piece, work as shown here, bringing the needle up at 1 and inserting it at 2. Otherwise, turn the work, and stitch the next row from top to bottom as before.

Backstitch is mainly used for outlining, adding emphasis and detail to areas of color or pattern, often in black or a dark shade. Lines may be straight or stepped, or given the appearance of a curve by graduating the slopes of the stitches.

Each stitch is normally worked along one side of a square or diagonally across a square. For graduated slopes, stitches are sometimes worked at an angle across two squares, making a longer stitch.

Backstitch is usually indicated on a chart by straight lines showing exactly where to place the stitches. For cross stitch (page 26) and blackwork (pages 36–41), backstitch outlines and details are normally worked after the other stitching is complete.

For Assisi work (pages 74–75), the backstitch outline of the motif is worked before the background.

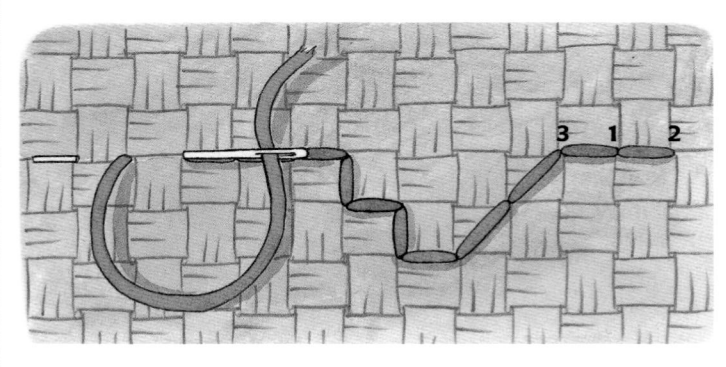

Work from right to left. Bring the needle up at 1, insert it to the right at 2 and bring it out again at 3. To begin the next stitch, insert the needle in same place as 1 (the end of the previous stitch). Repeat as required.

HOLBEIN STITCH

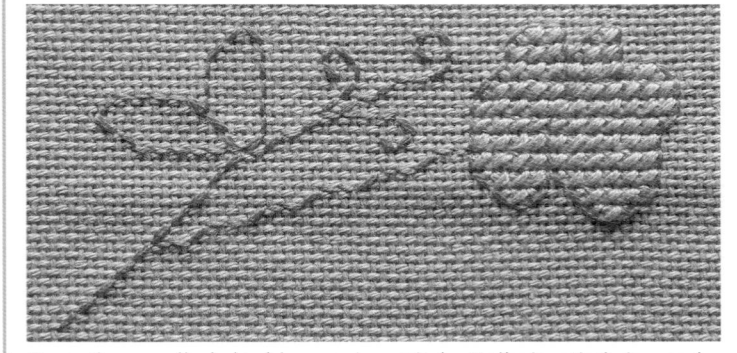

Sometimes called double running stitch, Holbein stitch is used for the same purposes as backstitch: outlines and details, normally worked after the completion of cross stitch or other stitches, to add details or to emphasize a shape. Again, lines may be straight or stepped, or graduated into curves.

The advantage of Holbein stitch is that the threads on the back of the work are less bulky. In fact if neatly worked Holbein stitch can be reversible. The threads are not carried across the back behind unstitched fabric, so dark thread may be used on an open-weave fabric without "shadowing."

Use Holbein stitch to work designs including lines that do not completely enclose a space, such as the little "sprigs" shown above.

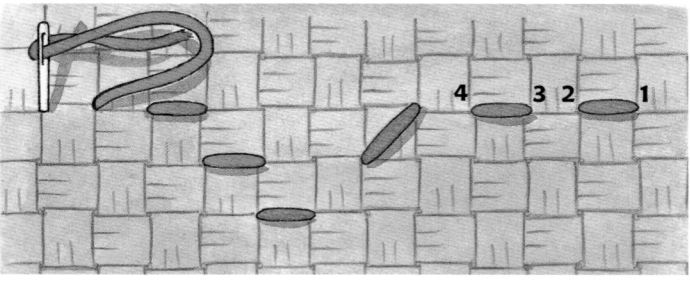

Each line is worked in two journeys:
Bring the needle up at 1, insert it at 2, then bring it up at 3, and insert it at 4. Repeat to form a line of running stitches. Stitches may be horizontal, vertical, or diagonal, as required.

Turn the work and stitch back along the line. Stitch through exactly the same holes, filling the spaces between the running stitches. Do not split the stitches made on the first journey. For a neat appearance, always bring the needle up through the hole above the thread of the first journey and insert it below, or vice versa.

This second journey may be worked in a contrasting color if desired.

"Sprigs" are usually worked on the first journey, stitching out to the end of the sprig and back again.

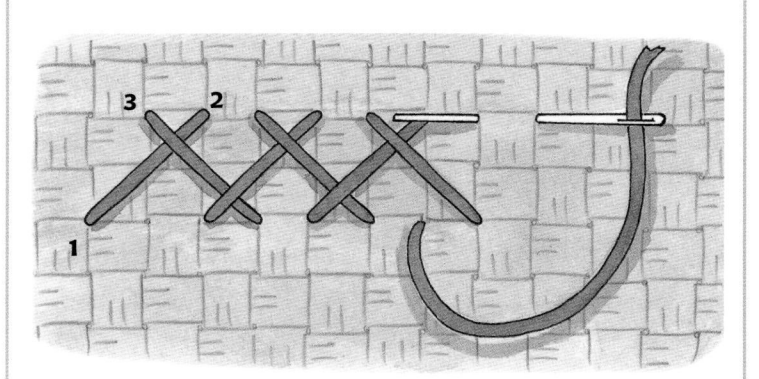

Special Cross Stitches

These stitches include variations on the basic cross stitch. Some were developed for various special purposes such as marking linen with neat stitching on both sides, while others are used essentially for their decorative qualities.

In the diagrams the stitch is shown worked in a line two squares deep, but the size and proportion may be varied as desired. As shown in the photograph, the texture will then vary from dense to open.

Always work from left to right:
Bring the needle up at 1. Insert it at 2, diagonally across two squares, and bring it out again at 3, one square left of 2.

HERRINGBONE STITCH

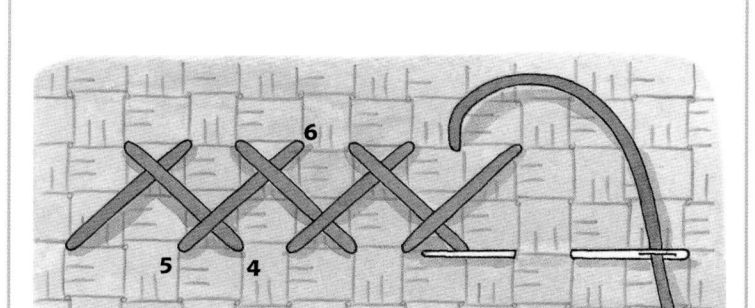

Insert the needle at 4, diagonally across two squares, and bring it out again at 5, one square left of 4, to begin the next repeat to the right. Insert the needle at 6, diagonally across two squares from 5, and two squares right of 2. Repeat to the right.

Sometimes called Russian cross stitch, this stitch is normally used as a border pattern or as a single decorative line. Lines of herringbone stitch may also be worked closely together to fill an area with a textured pattern.

MARKING CROSS STITCH

This is a reversible stitch, forming a line of crosses on the front of the work and a line of squares on the back. It was often used in the past for marking household linen with lettering or personal symbols. Such lettering would of course be back to front (but still clearly recognizable) on the wrong side, whereas a symbol such as a coronet or heart could be symmetrical. When ironing and storing items such as bed linen, it was easy to identify the wrong side because of the different appearance of the stitch.

When working such designs requiring lines in several directions, it is often necessary to work more than once over one or two stitches when turning the corners. For this reason, fine thread was traditionally used, to avoid making the corner stitches too bulky. In the past, this stitch was worked on linen by counting the threads, but it is shown here on Aida fabric.

To work a line of stitches from top to bottom:

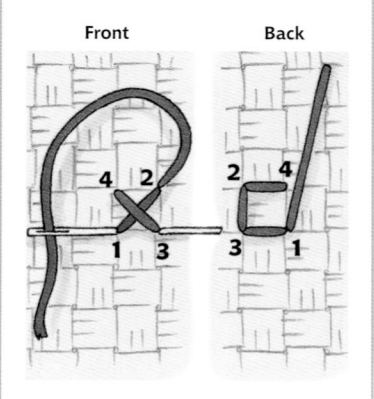

Front   Back

Using the away waste knot method (page 63) bring the needle up at 1, leaving a tail of at least 2 inches (50mm) at the back of the work; this will be run in later to complete the first square on the back.

Insert the needle at 2 across one square, bring it up at 3, and insert it at 4, making a cross stitch on the front of the fabric. Bring the needle up again at 2 and insert it at 1.

Bring the needle up again at 3. On the back of the work, three sides of the first square are complete.

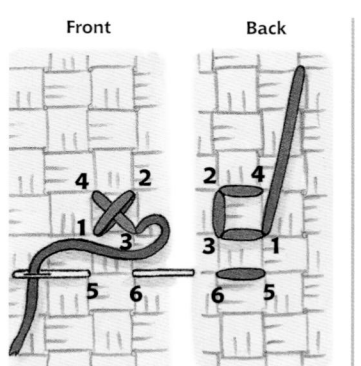

Front   Back

Insert the needle at 5, one square below 1, and bring it up at 6, one square below 3.

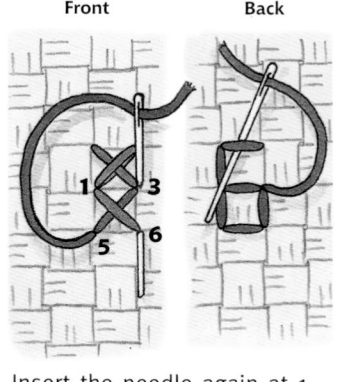

Front   Back

Insert the needle again at 1, bring it up at 5, and insert it at 3.

Bring the needle up again at 6 in order to begin the next repeat.

A second cross stitch is complete on the front, and a second square on the back.

Repeat this last cross stitch as required.

When turning corners, remember the working rule: all stitches on the front of the work are diagonal, and all those on the back run along one side of a square. If necessary, make extra stitches at corners to bring the needle into the correct position for the next line of crosses. Turn the work as required to work each line of crosses from top to bottom.

When the line is complete, cut the knot at the start, thread the tail into the needle, and neaten the end by running it in along the back of the stitches of the first square, as shown in the previous column.

DOUBLE-SIDED CROSS STITCH

This version of cross stitch produces identical cross stitches on both sides of the fabric, making the work reversible. It was often used in Assisi work to make banners and other articles designed to be seen from both sides, and is therefore sometimes called Italian cross stitch.

Double-sided cross stitch may also be used for linear designs on fine and translucent fabrics, where threads across the back of the work might show through on the surface.

Extra half-diagonal stitches are worked at the ends of lines and when turning corners, so the thread used should be quite fine, to avoid excess bulk.

All stitches made, on both front and back, should be either diagonal or half-diagonal.

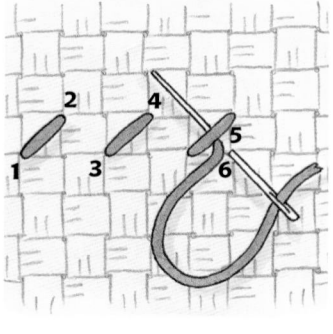

Each line of crosses is worked in four journeys. Work the first journey from left to right: Bring the needle up at 1 and insert it at 2, making a diagonal stitch across one square. Bring the needle up at 3, so forming a diagonal stitch on the back. Insert the needle at 4. Repeat to the end of the line, ending with a diagonal stitch on the right side of the work. Bring the needle up at 5, underneath the center of the last stitch made, and insert it at 6. Bring the needle up again at 5, through exactly the same hole.

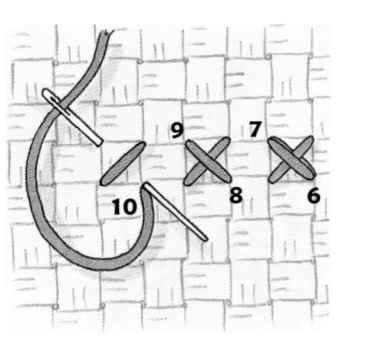

Insert the needle at 7, making another half diagonal stitch, then bring the needle up again at 6 and insert it at 7, making a complete diagonal stitch as the top thread of the end cross. In this way a correct cross is formed on both front and back, with the extra half-diagonal stitches hidden.

Now work the second journey from right to left: bring the needle up at 8, completing the next cross on the back. Insert the needle at 9, completing the next cross on the front. Repeat to the left end of the line. After crossing the last stitch on the front, bring the needle up at 10 to begin the third journey.

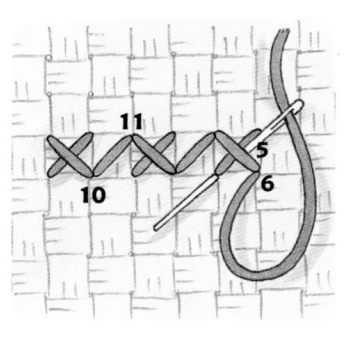

Work from left to right. Insert the needle at 11, making a diagonal stitch across the first space. Repeat in each space to the right to the end of the line. At the right end of the line, bring the needle up at 6 and insert it at 5, as before, hiding this half stitch underneath the previous diagonal, then bring the needle out at 12 as shown to begin the fourth journey. Work the fourth journey from right to left, crossing each diagonal stitch made on the previous journey. Each side of the work should show a line of complete crosses.

STAR STITCH

Also known as devil stitch or double cross stitch, star stitch is very simple to work and may be worked singly or in lines, arranged in a regular pattern, or scattered randomly as a decoration. It is often used in blackwork, or sometimes as part of a border.

Star stitch is usually worked across more than one square of Aida fabric, such as two or four squares in each direction, or across several threads of evenweave. The number of squares or threads must be an even number.

Begin with a cross stitch. Bring the needle up at 1 and insert it at 2, bring it up at 3, and insert it at 4.

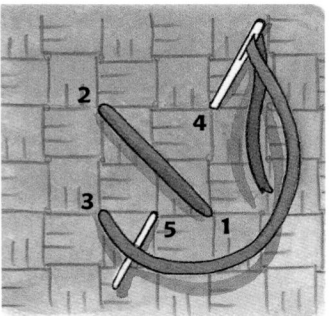

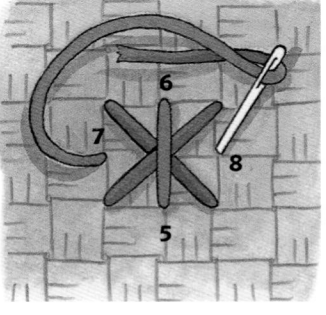

Bring the needle up again at 5, midway between 1 and 3. Complete the star with an upright cross stitch: insert the needle at 6, and bring it out again at 7, midway between 2 and 3, then insert it at 8. Repeat as required.

UPRIGHT CROSS STITCH

Another name for this stitch is St. George's cross stitch. It may be used as a substitute for cross stitch to work any design or pattern, although it will not cover the fabric so completely. The stitch may be worked singly or in lines, scattered or repeated closely as a solid filling. It is often used in blackwork patterns.

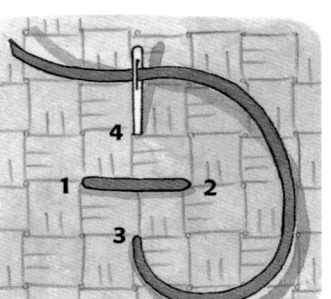

Single upright cross stitch
Bring the needle up at 1 and insert it at 2 across two squares (or threads) making a horizontal stitch. Then bring the needle up at 3 and insert it at 4, making a vertical stitch. Repeat as required.

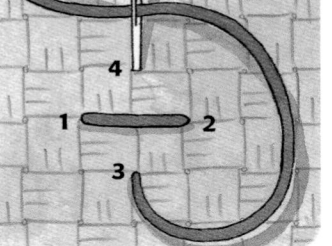

Upright cross stitch in lines

Work the first journey from right to left. Bring the needle up at 1 and insert it at 2 making a horizontal stitch. Repeat to the left as required.

Work the second journey from left to right. Bring the needle up at 3 and insert it at 4, so crossing the horizontal stitch with a vertical. Repeat the process to the right.

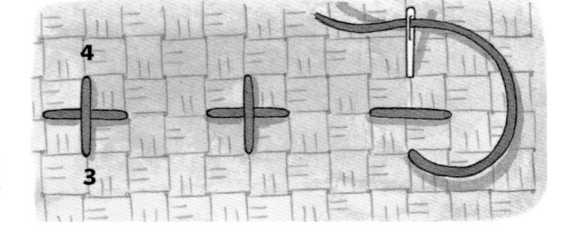

Blackwork Filling Patterns

These patterns are used to fill different areas of a blackwork design, as described on pages 78–81. There are an infinite number of blackwork filling patterns, and most of the individual stitches within this Stitch Library may be used to work them. Some patterns utilize only one type of stitch (such as Holbein stitch, page 31); others use combinations of two or more stitches to complete the pattern.

Each blackwork pattern consists of a small to medium-sized repeating unit. For a consistent appearance, it is important to work each pattern repeat always in the same order.

When working on light fabric with dark thread it is advisable to avoid passing the thread behind unstitched fabric, to prevent it showing as a "shadow." For this reason Holbein stitch is usually preferable to backstitch and patterns with isolated stitches may be unsuitable on open or lightweight fabrics. Sometimes it is possible to pass the thread through the stitches at the back of the work (instead of across a gap) to reach the position for the next stitch.

Blackwork was traditionally worked in black thread on white linen, but any strong color contrast will suit these patterns. Some of the samples in the photographs are worked on evenweave fabric, and some on Aida fabric; on the diagrams one square represents one square of Aida fabric. The proportions of all these stitches may be varied as desired: plan your variations carefully on graph paper.

Patterns made with single stitch types

HOLBEIN TRELLIS
Begin at right. Work the first line of Holbein stitch (page 31) from right to left and back again.

Work a second line of Holbein stitch in a similar way, positioned as shown.

Repeat these two lines to form an allover pattern.

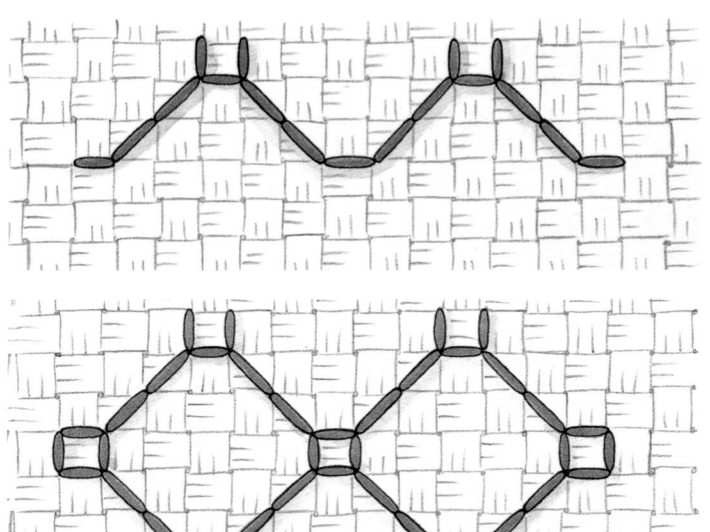

HOLBEIN SPRIGS
Work the first line of Holbein stitch (page 31): on the first journey (right to left) complete all the sprigs by working out to the end and back again. Then work the second journey from left to right to complete the central line.

Repeat the line, positioned as shown.

DARNING BLOCKS

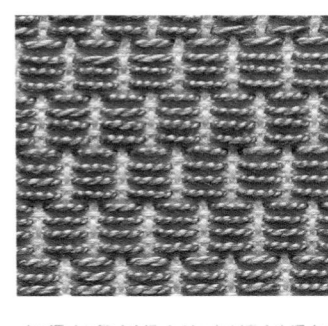

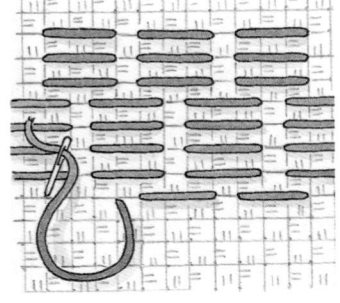

Begin at right. Work the top line of darning stitches (page 52) from right to left, then work the second line from left to right. Continue working lines to form the pattern shown.

DARNING HOURGLASS

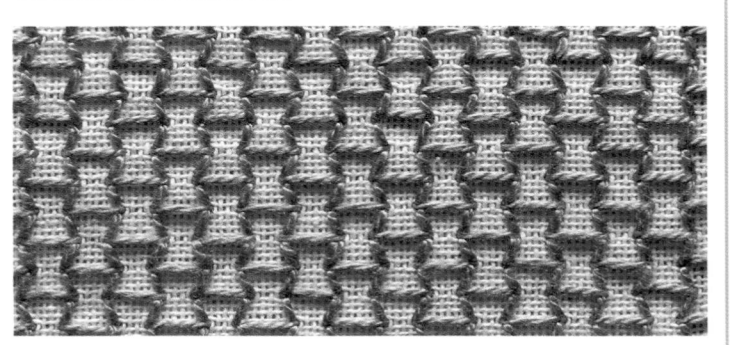

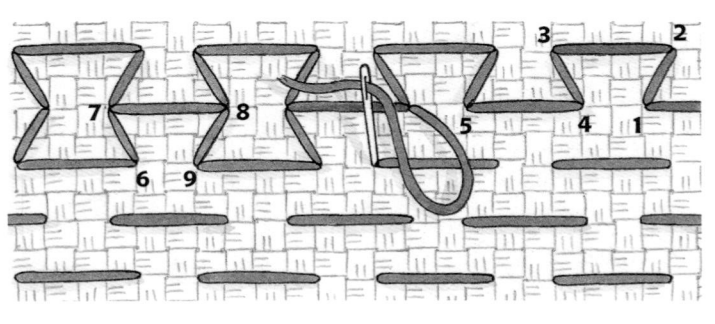

This type of darning pattern is sometimes called Japanese darning.

Begin at right. First work all the horizontal stitches positioned as shown, working lines of darning stitch (page 52) back and forth in the same way as for the darning blocks pattern above.

Then add the sloping stitches to complete the pattern: begin again at top right. Bring the needle up at 1, down at 2, up at 3, and down at 4. Repeat to the left, beginning at 5. Work the next line from left to right: bring the needle up at 6, down at 7, up at 8, down at 9. Repeat to the right. Repeat these two rows to complete the pattern as required.

DARNING ZIGZAG

Begin at right. First work all the horizontal stitches positioned as shown, working lines of darning stitch (page 52) back and forth. Then add the sloping stitches to complete the pattern: begin again at top right. Bring the needle up at 1, down at 2, up at 3, and down at 4. Repeat to the left.

Then work from left to right: bring the needle up at 5, down at 6, up at 7, down at 8. Repeat to the right.

Repeat these two rows to complete the pattern as required.

UPRIGHT CROSS FILLING

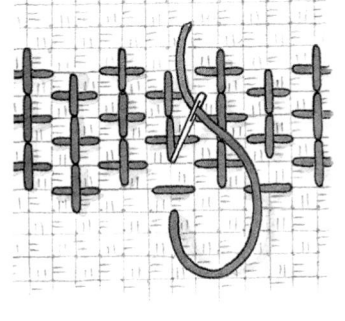

Beginning at top right, work the first line of upright cross stitch (page 39) from right to left and back again. Then work the second line, placing the crosses as shown. Repeat these two lines as required.

ALGERIAN EYE FILLING

Beginning at top right, work the first line of Algerian eye stitch (page 52) from right to left. Then work the second line from left to right, positioned as shown. Always work each unit of eight stitches in exactly the same order throughout. Repeat these two lines as required.

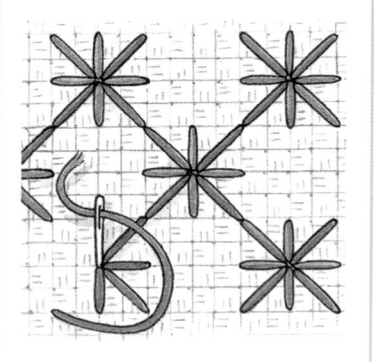

SATIN STITCH FLOWERS

Each unit consists of four blocks and each block consists of three satin stitches (page 51).

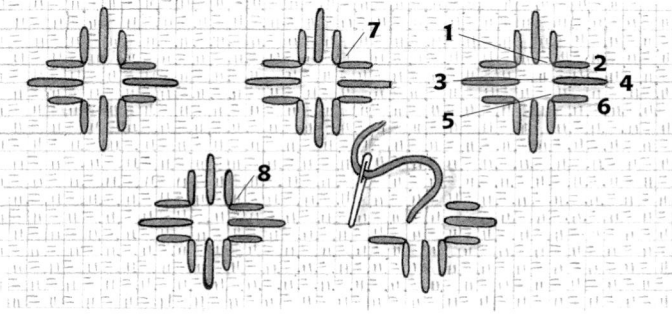

Begin at top right with the right-hand block of the unit: bring the needle up at 1 and down at 2, then make two more satin stitches 3–4 and 5–6 as shown. Work clockwise: bring the needle up again at 5 to begin the lower block. Work the remaining two blocks in the same way, ending with the top block. Run the thread through the back of the top block and bring it out at 7 to begin the next block to the left. Repeat to the left. Work the second row of units from left to right: bring the needle up at 8 and work all the stitches of each block in exactly the same order. Repeat to the right.

Repeat these two rows of blocks.

Patterns made with stitch combinations

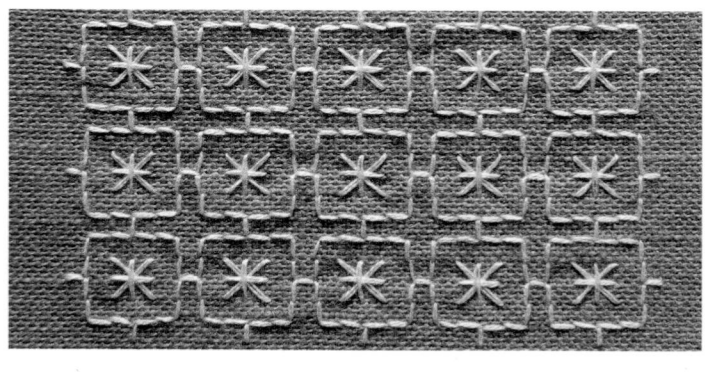

HOLBEIN AND STAR STITCH

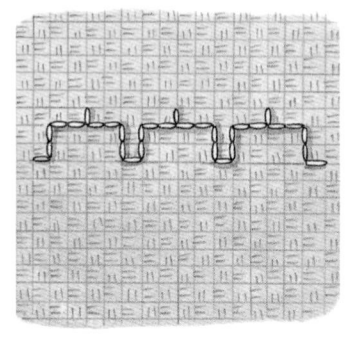

Begin at right and work the first line of Holbein stitch (page 31) as shown, from right to left and back again.

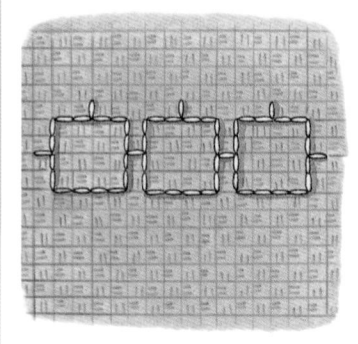

Work a second line of Holbein stitch to complete

the squares. Repeat these two lines to fill the area. Begin again at top right and work a star stitch in each square as shown, working back and forth in rows. Work the individual stitches of each star in the same order throughout.

CROSS STITCH AND UPRIGHT CROSS

Work the first row from right to left: bring the needle up at 1 and insert it at 2, then bring it up at 3 and insert it at 4, making a large cross stitch.

Then bring the needle up at 5, insert it at 6, bring it up at 7, and insert it at 8, making a small upright cross stitch.

Repeat to the left as shown.

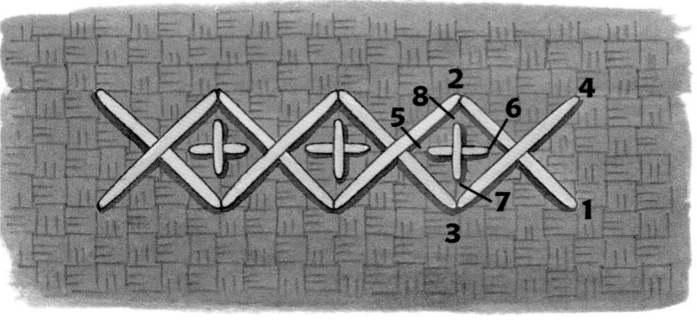

Work the next row from left to right, making only upright cross stitches, as shown. Repeat these two rows.

For a more open pattern, omit the second row of upright crosses, and work the second row to match the first, as shown in the lower half of the photograph.

BACKSTITCH AND ALGERIAN EYE

Begin at right and work a line of backstitch (page 30) as shown, repeating to the left.

Complete the backstitch motifs and stitch an Algerian eye in each space, as shown. For the variation in the lower half of the photograph, elongate the diagonals of each Algerian eye in the same way as the variation shown in the next column.

ALGERIAN EYE VARIATION

Here, two variations of Algerian eye stitch (page 52) are used: the Algerian eye at top right has elongated horizontals and verticals, while the next Algerian eye has elongated diagonals. Work the first row of units from right to left and the next row from left to right, always working the stitches of each unit in the same order. Repeat these two rows as required.

DARNING AND UPRIGHT CROSS

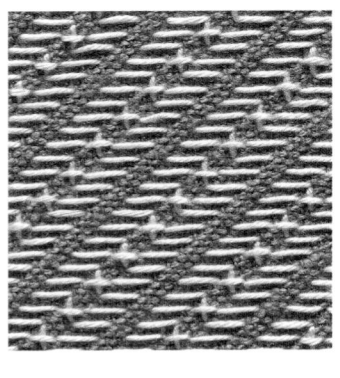

First work all the horizontal lines of darning stitch (pages 52–53) spaced as shown to make a pattern of sloping lines. Then add the upright cross stitches (page 35). Work these in diagonal lines down and up the area: begin with the first cross 1–2 and 3–4, then bring needle up at 5 to begin next cross.

Note that these upright crosses have the horizontal thread (not the vertical) as the top thread, to correspond with the horizontal darning stitches; change to a vertical top thread for a slightly different appearance.

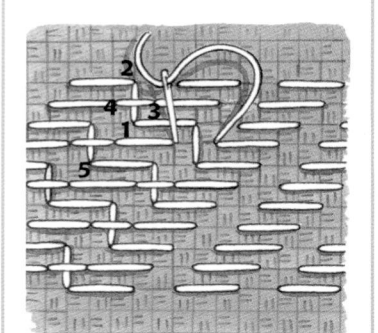

HOLBEIN AND CROSS

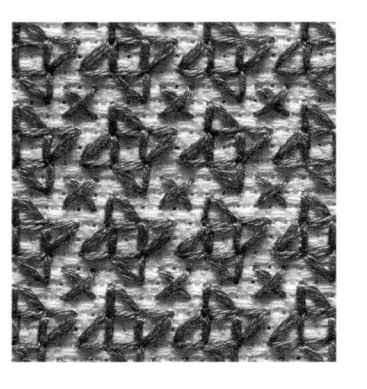

First work a row of motifs in Holbein stitch, beginning at right. Each unit is made up of four triangles.

Bring needle up at 1, insert it at 2, bring it up at 3, and insert it again at 1, then bring it up at 2, and insert it at 3. Bring the needle up again at 4 to begin the next triangle. Work the four triangles clockwise around the shape, ending with the top triangle. Repeat the motif to the left as shown.

Work a row of cross stitches from left to right, bringing needle up at 1, down at 2, up at 3, and down at 4. Repeat to the right as shown. Repeat these two rows as required.

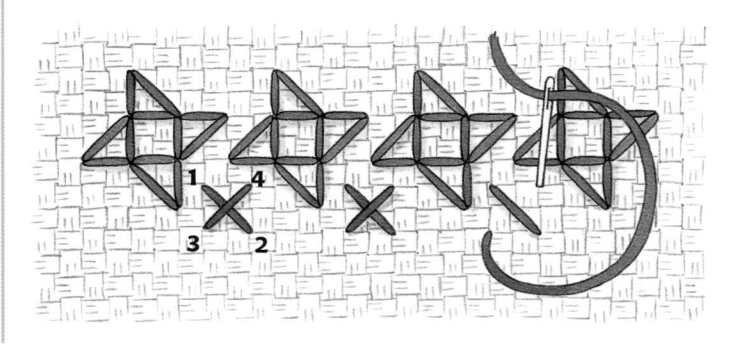

SATIN AND BACKSTITCH

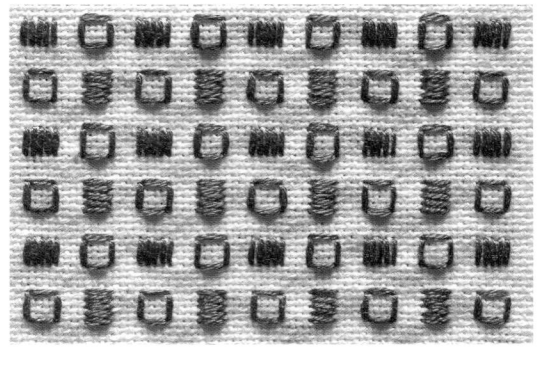

Begin at right: bring needle up at 1 and insert it at 2, making a single vertical satin stitch (page 51). Repeat this stitch four more times as shown, making a block of five stitches. Bring needle up at 3, down at 4, up at 5, down at 3, up at 6, down at 5, up at 4, and down at 6, making a square of backstitch. Bring needle up again at 7 to begin next repeat to the left.

Work the next row from left to right: place a square beneath each block, and a block beneath each square. Bring needle up at 8, down at 9, up at 10, down at 8, up at 11, down at 10, up at 9, and down at 11, to make a backstitch square. Bring needle up again at 12 and insert it at 13, making a horizontal satin stitch. Repeat this stitch four more times as shown to complete the block. Repeat to the right.

Repeat these two rows.

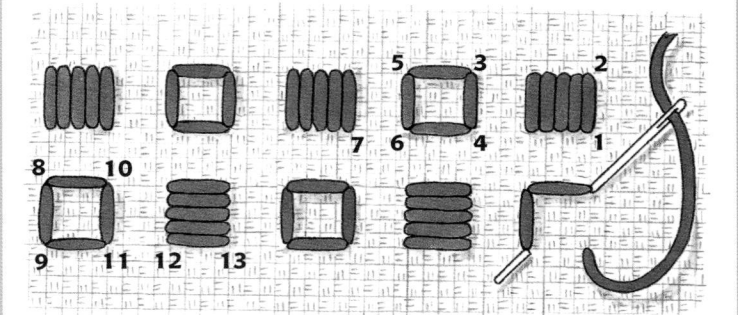

Hardanger Stitches

The stitches in this group are commonly used for Hardanger work, which is described in more detail on pages 82–84. Hardanger work involves cutting and withdrawing certain threads from the fabric; before this, the threads must first be secured with Kloster blocks. The remaining threads may then be overcast or woven into bars, and the open spaces between them decorated with various fillings.

◀ TRADITIONAL ANTIQUE BAND SAMPLER
Coats Crafts
19 x 10 in
(480 x 250mm)
Cross stitch, back-stitch, satin stitch, overcast bars, and herringbone stitch using coton à broder on Hardanger fabric
A variety of motifs are repeated in simple bands in the manner of a traditional stitch sampler.

KLOSTER BLOCKS

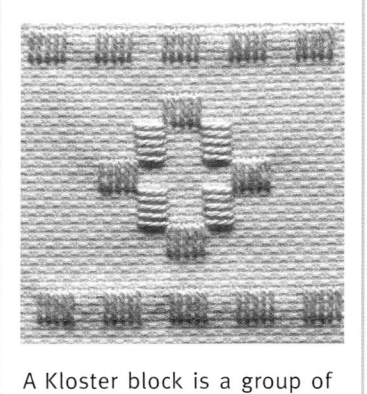

A Kloster block is a group of five satin stitches, worked over four squares of Hardanger fabric. Blocks may be worked in straight rows, or in diagonal steps. The exact placing and direction of each Kloster block is crucially important because threads may only be cut along the ends of the satin stitches, and only where there is another Kloster block directly opposite, so that the cut thread ends are enclosed on each side of the space. A fairly heavy thread (such as Pearl cotton no. 5) is usually required, to cover the fabric and to hide the ends when the fabric is cut. It is important to work the blocks in the correct order, to prevent the thread from showing through where it passes from one block to the next. The thread ends should be well secured by running them in along the back of several blocks.

To work Kloster blocks in straight rows

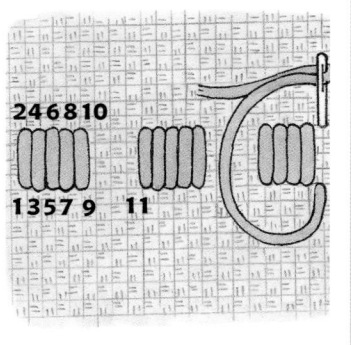

Secure thread at left with several waste backstitches. (Unpick these later and run in thread end [see page 83].) Bring the needle up at 1 and down at 2, over four fabric squares, making one satin stitch. Repeat this stitch four more times, from 3–4, 5–6, 7–8, and 9–10. Bring needle up again at 11, four squares right of 9, to begin the next repeat to the right.

To work Kloster blocks in diagonal steps

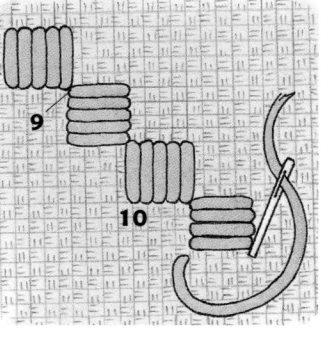

Begin at top left and work downward, to the right. Stitch the first block in same way as above, then bring the

needle up again at 9 to begin the second block, which is worked horizontally as shown.

At the end of the second block, bring the needle up again four threads below the end of the previous satin stitch at 10, to begin the next block down and to the right. Repeat the blocks as required, alternating the direction of the blocks down the stepped line.

KLOSTER BLOCKS WITH THREADS WITHDRAWN

After working Kloster blocks around the edges of a shape, certain fabric threads may be cut and withdrawn as on page 83. The remaining fabric threads may then be worked as overcast or woven bars, and the square spaces may then be filled with one of the fillings on pages 44–45.

OVERCAST BARS

These bars are worked on a bundle of fabric threads running in one direction only, after threads in the other direction have been withdrawn.

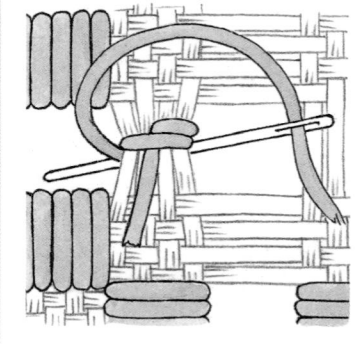

Hold the end of the thread along the bundle of threads to be overcast and pass the needle under the bundle from right to left.

Repeat until the bundle is completely covered. After the first two or three coils, pull the thread firmly. Use the needle tip to stroke the coils into place, so they lie closely side by side. When the bundle is completely covered, pull gently on the starting end and trim the thread tail. The needle may then be passed under the next bundle diagonally down and to the right, as shown, to begin overcasting in the same way. To fasten off the thread, run the needle through the back of the overcasting.

WOVEN BARS

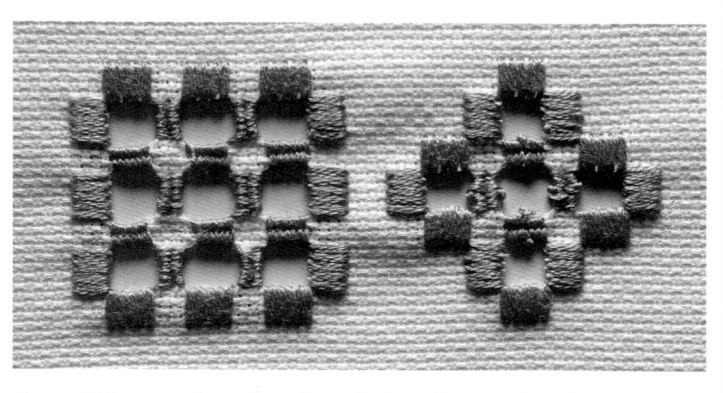

For a different effect, bundles of threads may also be worked as woven bars, with or without picots (see page 44).

Basic woven bar

Hold the end of the thread along the bundle to be woven and pass the needle under the right half of the bundle from right to left.

Then pass the needle under the left half of the bundle from left to right, enclosing the tail of the thread at the same time.

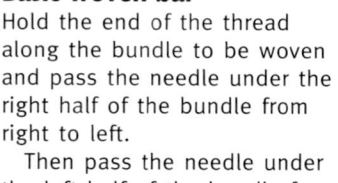

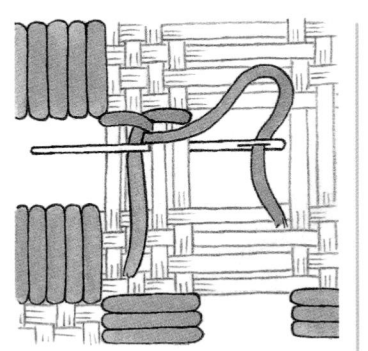

Repeat these two steps down to the base of the bar.

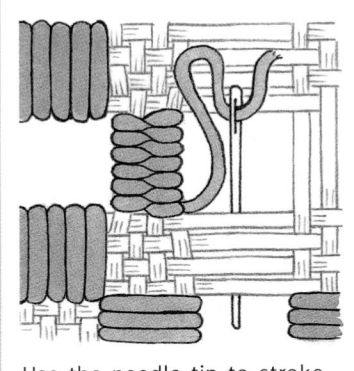

Use the needle tip to stroke the weaving into place. The stitches should be fairly close together so the bundle is completely covered. The needle may then be passed to the next bundle down and to the right, in the same way as for the overcast bar. Pull gently on the starting end to tighten the first stitch and trim off the thread tail. To fasten off, run the needle up the back of the bar and trim.

Woven bar with picots

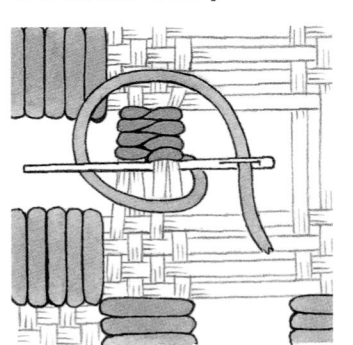

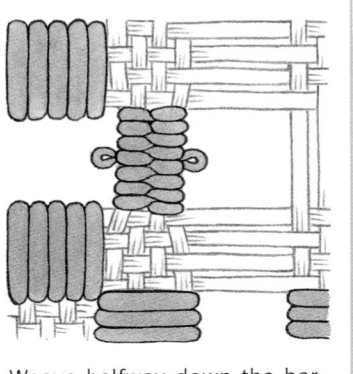

Weave halfway down the bar as above, then pass the needle under the right half of the bundle and loop the thread around the needle as shown. Pull through to make a picot knot.

Make another picot knot to match on the left side of the bar in a similar way, then complete the weaving down to the bottom of the bundle.

STRAIGHT LOOPSTITCH FILLING

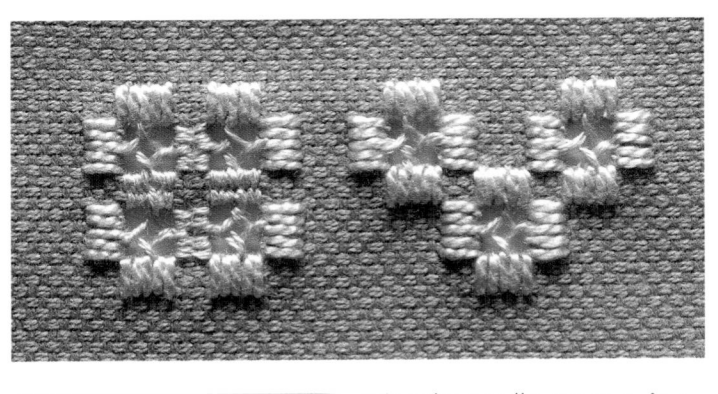

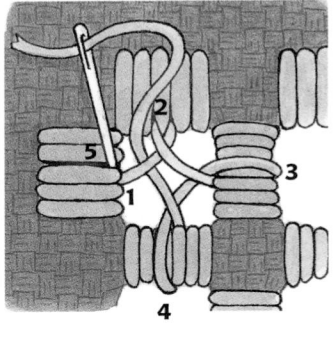

Bring the needle out at 1. At a Kloster block, pass the needle underneath the central stitch (as at 2); at an overcast bar, pass the needle around the bar as shown at 3; at a woven bar, insert the needle at the center of the bar. Bring the needle over the previous loop and repeat at 3 and at 4. Pass the needle under the first loop made and insert it at 5, then along the back of the stitches for the next stitch.

◀ **LAVENDER SACHET BAG Coats Crafts**
6¼ x 6¼ in (160 x 160mm) *Cross stitch, backstitch, woven bars, and dove's eye filling using Pearl and stranded cottons on Hardanger fabric* The stitched edging enables the heart to be cut to shape.

DOVE'S EYE FILLING

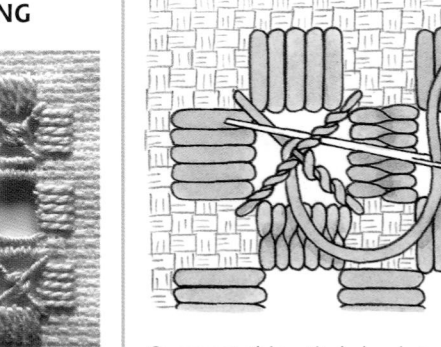

Overcast this stitch back to the center, then pass the needle under and over the "spokes" until the central spiral is the size required, ending at the single thread leading to point 3. Overcast the remaining thread back to 3 and insert the needle at 3. The needle may then be passed along the back of the stitches to the position required for the next stitch.

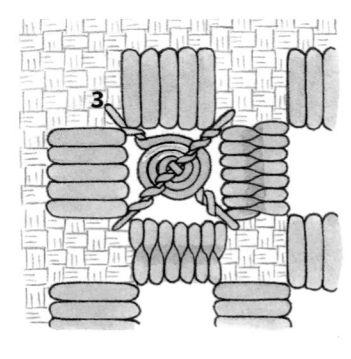

Bring the needle up through the fabric at 1, then insert it at 2, at the opposite corner. Pull quite firmly. Bring the needle out from below the fabric and pass it around the first stitch several times, overcasting it neatly back to 1. Insert the needle at 1 and pass it through the back of the stitches to 3. Bring it up through the fabric at 3 and insert it at 4, making another firm stitch.

OBLIQUE LOOPSTITCH FILLING

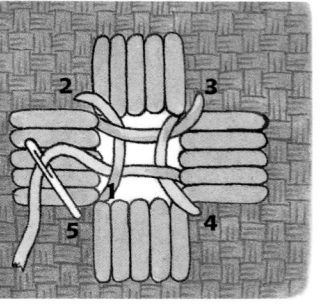

The sides of the square may be bordered by Kloster blocks, overcast bars, or woven bars.

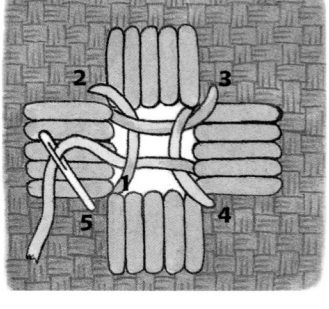

Bring the needle out from below the fabric at 1. Insert the needle at 2 and bring it out from below the fabric, inside the loop of thread. Repeat at 3 and at 4. Pass the needle under the first loop made, as shown, and insert it at 5 through the fabric. The needle may then be passed along the back of the stitches to the position required for the next stitch.

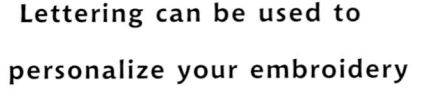

ALPHABETS

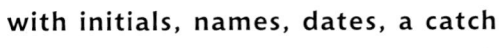

Lettering can be used to personalize your embroidery with initials, names, dates, a catch phrase, a quotation, or even a poem. The alphabets given here show some of the different styles you can choose from.

ALPHABET 1

This alphabet is worked entirely in cross stitch (page 26). The tall letters and capitals are ten squares high, so on 14-count fabric they will measure approximately ¾ inch (19mm), on 18-count fabric just over ½ inch (13mm).

ALPHABET 2

This alphabet is worked in backstitch (page 30) or Holbein stitch (page 31), with French knots (page 50) for the dots on small letters i and j. The tall letters require six squares in height, so on 14-count fabric they will measure just under ½ inch (13mm), and on 18-count fabric ⅓ inch (9mm).

TIPS

• To add lettering to a chart, copy the letters you require onto graph paper, then count the number of squares needed for the whole message. You can then center the lettering or position it where required.

• For a neat finish, do not pass the thread across the back from one letter to the next, but finish off the thread and begin the next letter anew.

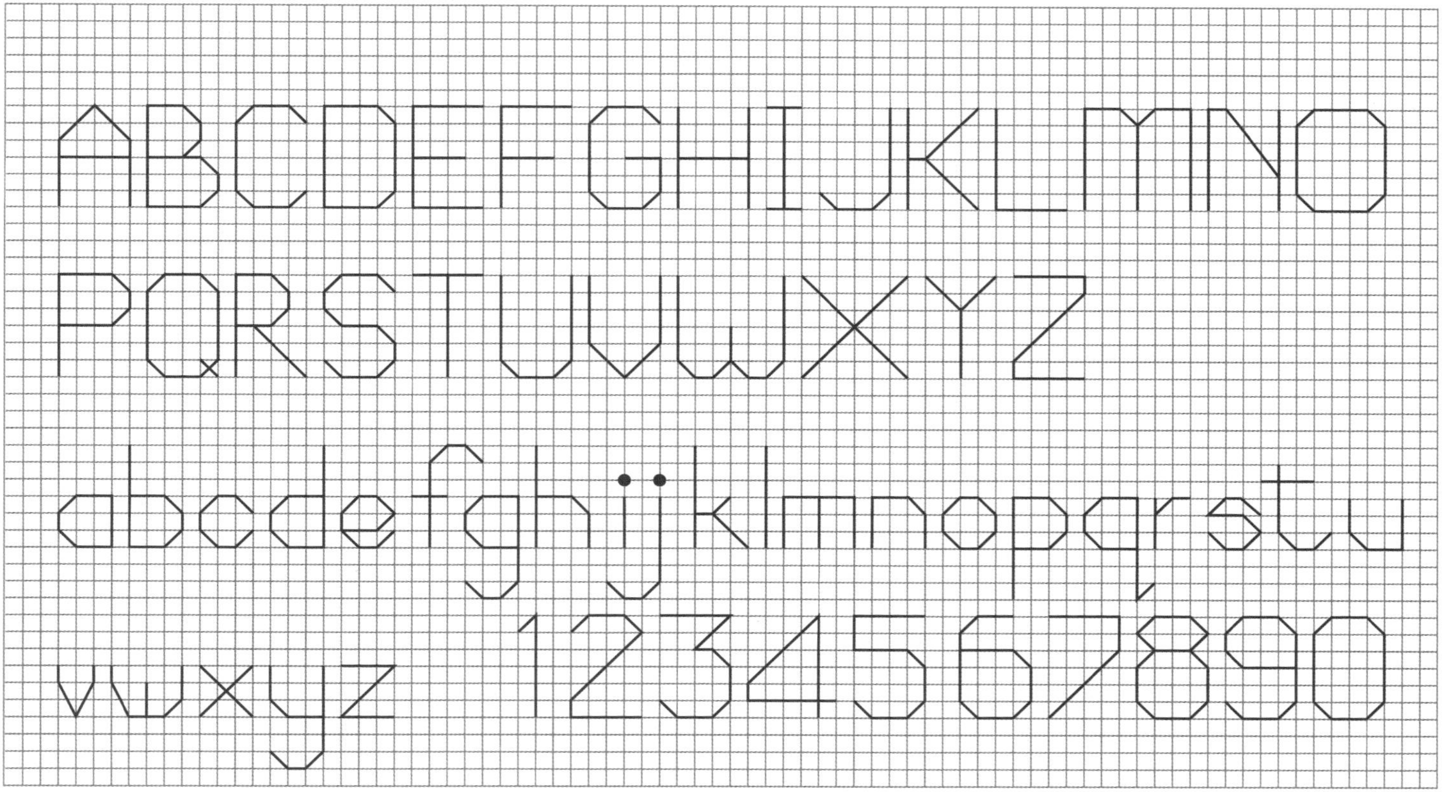

ABCDEFGHIJKLMNO
PQRSTUVWXYZ

abcdefghijklmnopqrstu
vwxyz 1234567890

ALPHABET 3

Here the letters are worked in backstitch (page 30) or Holbein stitch (page 31), with cross stitch (page 26) and quarter cross stitch (page 28) filling the wider parts. As a variation, you could omit the cross stitch and quarter cross stitch, working only the outlines.

The maximum height of letters is eight squares, so measuring just over ½ inch (13mm) on 14-count fabric and just under ½ inch (13mm) on 18-count fabric.

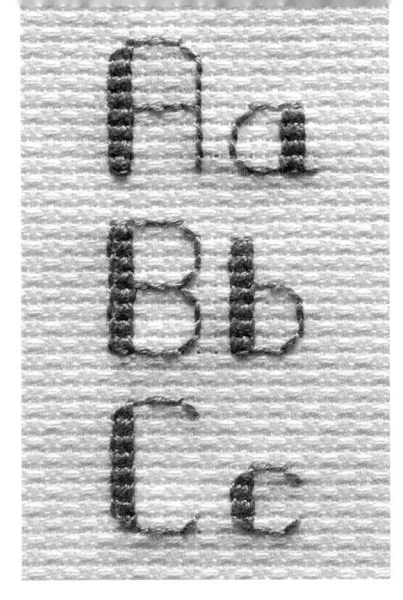

ALPHABET 4

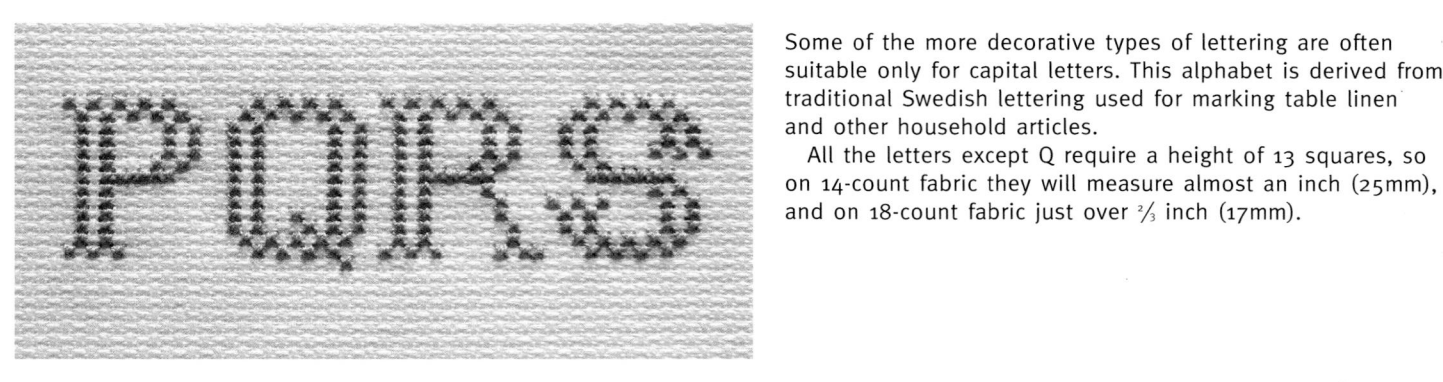

Some of the more decorative types of lettering are often suitable only for capital letters. This alphabet is derived from traditional Swedish lettering used for marking table linen and other household articles.

All the letters except Q require a height of 13 squares, so on 14-count fabric they will measure almost an inch (25mm), and on 18-count fabric just over ⅔ inch (17mm).

Other Useful Stitches

The stitches in this group may be used to add details, outlines, or borders to various types of counted thread embroidery.

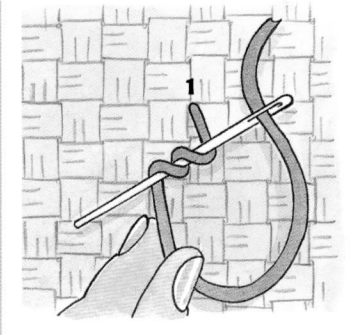

FRENCH KNOTS

A single French knot is often used to represent an eye in a pictorial design. Other uses include dots on letters such as i or j, or full stops. Groups of French knots can be used to represent tiny flowers. All or part of any charted design may be interpreted using French knots in different colors, for a boldly textured effect.

Bring the needle up at 1 and wind the thread twice around the needle tip as shown.

Hold the thread taut with your finger and thumb and insert the needle a small distance away at 2. Keep the thread taut as you pull the needle through to the back of the work. The French knot will form at 2.

TIPS

- *To make French knots larger, don't wind the thread more than twice around the needle tip, as this makes it difficult to form the knots smoothly. Instead, change to a heavier thread (or more strands, if using stranded cotton).*
- *If you want the knot to be at the center of an Aida square, bring the needle up through a hole as shown and insert it at the center of the square.*
- *If you want the knot to be over a hole, bring the needle up at the center of a square and insert it through the hole. If the knot disappears through the hole, change to heavier thread.*
- *If working on evenweave, points 1 and 2 are normally spaced one thread or intersection apart.*

SATIN STITCH

When worked correctly, satin stitch covers the fabric completely, with no fabric showing between the stitches, so a relatively heavy thread is often required. Small areas of satin stitch are often used in blackwork for solid details. Blocks of satin stitch called Kloster blocks (page 42) are the basis of Hardanger work.

In counted thread embroidery, satin stitches are normally worked vertically, horizontally, or diagonally.

To work satin stitch vertically

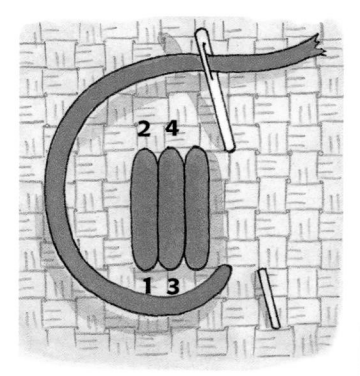

Begin at left. Bring the needle up at 1 and insert it at 2, then bring it up at 3 and insert it at 4. Repeat to the right.

To work satin stitch diagonally

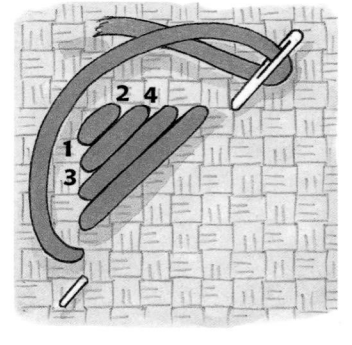

Begin at top left. Bring the needle up at 1 and insert it at 2, then up at 3 and down at 4. Repeat downward and to the right.

▼ SEA VIEW
Betty Barnden
11½ x 8 in (300 x 200mm)
Satin stitch using tapestry wools on canvas
Satin stitches of varying lengths (often called long stitch) may be used to complete designs. This technique is also useful for filling background areas around a cross stitch motif.

ALGERIAN EYE STITCH

This decorative stitch forms a star shape, and the central hole may be emphasized by pulling the stitches firmly to open it up. Algerian eye stitch may be used as a single detail, or repeated in a border pattern or a blackwork filling (pages 36–41).

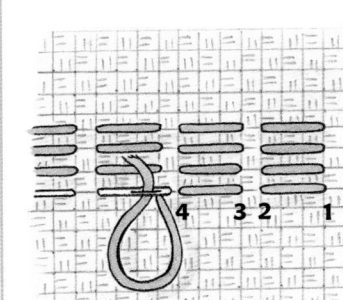

Bring the needle up at 1 and insert it at 2 (the center of the eye). Bring the needle up at 3 and insert it again at 2. Bring it up at 4, 5, 6, 7, 8, and 9 in turn, always inserting it at 2.

When working a repeating pattern, the eight stitches of each unit should always be worked in exactly the same order to maintain an even appearance.

DARNING STITCH AND VARIATIONS

This simple stitch can be used in several ways. Lines of darning can be used for blackwork fillings (pages 36–41). One or more lines of darning stitches may be decorated with another thread, for decorative border patterns.

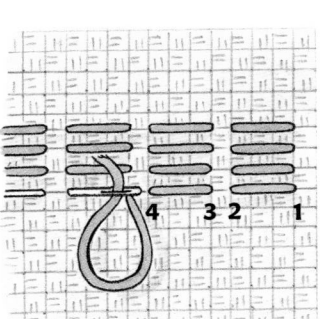

Work from right to left. Bring the needle up at 1 and insert it at 2, then bring it up at 3 and insert it at 4. Repeat to the left.

To work several lines, turn the work at the beginning of each line and stitch again from right to left.

The length of the stitches and the intervals between them may be varied as desired, but the stitches on the surface are normally longer than the spaces between.

Stitches may be arranged to form simple patterns as shown in the photograph and on pages 37 and 40.

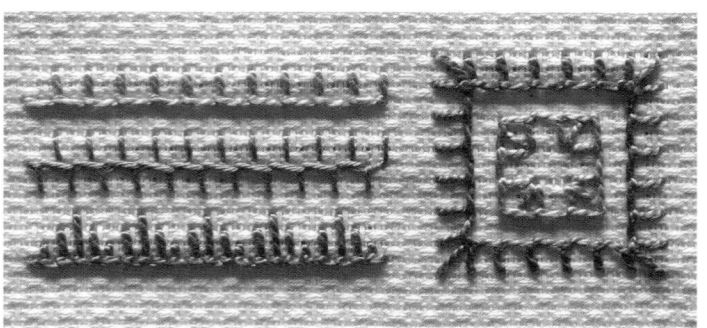

Laced darning

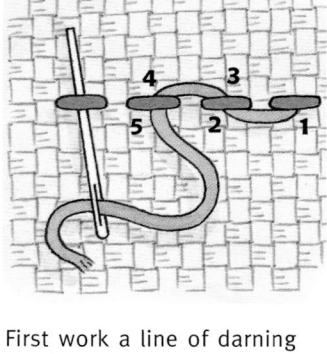

First work a line of darning stitches. Bring another thread in a blunt needle up through the fabric at 1. Without piercing the fabric, pass the needle upward from 2 to 3 under the second darning stitch, then downward from 4 to 5 under the third darning stitch. Repeat to the left. End by inserting the needle through the fabric at the center top or bottom of the last stitch.

Several lines of parallel darning stitches may be laced together in this way as shown in the photograph on the opposite page.

Whipped darning

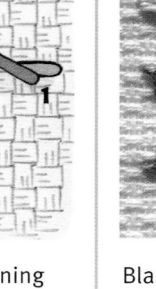

First work a line of darning stitches. Bring another thread in a blunt needle up through the fabric at 1, then pass the needle from 2 to 3 underneath the next darning stitch, without piercing the fabric. Repeat to the left. End by inserting the needle through the fabric at the center top of the last stitch.

BLANKET STITCH

Blanket stitch may be used in a single line as a decorative detail, or several lines of various proportions may be combined to form border patterns. At the corners of a border the stitches may be fanned out in radiating lines.

Work from left to right, when a solid line will form at the lower edge. Bring the needle up at 1 and insert it at 2, then bring it up again at 3 inside the looped thread as shown. Pull through. Insert the needle at 4 to begin the next repeat to the right.

At the end of a line of blanket stitch, hold down the last loop with a tiny stitch as shown.

As shown in the photograph, two lines of blanket stitch may be worked back to back to form a spiky line, or the lengths of the stitches may be varied in steps. Borders may be worked with the solid line to the inside or outside, when different effects will form at the corners.

STEM STITCH

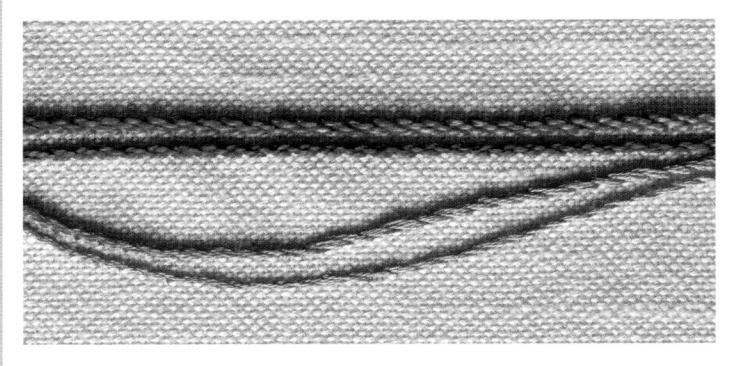

Stem stitch is often used for outlines. When worked through the holes of Aida or evenweave fabric, lines may be horizontal, vertical, or sloping, but should always be straight.

Stem stitch is sometimes worked without counting threads as an outline for blackwork, when a sharp needle should be used, and lines may then be curved as required.

CHAIN STITCH

This stitch may be used in straight lines (horizontal, vertical, or diagonal), often as part of a border design.

It may also be worked without counting threads as an outline for blackwork, and then may be curved.

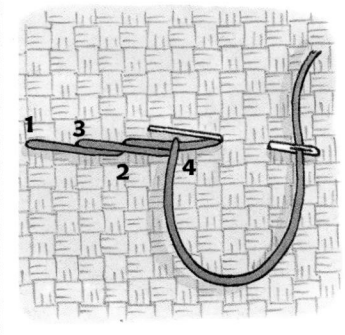

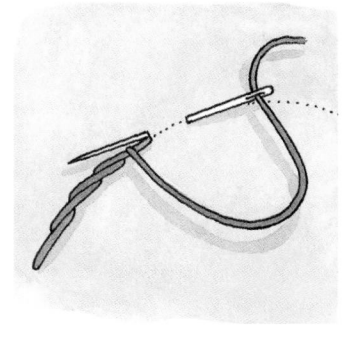

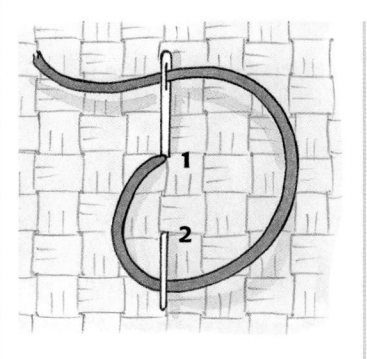

Work from left to right. Bring needle up at 1 and insert it at 2. Bring it out at 3, above the previous stitch, and insert it at 4. Bring it up again at 2, above the previous stitch, to begin the next repeat to the right.

The length of the stitches may be varied as desired but should always be equal.

When working without counting threads, use a sharp needle. It is helpful to mark the required line with a series of evenly spaced dots. For tight curves use small stitches.

Work from top to bottom. Bring the needle up at 1. Form a loop with the thread as shown, insert the needle again at 1, and bring it up at 2, inside the loop. Pull through gently.

Repeat downward, always inserting the needle inside the previous loop.

BASIC COUCHING

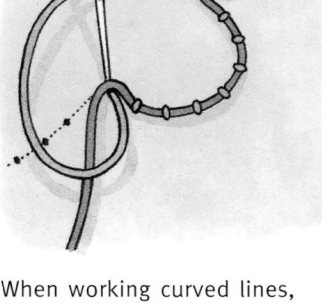

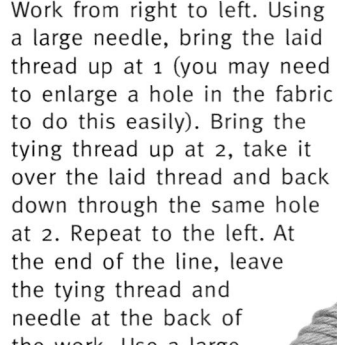

At the end of the line, hold down the last loop with a tiny stitch as shown.

When working without counting threads, use a sharp needle. It is helpful to mark the required line with a series of evenly spaced dots.

Decorative threads that are too heavy to be stitched through the fabric may be added using this technique. This stitch is also used as an outline for blackwork, when lines may be curved without counting the threads.

The heavy thread to be couched is called the "laid thread" (it lies on the fabric surface), and the second, finer thread is called the "tying thread" or "couching thread."

Work from right to left. Using a large needle, bring the laid thread up at 1 (you may need to enlarge a hole in the fabric to do this easily). Bring the tying thread up at 2, take it over the laid thread and back down through the same hole at 2. Repeat to the left. At the end of the line, leave the tying thread and needle at the back of the work. Use a large needle to take the laid thread through to the back. Fold it back along the wrong side of the stitching line and use the tying thread to catch it down to the back of the stitches for about 1 inch (25mm) before trimming it off.

When working curved lines, use a sharp needle. Tying stitches are normally worked at right angles to the laid thread, but may also be worked at an angle if desired. They need not pass down through exactly the same hole; make them a little longer if you wish. It is helpful to mark the required line with a series of evenly spaced dots.

For sharp corners, space the tying stitches so that a stitch will be placed exactly at a corner to hold it precisely in place.

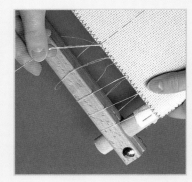

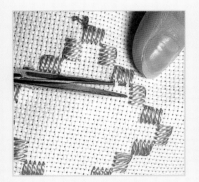

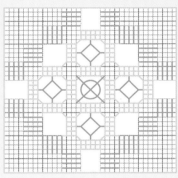

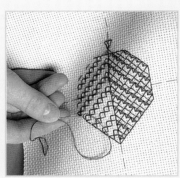

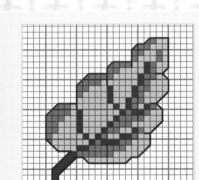

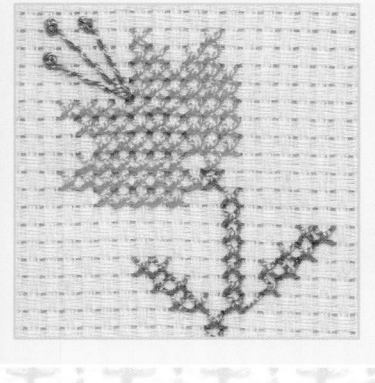

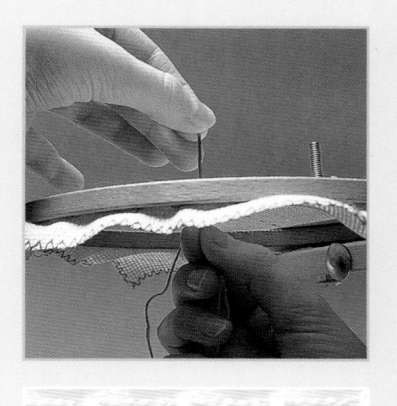

CHAPTER 3

Working Practice

Here you will find all the information you need to start stitching, beginning with general guidelines for preparing and choosing materials and equipment, starting and finishing a thread, and pressing or blocking your finished work.

Special techniques for cross stitch, Assisi work, blackwork, and Hardanger work are described in detail, together with various types of repeating patterns.

At the end of this section you will find ideas for adapting charted designs in different ways, using unusual materials and different stitches.

General Guidelines

Some techniques are common to all types of counted thread embroidery. In this section you will find the information you need to prepare your fabric or canvas correctly, choose suitable needles and thread, begin and end your stitching neatly, and press or block your finished piece.

PREPARING FABRIC AND CANVAS

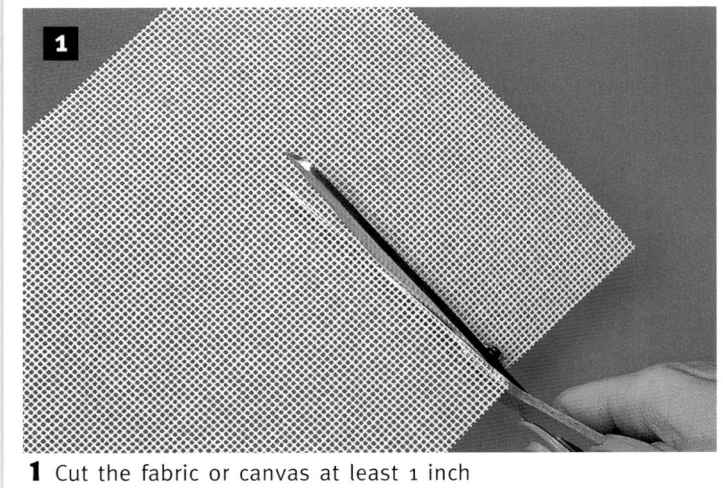

1 Cut the fabric or canvas at least 1 inch (25mm) larger all round than the size required. If you are stretching the material in a frame or hoop, you may need a larger size.

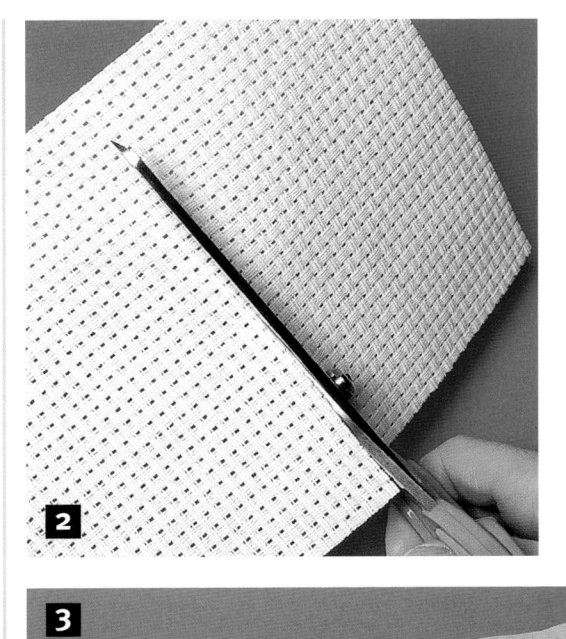

2 Always cut along straight rows of holes.

3 Raw edges of fabric and canvas will tend to fray as you stitch unless they are treated in some way. Frayed canvas edges are liable to catch on the embroidery thread and spoil it. There are several ways to prevent edges from fraying: one way is to oversew them with ordinary sewing thread.

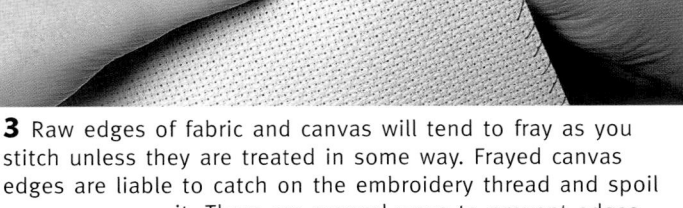

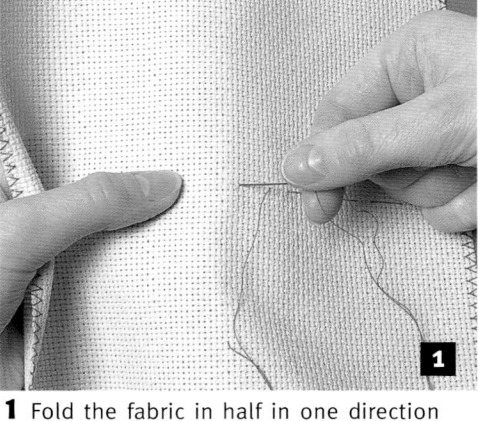

MARKING CENTER LINES

If you are working from a chart, you usually need to mark your fabric or canvas with center lines to match the chart, so that your stitching will be placed correctly.

1 Fold the fabric in half in one direction along a straight row of holes. Thread a small tapestry needle with ordinary sewing thread and work a line of basting along the fold, through the holes.

2 Repeat this operation in the other direction. Where the two threads cross marks the center of the fabric.

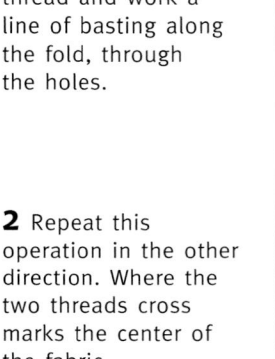

4 Alternatively stitch them with a zigzag stitch on a sewing machine.

5 Another option is to bind them with masking tape.

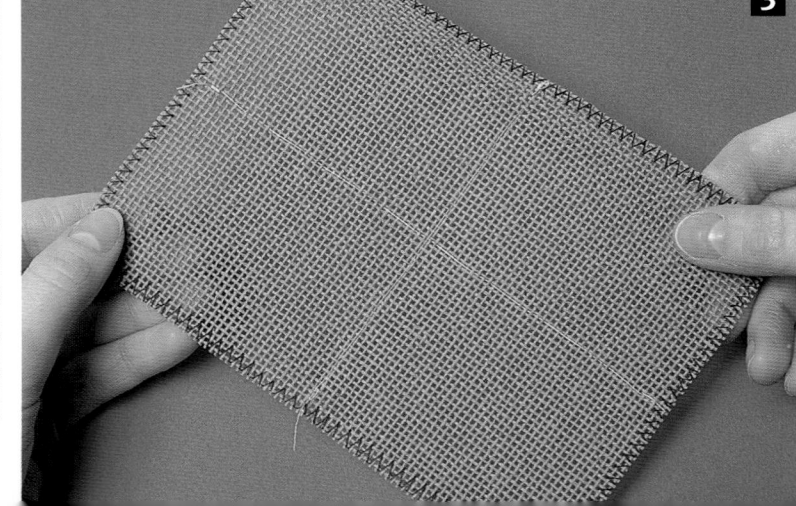

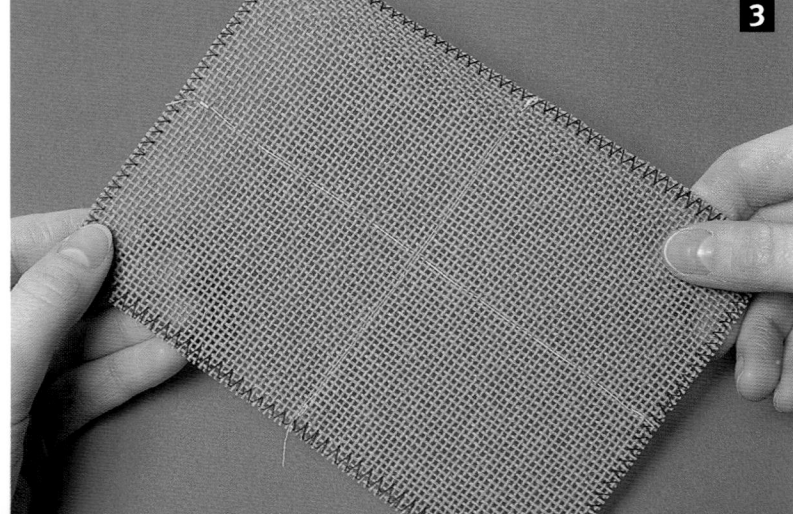

3 Center lines on canvas are marked in exactly the same way.

STRETCHING IN A HOOP OR FRAME

As a rule, a hoop (page 21) may be used for any design that fits inside it completely, so that the hoop will not need to be repositioned over completed stitching. A slate frame (page 22) is advisable for larger pieces of work: the width of the fabric must fit inside the frame, but excess length may be wound around the rollers. For stiff or heavy canvas a slate frame is more suitable than a hoop.

1 Iron the material flat and square. Set the iron to a suitable heat (medium-hot for cotton, hot for linen) to make sure all creases are removed. You can use gentle steam on Aida or evenweave fabric. Canvas rarely requires ironing, but if it does, do not use steam as the canvas will soften and stretch.

TIP *To protect delicate fabrics, use two or three layers of tissue paper at each side of the fabric. Position the hoop in the usual way then tear away the tissue at the center of the hoop, above and below the fabric, to reveal the working area.*

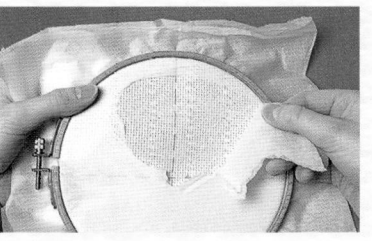

To stretch material in a hoop

2 First adjust the size of the outer ring to fit neatly over the inner ring. Lay the inner ring on a flat surface. Lay the fabric over the inner ring, then push the outer ring into position, loosening it slightly if necessary.

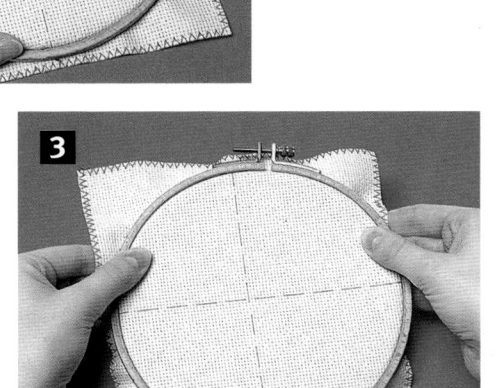

It should be a snug fit, stretching the fabric tightly. To avoid damaging the fabric, never tighten the outer ring with the fabric in position.

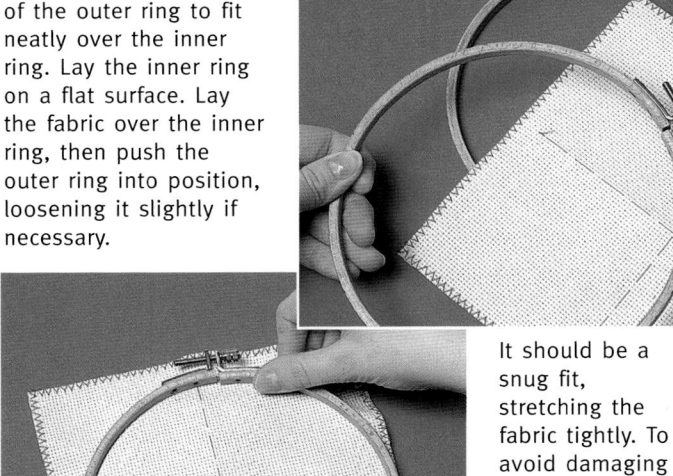

3 To release the fabric, simply push out the inner ring with both thumbs. It is a good idea to remove your work from the hoop whenever you put it aside for more than an hour or so, otherwise the mark left by the hoop may be difficult to press out.

To stretch material in a slate frame

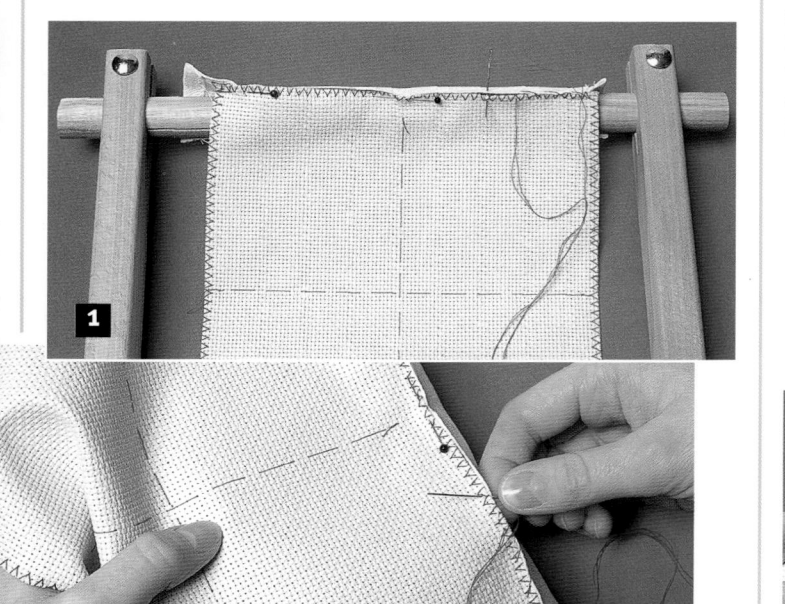

3 Wind the rollers so the working area is at the center, then tighten the fixings on the rollers to hold them in place.

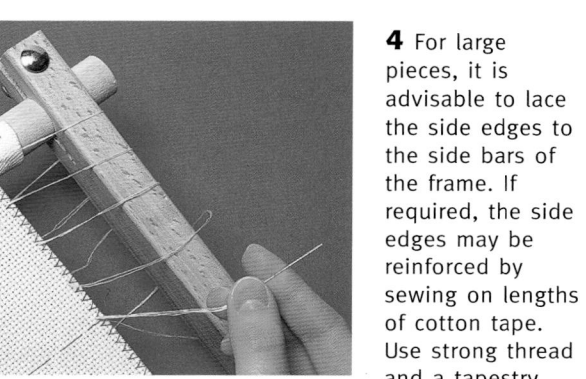

1 Mark the center of the webbing on each roller. Pin two opposite sides of the fabric or canvas to the webbing on the rollers, matching the center line to the centers of the rollers.

2 Then use a sharp needle and sewing thread to baste the fabric to the webbing. For large pieces, work from the center out to each side in turn.

4 For large pieces, it is advisable to lace the side edges to the side bars of the frame. If required, the side edges may be reinforced by sewing on lengths of cotton tape. Use strong thread and a tapestry needle. If the working area is longer than the frame, it is necessary to work one end of the design, undo the lacing, reposition the fabric by adjusting the rollers, then relace the sides in the new position.

The fabric is now ready to be stitched.

CHOOSING NEEDLE AND THREAD

For most counted thread work you need a tapestry needle (page 21) with a blunt tip to slip through the holes in the fabric. Choose the smallest size that easily takes your thread. As a guide:

stranded cotton	Pearl cotton	Persian yarn	needle size
1 or 2 strands	no. 12		26
3 strands	no. 8		24
4 strands		1 strand	22
6 strands	no. 5	2 strands	20
	no. 3	3 strands	18
		(= tapestry wool)	

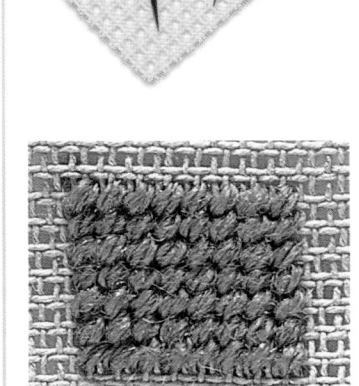

Choose the correct weight of thread to achieve good coverage on fabric, especially when working on canvas. Too thin a thread will make gappy, uneven stitches. Too heavy a thread will make a lumpy surface and be difficult to stitch. Try out small blocks of stitches in the margin of the work, or make a separate test piece using exactly the materials you intend to use.

Too thin thread   Too heavy thread

To thread the needle

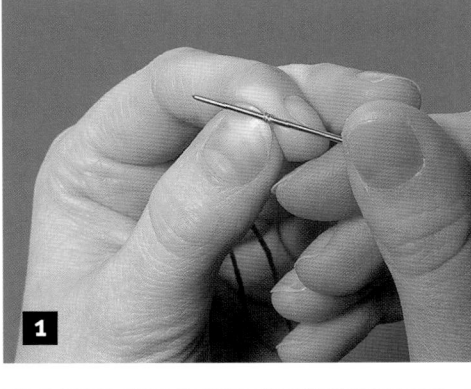

1 Never work with a thread longer than about 18 inches (450mm). Cut a length of the first color and divide the strands if necessary. Fold the smooth end over the needle and hold it tightly.

2 Withdraw the needle, then slip the loop of thread through the eye.

STARTING TO STITCH

Begin stitching at or near the center of the design, where the center lines cross, so that you will not miscount. Decide which area to stitch first.

Begin with an away waste knot

1 Knot the end of the thread, and pass the needle through the fabric, about 1 inch (25mm) away from where the first stitch will be, so that the thread on the back lies along the line of the first few stitches. Bring the needle up again as required for the first stitch.

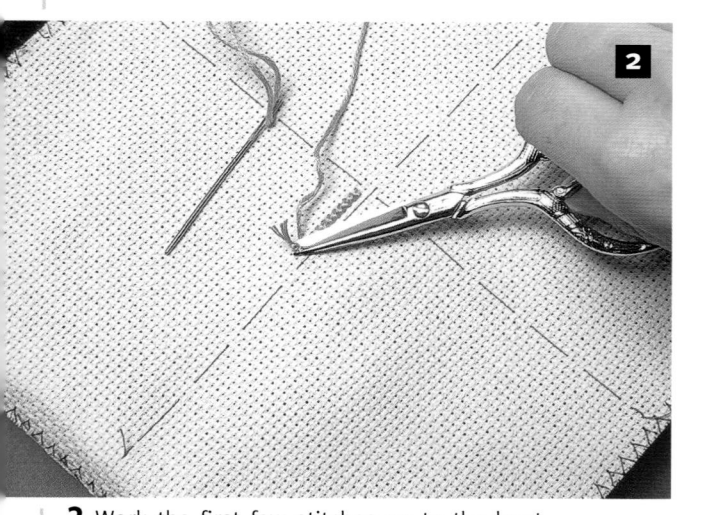

2 Work the first few stitches up to the knot, enclosing the thread end on the back, then snip off the knot.

To finish off a thread

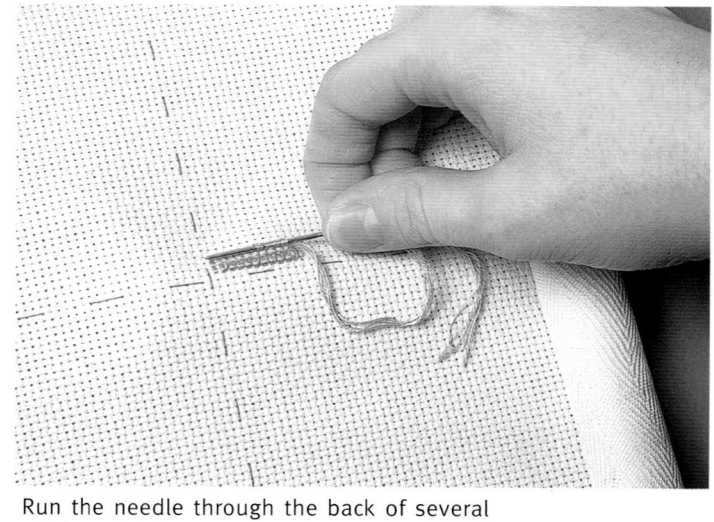

Run the needle through the back of several stitches (of the same color) on the wrong side of the work, then snip off the excess thread. Never leave tails of thread dangling at the back of the work as they will be caught up as you continue to stitch.

To begin another color

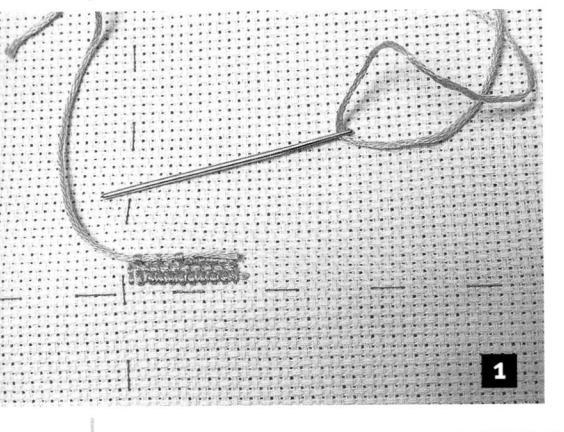

1 Once some stitching is complete, you can begin a new length of thread by running the needle through the back of several stitches up to the required position.

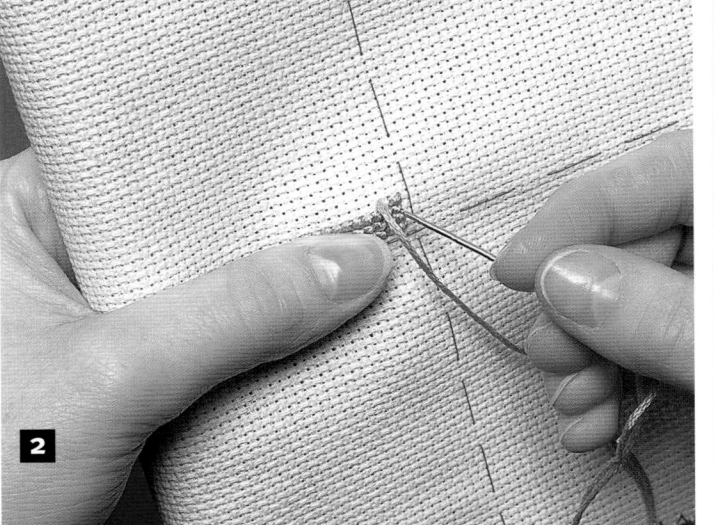

2 Bring the needle through to the right side, holding the enclosed end in place between your finger and thumb while you work the first couple of stitches.

To form stitches by the "stabbing" method

1 It is best to use this method when working in a hoop or frame. Run the needle tip across the back of the fabric to find the correct hole. Bring the needle up through the fabric and pull the thread through completely.

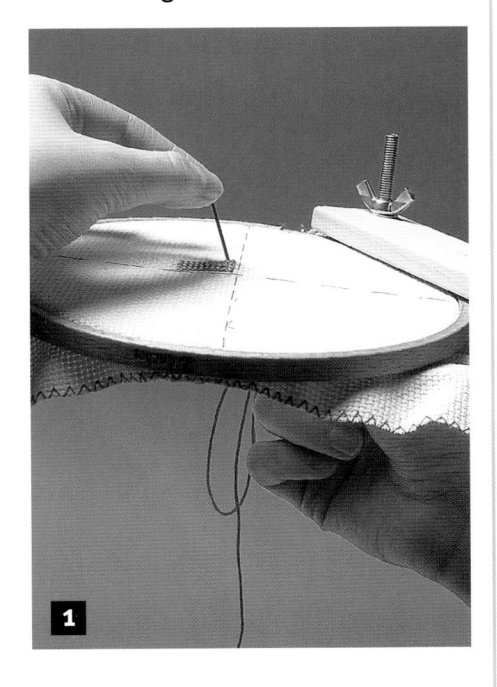

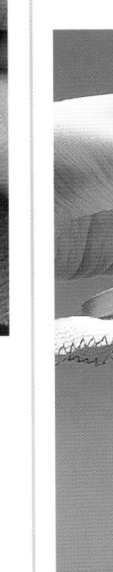
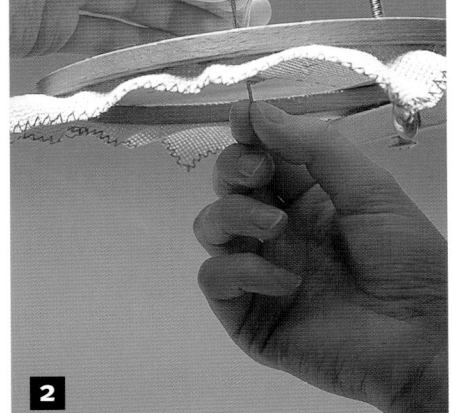

2 Then take the needle down where required and pull all the thread through to the back. The needle passes vertically through the fabric surface.

3 This method may seem slow, but it will give neat and accurate results. A hoop or frame mounted on a stand will leave both hands free, and with practice you can learn to use one hand below the work (the right hand, if you are right-handed) and the other above, and so stitch more quickly.

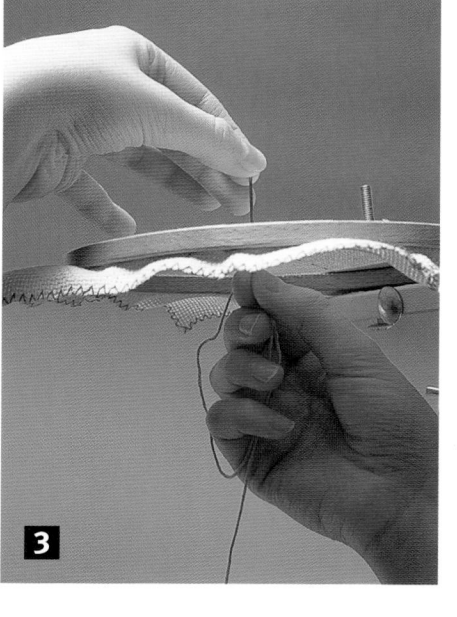

To form stitches by the "sewing" method

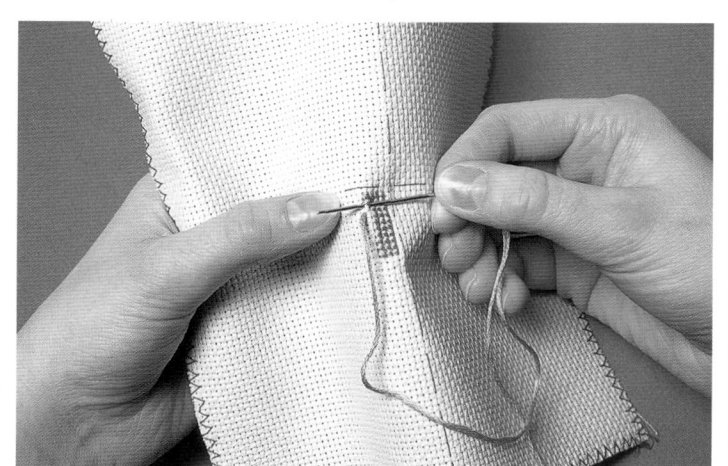

If you take the needle down and up again in one movement the stitches will tend to be less accurate and on canvas the thread will fray more quickly. However, for some purposes (such as stem stitch [page 54], used as a blackwork outline) this method gives a more fluid line.

TIPS
- *Try to keep the thread untwisted as you stitch: sometimes it is necessary to twirl the needle between your finger and thumb every few stitches to keep the thread flat and smooth.*
- *Try to plan the direction of working so that the needle is brought up through empty holes and inserted downward through holes that already contain thread. Sometimes this is impossible to arrange, so where you must bring a needle up through a "busy" hole, take care not to split the threads.*

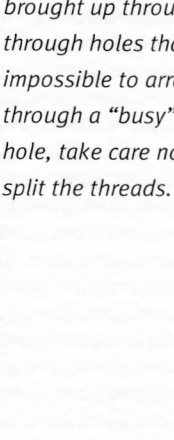

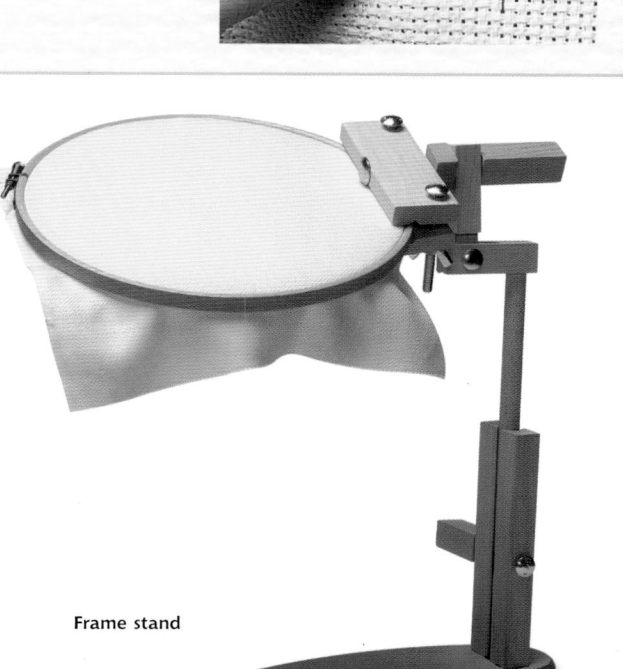

Frame stand

CORRECTING MISTAKES
To unpick just a few stitches

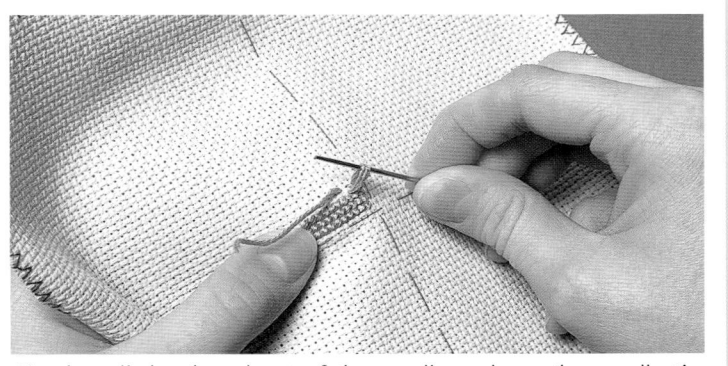

Simply pull the thread out of the needle and use the needle tip to unpick the stitches back to the last correct stitch. The thread will probably be frayed, so it is best to fasten it off and begin again with a new length.

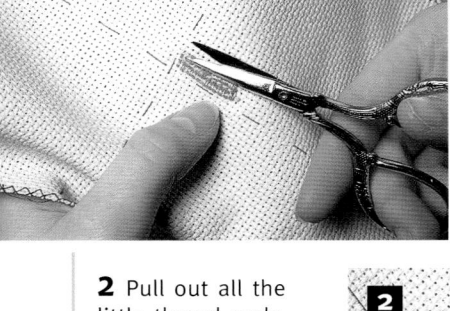

To unpick a lot of stitches
1 Use small scissors to snip carefully through most of the stitches at the back of the work. Unpick the last few with the needle as above so you are left with an end to run in.

2 Pull out all the little thread ends with tweezers.

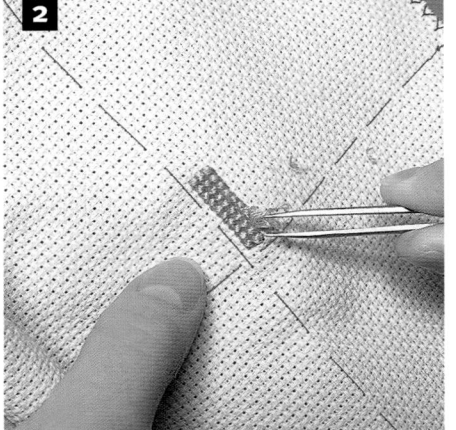

PRESSING AND BLOCKING

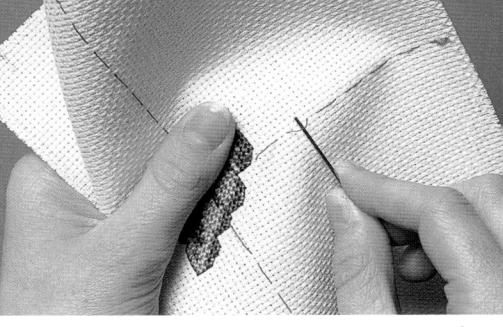

When the work is complete, remove the fabric from the hoop or frame and unpick the center basting lines.

Most types of embroidery require only pressing to finish them. Work on canvas will probably require blocking, especially when worked in a diagonal stitch such as tent stitch (page 29) or half cross stitch (page 28). If in doubt, press the work first; if it will not lie flat and square, block it.

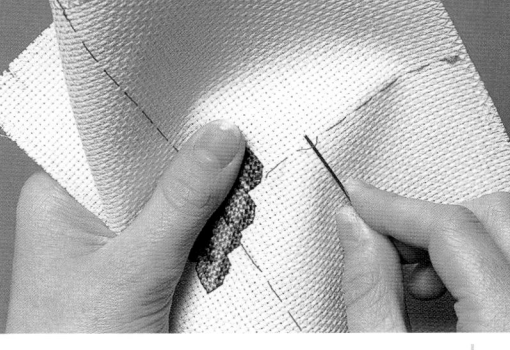

Pressing
Lay the work face down on a well-padded surface such as three or four layers of a folded towel. Heat the iron to a setting suitable for both fabric and threads: where several settings apply, choose the lowest. Gentle steam or a damp pressing cloth may be necessary. Iron the back of the work only.

TIP *Never split the thread of the center lines when stitching over them as this will make them difficult to remove.*

Blocking

For this you will need a blocking board (page 23) large enough to take the work flat, and a good supply of large-headed pins.

TIP *Seriously distorted pieces may require blocking two or three times until they will lie flat.*

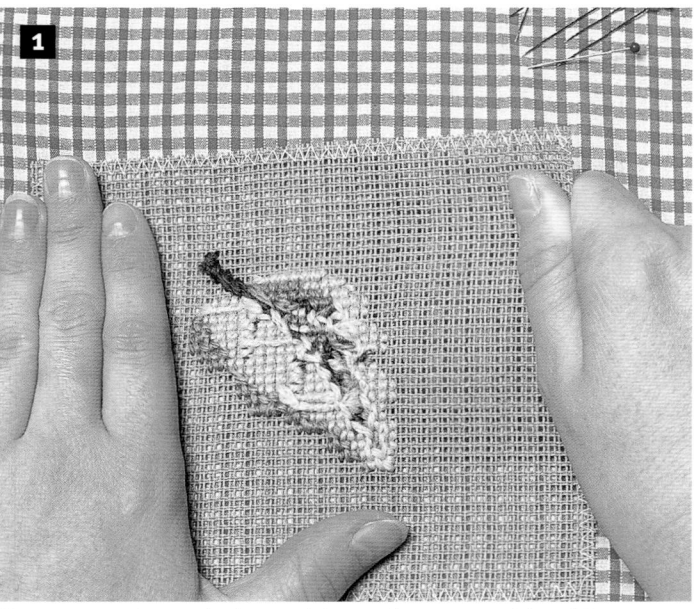

1 Dampen the work thoroughly on the wrong side with a sponge and lukewarm water, then lay it face down on the blocking board. Pat and pull it gently into shape. Use the pattern on the board as a guide.

2 Insert a pin at the center of each side, then insert more pins at intervals of about 1 inch (25mm) intervals, out toward the corners.

3 Leave the board flat until the work is completely dry.

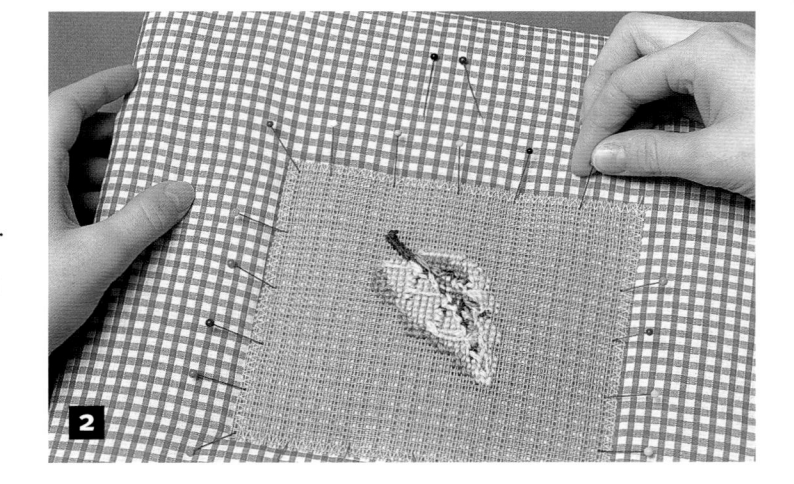

Cross Stitch from a Chart

This is the most popular type of counted thread embroidery, and most readers will have already tried it, but read this section anyway for helpful tips to make your stitching easier. Cross stitch from a chart is normally worked on Aida or evenweave fabric; on evenweave, crosses are usually worked over two threads in each direction. Depending on the fabric count, various weights of thread may be used. Stranded cottons are the most popular choice.

Follow the general guidelines on pages 58–67. It is not always necessary to use a hoop or frame, depending on the firmness of the fabric and how tightly you stitch. However, the result will be neater if the fabric is stretched, and will require less blocking or pressing.

READING THE CHART

A chart may be printed in color, or the different thread colors may be represented by symbols printed in the squares. Each colored square, or square with a symbol, represents one cross stitch worked on one square of Aida-type fabric, or one cross stitch worked over two threads of evenweave in each direction, or one cross stitch worked over one canvas intersection.

Chart printed in color

Key

□ Light green/blue
■ Mid green/blue
■ Dark green/blue
/ Holbein stitch in dark green/blue

Chart printed in symbols

Key

○ Light green/blue
+ Mid green/blue
■ Dark green/blue
/ Holbein stitch in dark green/blue

One cross stitch on Aida, on evenweave, and on canvas

Aida   Evenweave   Canvas

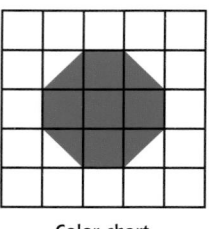
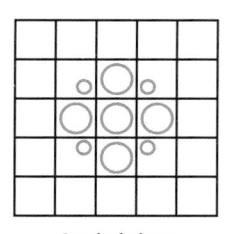
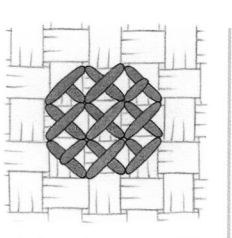

Color chart	Symbol chart	Stitches shown on Aida

Part stitches (three quarter and quarter crosses, page 28) are normally indicated by a square colored across one corner, or by a tiny symbol in the corner of a square.

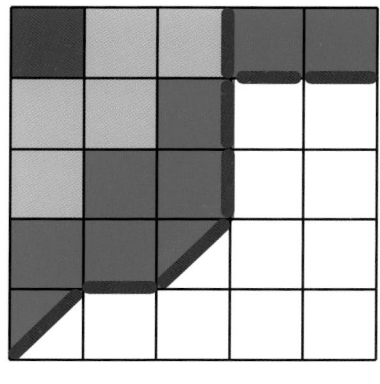

Straight stitch outlines and details (in Holbein stitch or backstitch) are shown as straight lines which may follow the sides of the squares or cross the squares diagonally. They may also be shown on top of a square in another color.

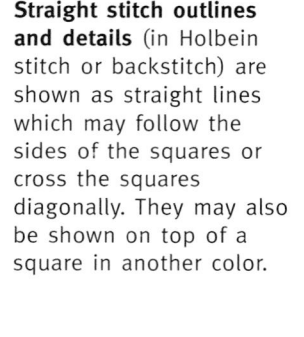

Detail from color chart showing straight stitch outline and detail

PREPARING THE THREADS

If you are working in several colors from a chart, identify each color on the chart key with the corresponding shade of thread. To avoid confusion, tape a small length of each color to the chart key.

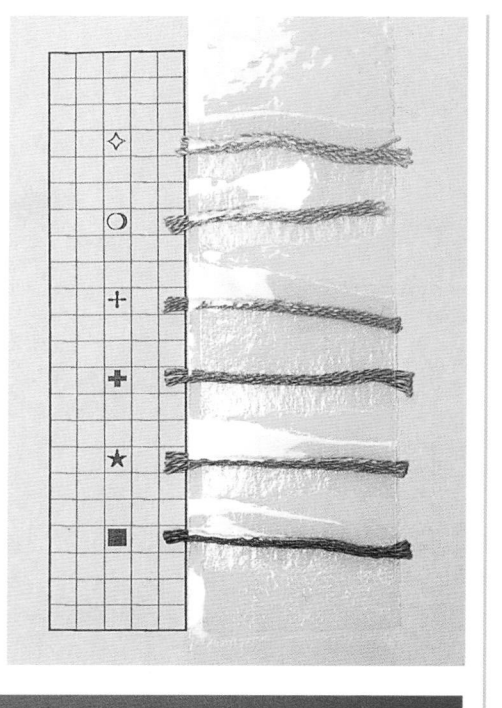

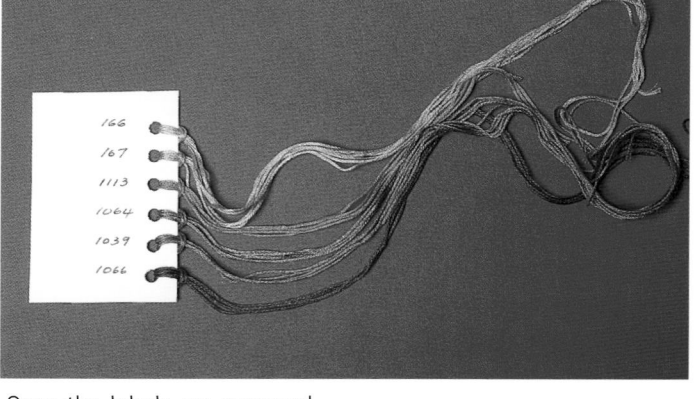

Once the labels are removed from skeins of thread the colors can be difficult to identify. Make a thread holder: punch holes in a piece of card, attach your threads, and label each one with the correct shade number.

STITCHING THE DESIGN

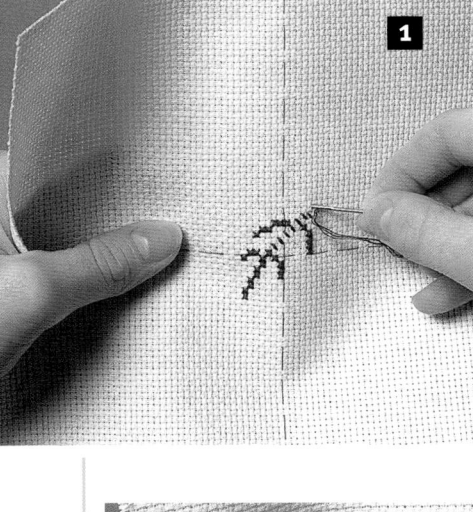

1 It is usually easier to work small intricate details before filling in the area around them. This example was begun near the center by working the leaf veins down to the end, then returning to the center and working the veins up to the top of the stalk. Count these first stitches very carefully and check their position relative to the center lines.

3 Work all the cross stitch, then add any outlines and details in backstitch (page 30) or Holbein stitch (page 31). Such straight stitches are usually worked in a finer thread, or with fewer strands. Some are worked along the edges of the squares and some diagonally across squares. They may also be worked on top of cross stitches in another color.

When all the stitching is complete, remove the work from the frame or hoop, and press or block it (pages 66–67).

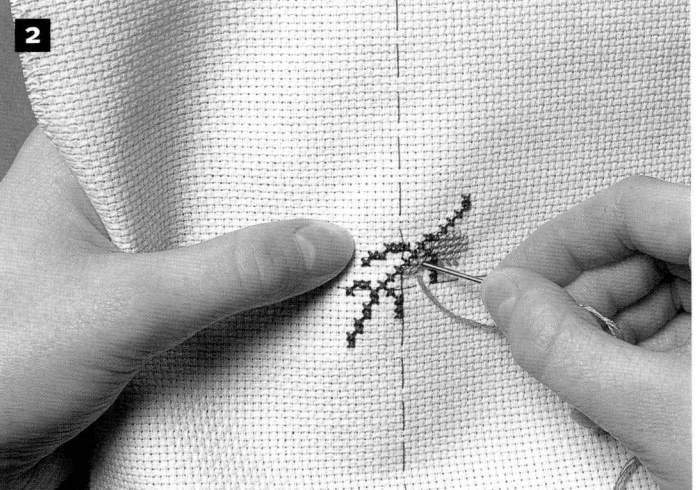

2 Work the adjacent areas of color as required. Work any part stitches (page 71) as they occur. The part stitches in this design are all worked as quarter cross stitches, because the outline stitches added later will complete the shape.

Try to work each new area touching a previous one so you will not miscount.

TIPS

- *Make sure all the top threads of the crosses lie in the same direction (page 26). As a reminder, sew a large diagonal stitch in one corner of the fabric, to represent the direction of the top thread.*

- *Cross stitch may be worked in exactly the same way on canvas, using a suitable thread such as tapestry wool.*

COLOR BLENDING

Subtle color effects may be introduced by blending colors in one of two ways. If the colors used are close in shade and tone, the effect will be to make a third color midway between the two. If the colors used are more contrasting, interesting textures can be achieved.

Part stitching

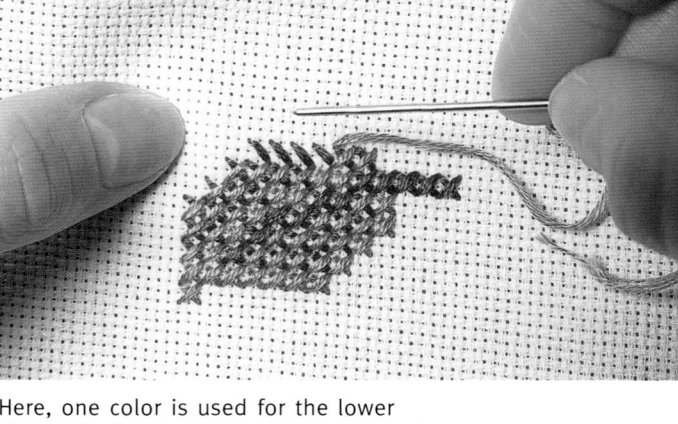

Here, one color is used for the lower diagonal of each cross stitch, and another color for the top diagonal. This method is useful when working with threads unsuitable for stranding, and quick to work when stitching crosses in rows (page 29). The effect is not quite such a close blend as at left, but the added texture can be an advantage, adding depth to the surface.

Combining threads

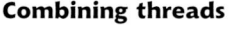

When working with stranded threads, you can combine single strands of two (or more) different colors together in the needle. Here the leaf shape is worked in three areas: blue, blue with green, and green. The blue and green threads give the effect of an intermediate shade between the two.

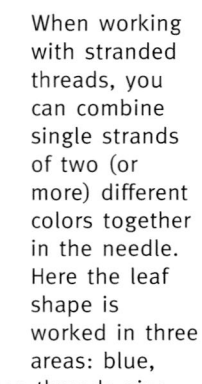

Designs Printed on Fabric and Canvas

Designs for cross stitch, tent stitch, and half cross stitch are widely available as preprinted fabrics or canvases, where each printed color corresponds to a different shade of thread. You can also paint your own designs onto canvas (page 100), or transfer photographs and other images onto fabric or canvas (pages 100–101).

It is not always necessary to use a hoop or frame, especially when working in cross stitch on firm canvas. However, it is best to use a frame or hoop for designs in tent stitch or half cross stitch, to avoid pulling the material out of shape.

Designs on Aida fabric or evenweave are normally worked in stranded cottons and similar threads, and designs on canvas in stranded Persian wool or tapestry wool.

Follow the general guidelines on pages 58–67. Center lines are not required.

IDENTIFYING THE THREADS

The color key is usually printed on the margin of the canvas or fabric. Attach a small piece of each color to the key to avoid confusion.

STITCHING THE DESIGN

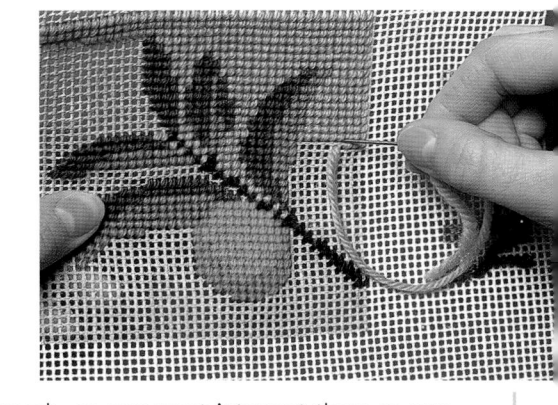

You can work the different areas of color in any order you please, but it is a good idea to begin with the main parts or foreground and fill in the background last. The edges of the printed color areas may not exactly correspond with the fabric squares or canvas mesh, so you must interpret them as you think best. You may wish to smooth the outline of a shape or slightly alter a sloping line to make even steps.

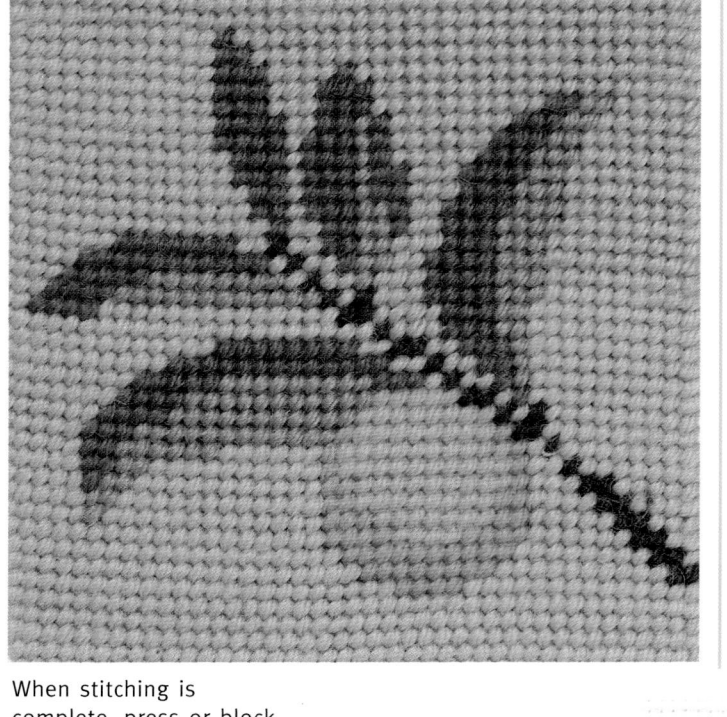

When stitching is complete, press or block the work (pages 66–67). This orange branch was worked in tent stitch using tapestry wool on a 10-gauge canvas.

Some designs printed on fabric need not always be completely stitched; the printing forms a background, and the important elements are emphasized with stitching.

▶ The floral spray was worked in cross stitch using stranded cottons on 14-count Aida fabric.

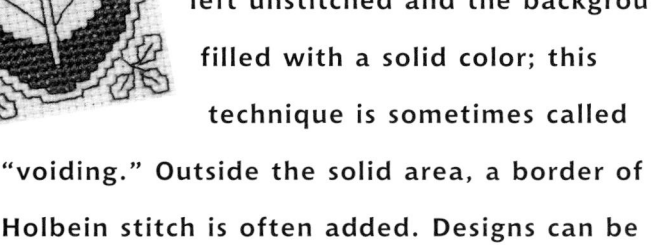

Assisi Work

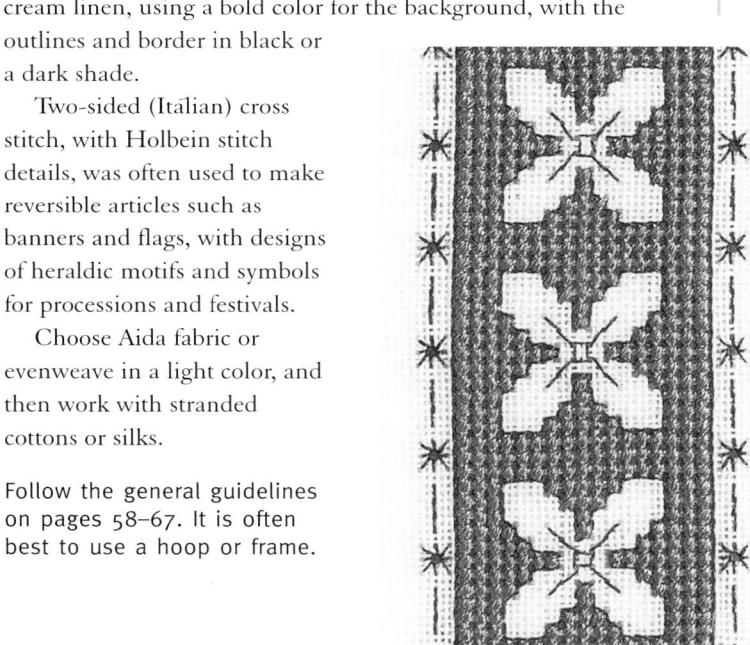

Assisi work is a particular type of cross stitch where the main motif is left unstitched and the background filled with a solid color; this technique is sometimes called "voiding." Outside the solid area, a border of Holbein stitch is often added. Designs can be repeated to form a ribbon of color interspersed with motifs.

This work first developed in the town of Assisi, Italy, at the time of the Renaissance. Traditionally, the work was stitched on white or cream linen, using a bold color for the background, with the outlines and border in black or a dark shade.

Two-sided (Italian) cross stitch, with Holbein stitch details, was often used to make reversible articles such as banners and flags, with designs of heraldic motifs and symbols for processions and festivals.

Choose Aida fabric or evenweave in a light color, and then work with stranded cottons or silks.

Follow the general guidelines on pages 58–67. It is often best to use a hoop or frame.

STITCHING THE DESIGN

Chart

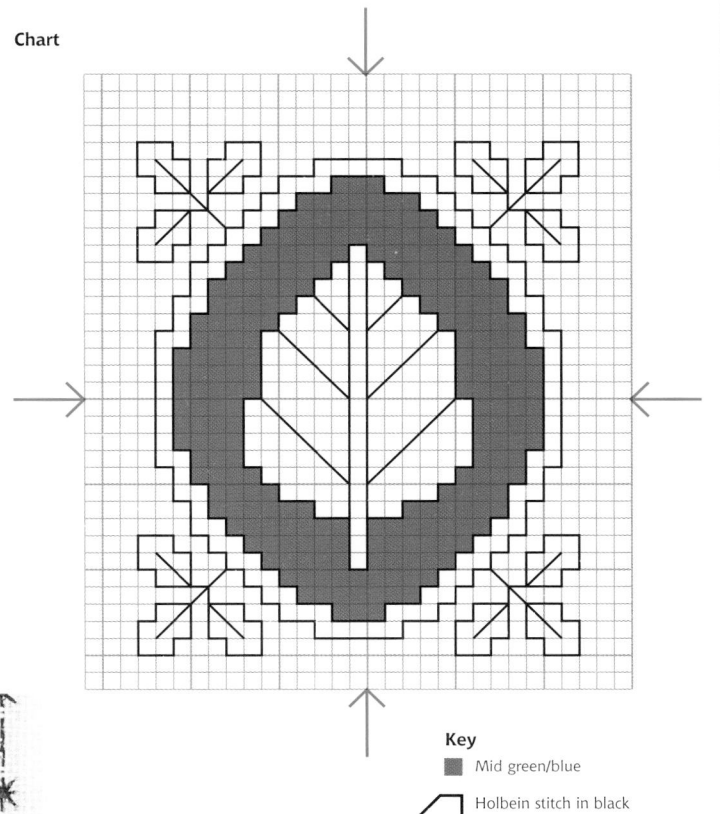

Key

■ Mid green/blue

⌐ Holbein stitch in black

◄ A simple Assisi work flower motif, repeated in a band. The outer borders include Algerian eye stitch (page 52).

1 Work the outline of the central motif, using Holbein stitch (page 31) and a fine thread (such as one or two strands of stranded cotton) in a dark color. Add any details within this outline.

4 When stitching is complete, press or block the work as on pages 66–67.

2 Fill in the background area with cross stitch, using a heavier thread in a bright color. It is often convenient to work these cross stitches in lines.

3 Outline the background shape with Holbein stitch and add the border, if any.

Waste Canvas Technique

This technique may be used to work designs in cross stitch and other stitches (such as blackwork patterns) onto plain fabric, that is, fabric that is neither Aida nor evenweave. Special waste canvas is used (see page 20) as a guide to placing the stitches, and removed after the stitching is complete.

Follow the general guidelines on pages 58–67.

Chart

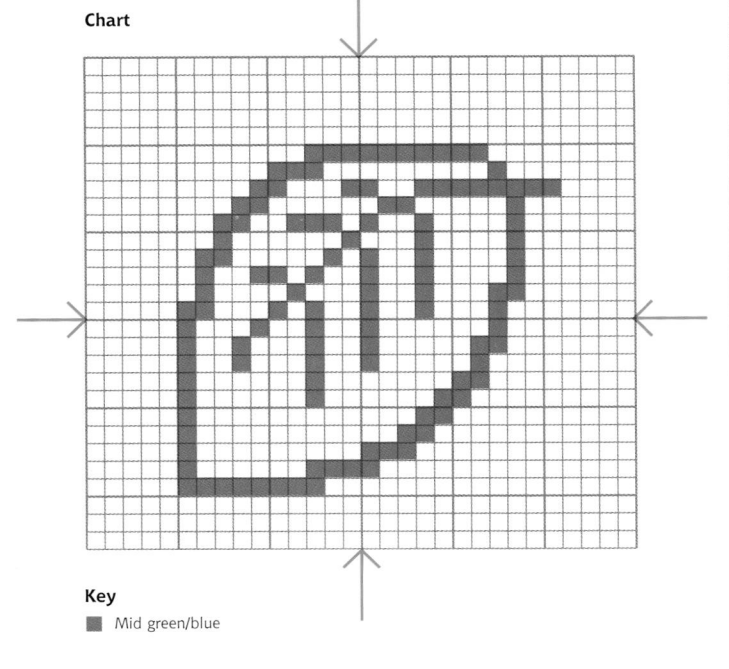

Key
■ Mid green/blue

PREPARING THE WASTE CANVAS

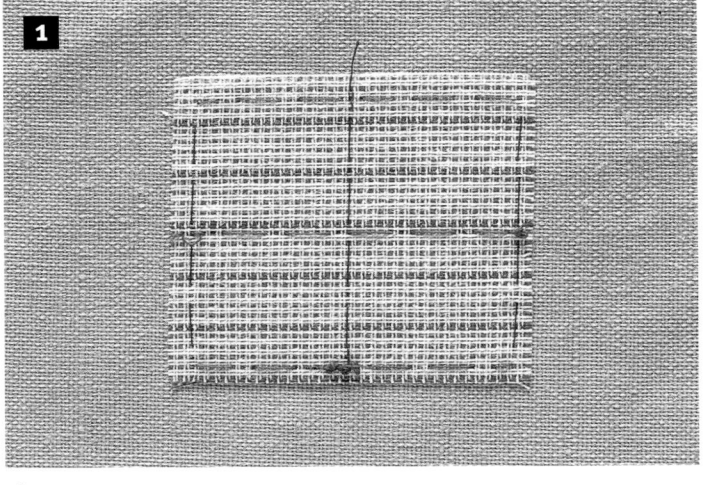

1

1 Count the squares on the charted design, and cut a rectangle of waste canvas three or four squares larger all round. Mark the center lines as on page 59 and pin the waste canvas to the fabric where required, matching the threads of the canvas to the grain of the fabric. Baste all round the edge.

TIP *For large motifs or slippery fabrics, baste the waste canvas with a grid of squares to hold it perfectly flat.*

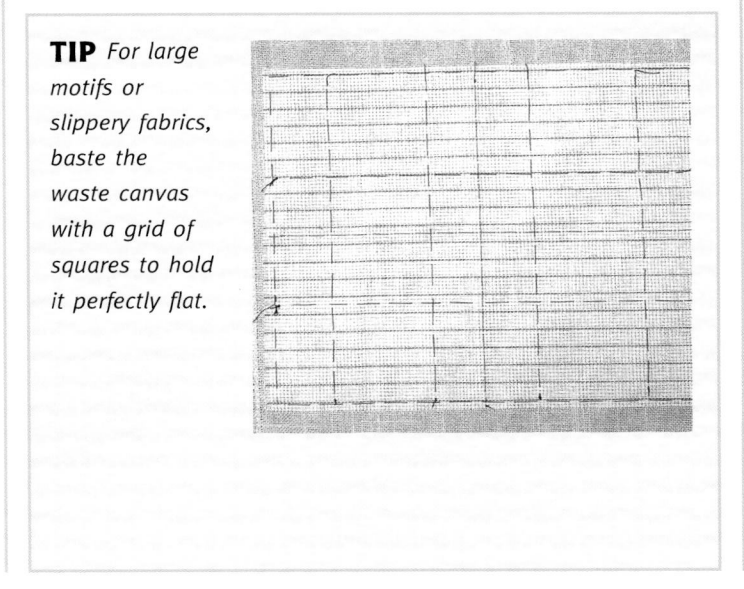

STITCHING THE DESIGN

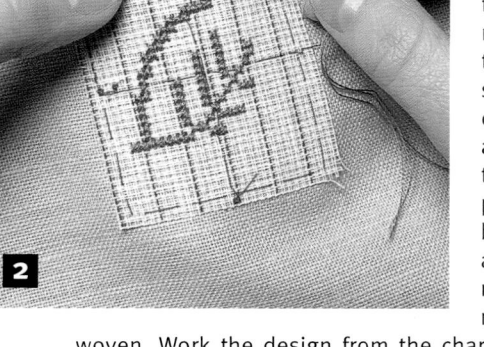

2 You may need to use a sharp needle to pierce the plain fabric. If so, take great care not to split any of the canvas threads. Some plain fabrics may be stitched with a small tapestry needle if they are not too closely woven. Work the design from the chart as required, stitching through the holes in the waste canvas.

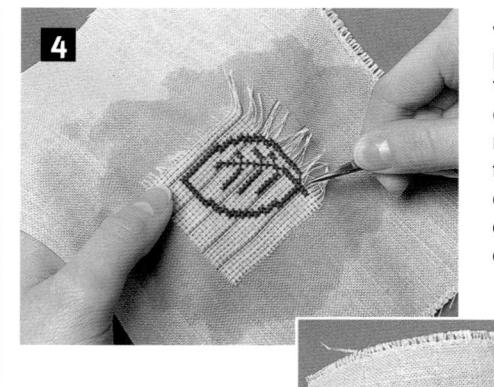

4 Use tweezers to pull the canvas threads gently out one by one, removing all the threads in one direction, then the other. Leave flat to dry before pressing.

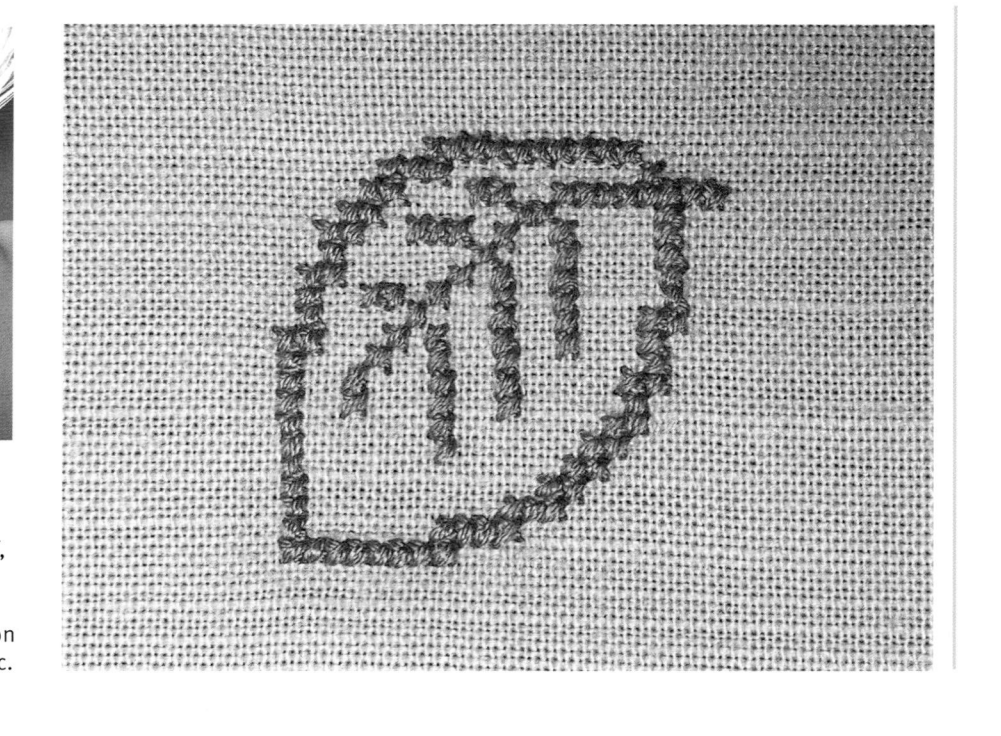

REMOVING THE WASTE CANVAS

3 When the stitching is complete, remove all basting. Dampen the canvas with a sponge and cold water to dissolve the stiffening.

▶ The leaf motif, worked in cross stitch using stranded cotton on plain cotton fabric.

Blackwork

The technique of blackwork is thought to have developed in Spain during the centuries of Moorish rule; it became popular across Europe during the sixteenth century. Different variations developed in different countries, used for clothing such as caps, collars, and sleeves as well as pillow covers and other bed linen. Blackwork was originally worked on natural white linen in black thread, or occasionally in red thread. Later designs were sometimes embellished with gold thread or sequins (known as "owes"), or worn beneath a layer of very fine linen gauze.

Blackwork is usually worked on Aida or evenweave fabric, using stranded cotton or silk, or a single firm thread such as Pearl cotton or coton à broder. Black thread on white or cream fabric is the traditional choice, but any strong contrast may be used: white thread on a dark fabric, or any strong color on a pale background.

For straight stitch patterns, use Holbein stitch (page 31) or backstitch (page 30). Holbein stitch is preferable unless the fabric is heavy enough to completely obscure any thread passing across the back of the work. Other suitable stitches include cross stitch (page 26), upright cross stitch (page 35), pattern darning (page 37), and Algerian eye stitch (page 52).

For small solid details, use satin stitch (page 51); details such as eyes may be represented by French knots (page 50), small beads, or sequins.

There are two types of blackwork design:

Charted designs
The fabric squares or threads are counted from a chart in the same way as for cross stitch (pages 68–69).

Free designs
The design outlines are drawn or transferred onto the fabric, then the different areas are filled with blackwork patterns. Each area may then be outlined with a non-counted stitch such as chain stitch (page 54), stem stitch (page 54), or couched lines (page 55). This method is often used for designs based on natural forms such as flowers and leaves.

Small repeating patterns (mostly made up of straight stitches) are used to fill different areas of a blackwork design, and the differing densities of these patterns create the tonal effect. Such patterns are shown on pages 36–41; you can create your own with pencil and graph paper.

◀ **CHESSBOARD**
Jill Cater Nixon for Coats Crafts
20 x 20 in (50 x 50 cm)
Blackwork using stranded cotton and metallic braid on evenweave fabric.
Small, repeating patterns are used to create the board for this traditional game.

STITCHING CHARTED DESIGNS

Chart

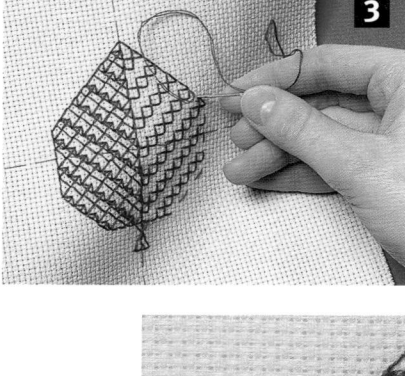

Key
Holbein stitch in black

Follow the general guidelines on pages 58–67.

1 Begin at or near the center point by working one line of pattern across one area. Fill the area by working down to the bottom, then return to the center and work up to the top of the area. Try to establish a logical working order for each pattern, always working the individual stitches of each repeating unit in the same order, to keep the appearance as regular as possible. Work the patterns in horizontal, vertical, or diagonal rows, as appropriate. Part stitches may be required at the edges of a shape.

2 Work all the pattern areas in this way. To carry the thread across the wrong side to begin another area, run it along the back of previous stitching; do not make long stitches on the wrong side across areas that are lightly stitched or unstitched, or dark thread may show as a shadow on the right side.

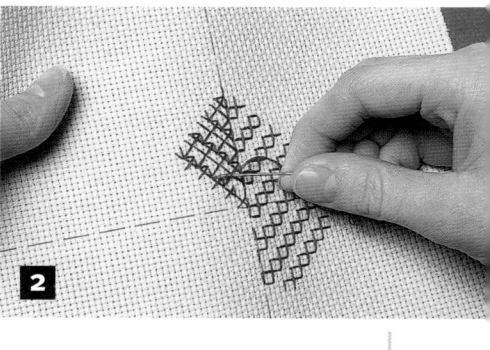

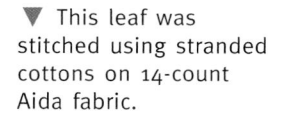

3 Work the outlines last, using a different weight of thread if desired.

▼ This leaf was stitched using stranded cottons on 14-count Aida fabric.

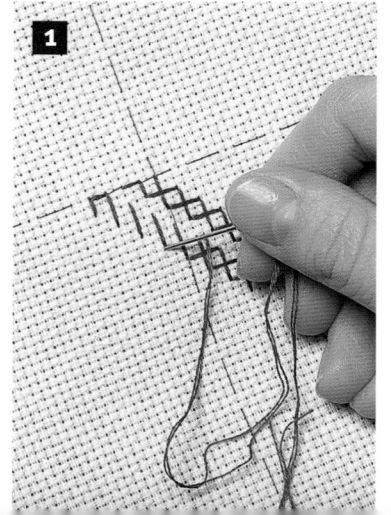

STITCHING FREE DESIGNS

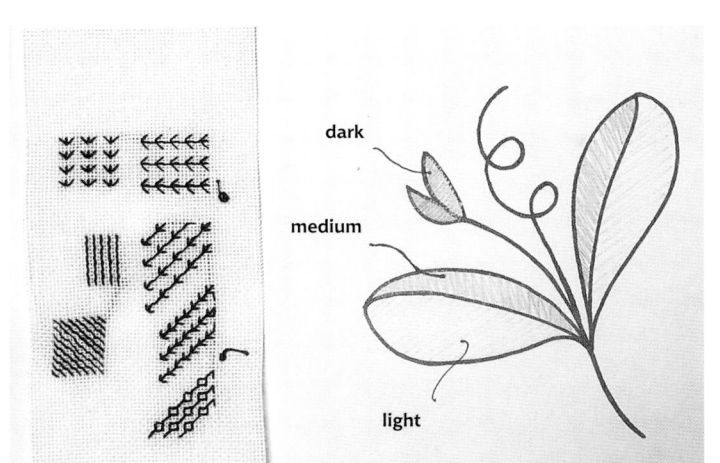

dark

medium

light

To plan the patterned areas, make a copy of the design and shade in the different areas with pencil in three or four shades from light to dark. Test the effects of different blackwork patterns on a sample piece using the same thread and fabric as you will use for the finished piece, stitching a small area of each pattern. Stand back and study the effect from several feet away to choose which pattern to use for each tone you require.

1 Trace or transfer the design outlines onto the fabric by one of the methods described on page 99. These lines will be covered by stitching so you can use permanent marks.

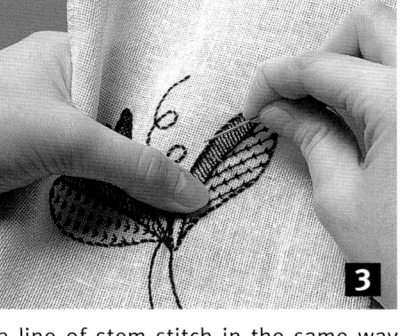

2 To stitch each pattern area determine the center of the area by eye and mark it with two basted lines if desired. Then stitch one line of pattern beginning at the center of the area and stitching out to each side in turn. Partial patterns or stitches may be required at the edges. Then use this first line as a reference, placing subsequent lines to fill the area. Fill all the pattern areas in the same way.

3 To work the outlining, you will probably need to change to a sharp needle. Use a flowing stitch such as stem stitch, chain stitch, or couched lines, working without counting threads. You can work these lines in gold or metallic thread, or whip a line of stem stitch in the same way as whipped darning (page 53). Stitch on any beads or sequins required.

SHADING BLACKWORK

Gradations of tone may be introduced within a pattern area to make a more realistic effect, either by using threads of different thicknesses or by gradually omitting elements of the stitch pattern. This technique may be used to adapt a charted design or add depth to a free design.

Shading with varying thread thickness

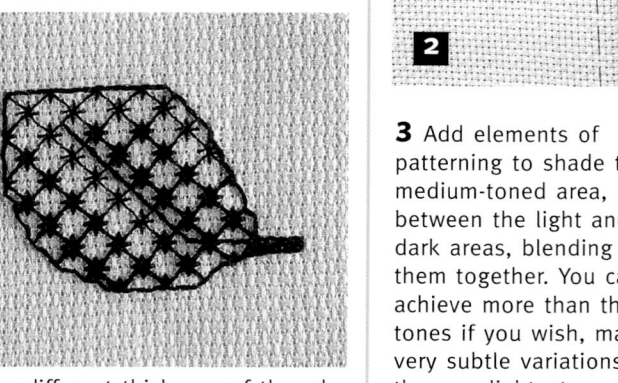

Stranded threads are useful for this method: by stitching with one, two, three, or more strands, the pattern will increase in density. Use a water-soluble pen to outline the different areas of shading, then stitch each area separately with a different thickness of thread, keeping the stitch pattern constant across the whole shape.

Shading by varying the stitch pattern

By successively eliminating elements of each stitch group, the pattern "breaks up" in the lighter areas. You can plan the varying pattern on graph paper before you begin, or work more freely:

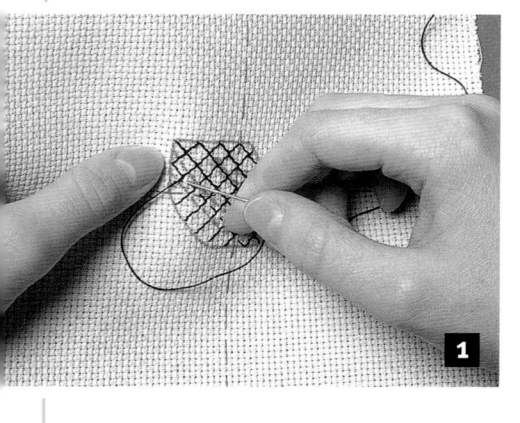

1 Use a water-soluble pen to outline the areas of different shades, then begin by working the lightest version of the pattern over the whole area.

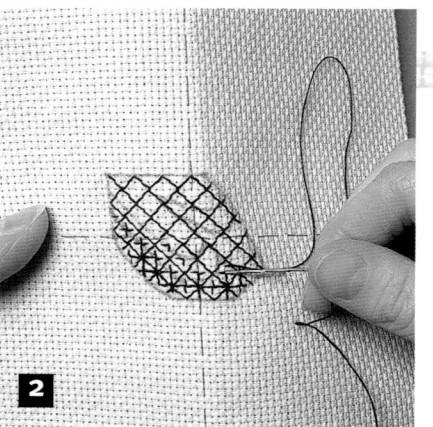

2 Then work the complete version of the pattern in the darkest area.

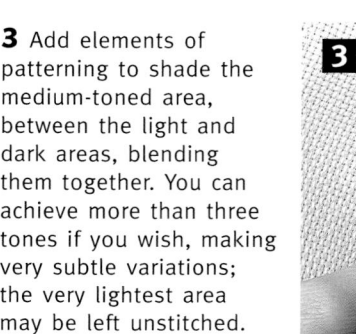

3 Add elements of patterning to shade the medium-toned area, between the light and dark areas, blending them together. You can achieve more than three tones if you wish, making very subtle variations; the very lightest area may be left unstitched.

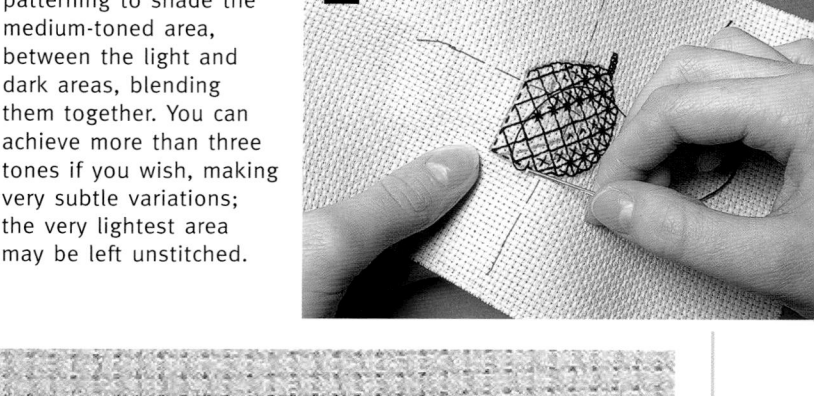

4 Work outlines and/or straight stitch details last.

Hardanger Work

This type of embroidery developed in the Norwegian district of Hardanger. Although the traditional geometric patterns appear quite simple they may be arranged in many ways, forming a variety of intricate effects.

Kloster blocks (page 42) are small blocks of satin stitch which secure the threads so they may be cut and withdrawn. Careful planning and perfect counting are necessary. After cutting and withdrawing threads, a grid of empty threads remains which may then be overcast or woven into bars. The square spaces in the grid may be decorated with various filling stitches, making intricate patterns contrasting the light fabric and thread with the dark spaces. Other stitching (such as satin stitch motifs) may be included in any design. Patterns are necessarily geometric but are often derived from stylized natural forms.

Hardanger fabric is commonly used for this work; this is a closely-woven evenweave, 22- and 24-count (page 19). Other evenweave fabrics may be used but they should be firmly woven. The fabric count determines the size of the motifs.

It is usual to work with two different threads: a heavy thread such as Pearl cotton no. 5 for the Kloster blocks and any satin stitch, and a lighter weight such as Pearl cotton no. 12, or two or three strands of stranded cotton, for the bars and fillings. The threads should be chosen to suit the fabric count. The heavy thread should give good coverage on the Kloster blocks otherwise the cut ends of the withdrawn threads will look untidy.

Hardanger work is traditionally stitched in white thread on white linen, but other colorways are often used today. Choose fabric and thread in close colors to help disguise the ends of the cut threads.

STITCHING A HARDANGER DESIGN
Follow the general guidelines on pages 58–67. Hardanger designs are worked from charts.

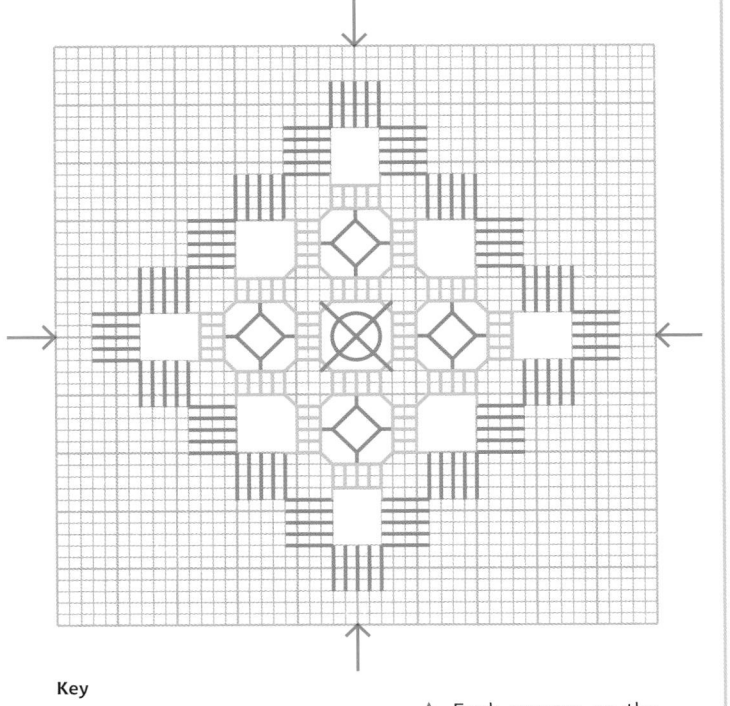

Key

|||| Kloster block

▥ Woven Bar

◇ Straight loopstitch filling

⊗ Dove's eye filling

▲ Each square on the chart represents one square of Hardanger fabric. The blank areas represent the spaces left after the groups of four threads have been cut and withdrawn, and after the woven bars have been worked over the remaining threads. Some of these spaces are then filled with a decorative filling stitch.

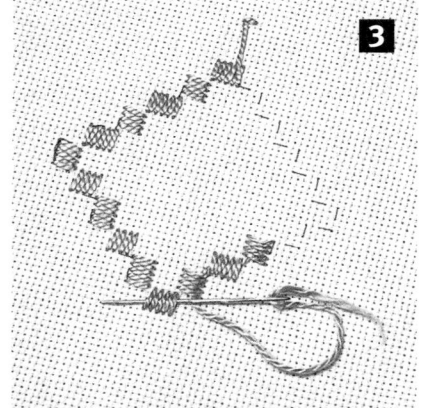

1 Baste any center lines and the outline of the design onto the fabric. Basting is more accurate than using a marker: place small basting stitches along straight rows of holes. The stitching must be accurate for the threads to be successfully cut and withdrawn.

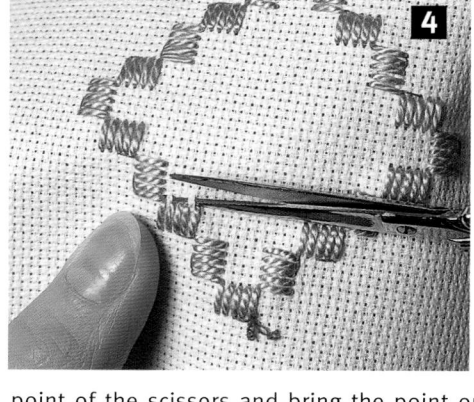

4 Use a tapestry needle to enlarge the holes at the base of a Kloster block, inside the shape. Use very sharp, pointed embroidery scissors to cut through the four threads (one at a time) at the base of a Kloster block: insert the point of the scissors and bring the point out again beyond one thread before closing the scissors, to avoid snipping into the Kloster block. Cut through the same four threads at the base of the block directly opposite. Cut only those threads that run in the same direction as the satin stitches.

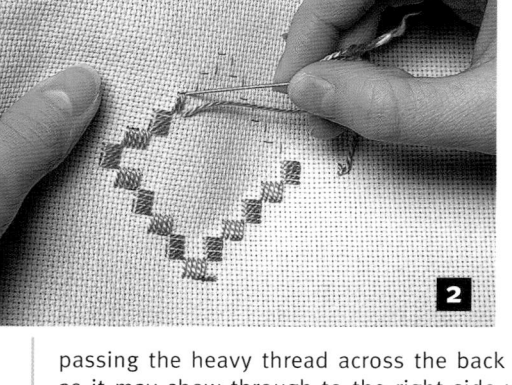

2 Work the Kloster blocks (page 42): use heavy thread and a small tapestry needle. For blocks that enclose a shape where threads are to be withdrawn, begin at one corner of the shape and work clockwise around it. Always avoid passing the heavy thread across the back of unstitched areas, as it may show through to the right side when the work is displayed. Blocks and other shapes in satin stitch are sometimes used as pattern elements without cutting threads. If so, work these next using the same heavy thread.

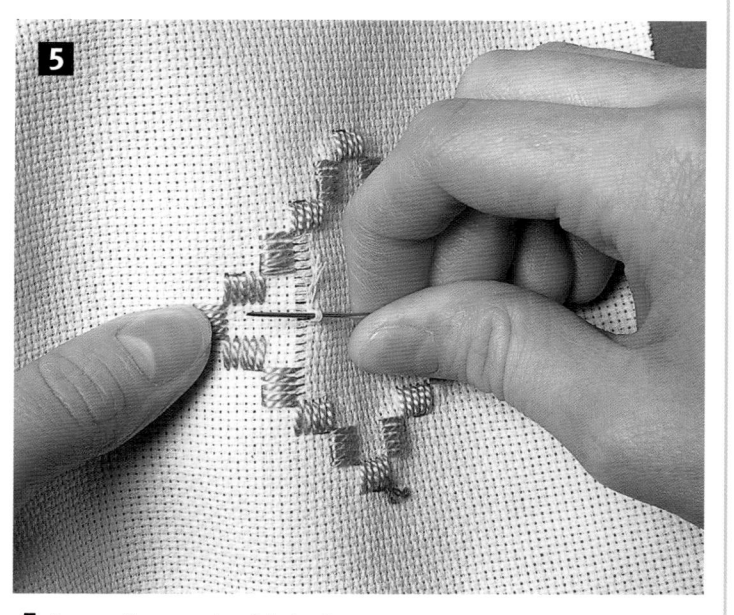

3 Unpick the waste backstitch and run in all the thread ends securely along the back of several blocks.

5 Depending on the fabric, it may help to loosen the threads with a tapestry needle.

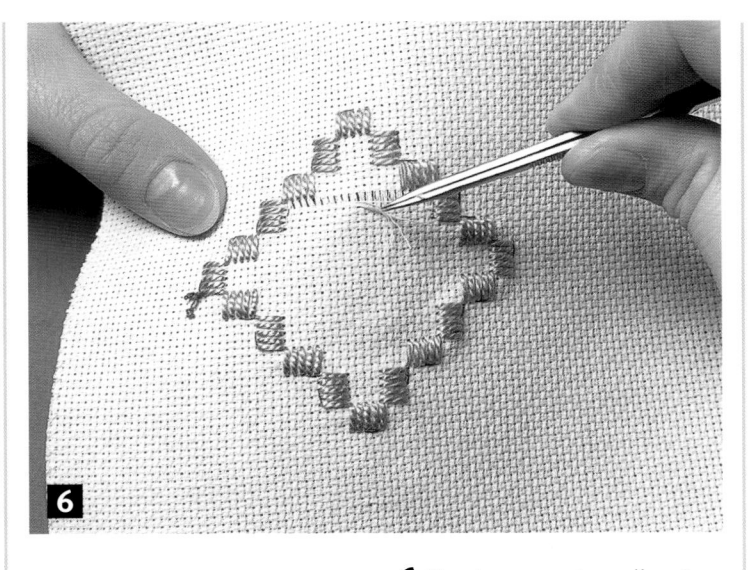

6 Use tweezers to pull out the cut threads one by one.

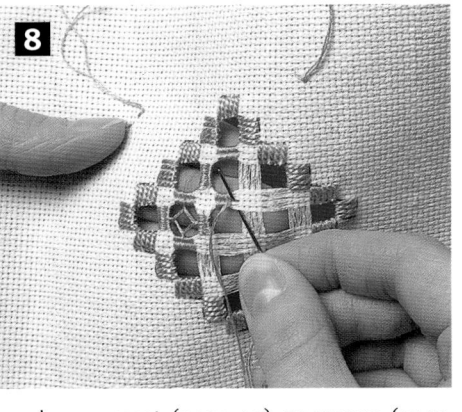

8 Change to a finer thread to work the bars and fillings. Bars are worked on the open grid of fabric threads, and fillings inside the empty squares. Bars may be overcast (page 43) or woven (page 43), or woven with picots (page 44). Empty squares may be filled with loop stitch (page 44), oblique loop stitch (page 45), or dove's eye filling (page 45).

Work in a logical order: begin at the top (or top left) of the shape and work diagonally down and then up the design, working the bars of each square (and its filling, if used) in turn. Where necessary pass the thread through the back of a Kloster block. Fasten off securely.

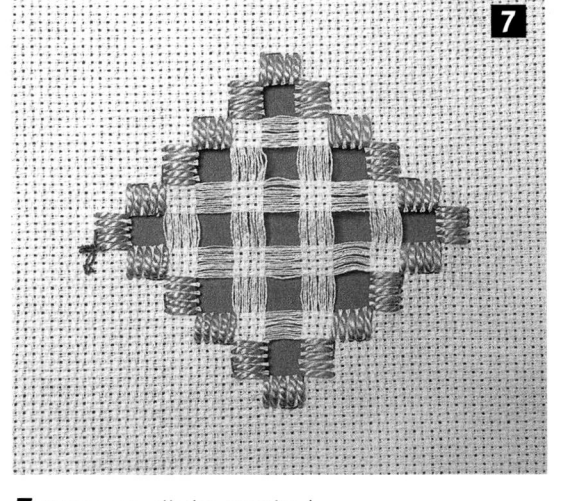

7 Draw out all the required threads in one direction, then the other, so that a grid of open threads remains.

Repeating Patterns

A motif may be repeated in several ways to make a pattern: as a border repeat, a straight arrangement, brick arrangement, or half-drop arrangement, in symmetrical halves (mirror image) or as a quartered repeat.

BORDER REPEATS

Count the number of squares required for the width of one repeat and calculate how many repeats you will need for the length of the border. Sometimes it is quite easy to adjust the number of stitches in each repeat by omitting or adding one or more background squares or stitches to make a perfect fit.

Odd number of repeats

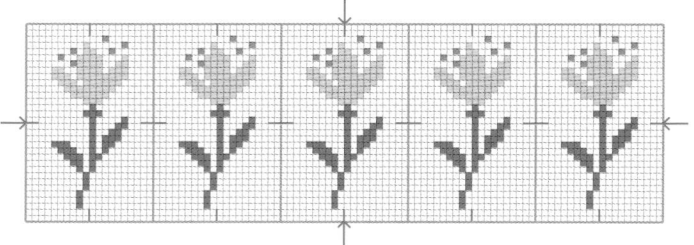

Place one motif at the center of the border, matching the vertical center line on the chart to the center line on the fabric or canvas. Then work the repeats out to each side.

Even number of repeats
Work one motif at either side of the center line on the fabric or canvas, then repeat the motifs out to each side.

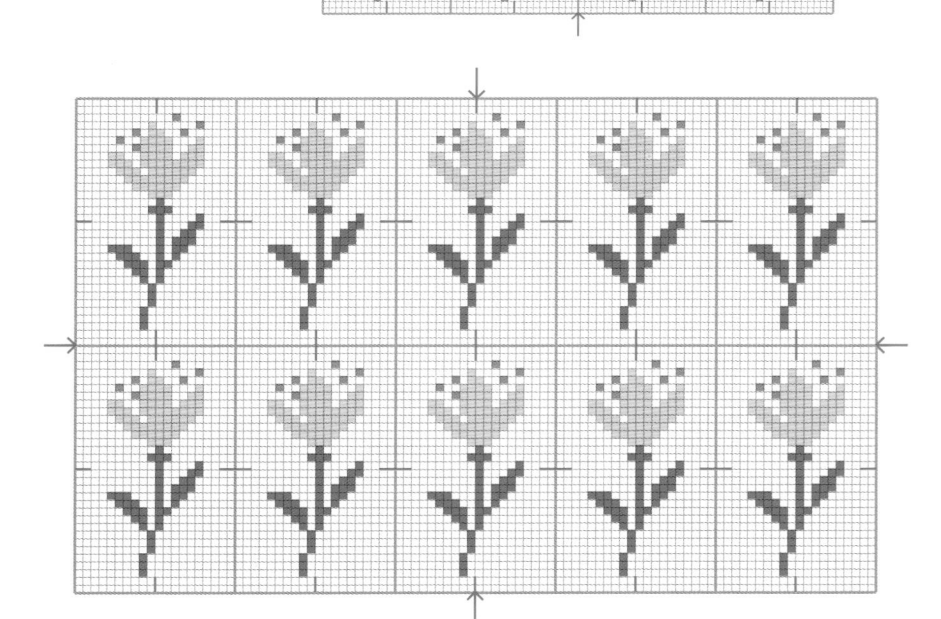

STRAIGHT ROW ARRANGEMENT

Calculate how many repeats you will need for the width, and how many rows of repeats for the height.

For an odd number of rows, work the central row first, as for a border repeat. Then repeat the row above and below.

For an even number of rows, place one row above the horizontal center line and one row below it.

BRICK ARRANGEMENT

Count how many repeats you need for the width, and how many rows for the height.

If you need an odd number of rows, work the central row first as for a border repeat.

If you need an even number of rows, work the first row either above or below the horizontal center line on the fabric or canvas.

Then match the center line of each repeat on the first row to the side edges of the repeats on the rows above and below. Repeat the two rows, above and below, outward from the center, alternating the repeats as shown. The repeats are arranged like bricks in a wall.

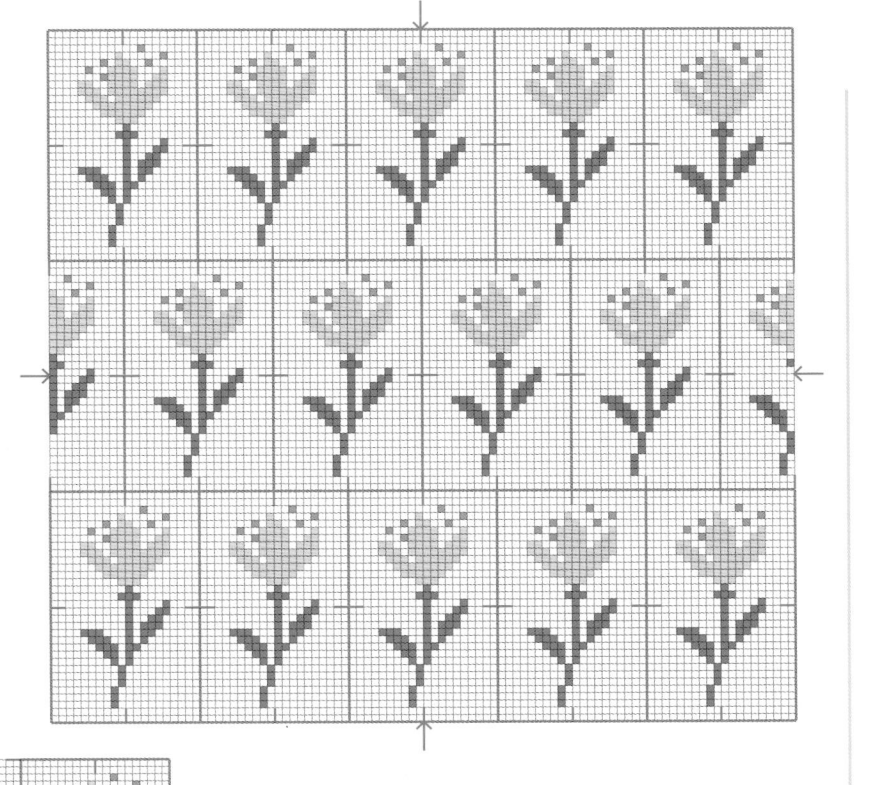

HALF-DROP ARRANGEMENT

Count how many vertical rows you will need for the width, and how many repeats within each row for the height.

If you need an odd number of vertical rows, work the central row first. If there are an odd number of repeats in the central row, match the center lines of the central repeat to the center lines on the fabric or canvas. If there are an even number of repeats in this row, work the first repeat above or below the fabric/canvas center line.

If you need an even number of rows, work the first row to right or left of the vertical center line on the fabric or canvas. Then match the center line of each repeat on the first row to the top and bottom edges of the repeats on the rows to right and left. Repeat the rows outward from the center, alternating the repeats as shown.

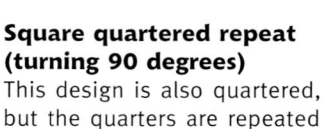

SYMMETRICAL HALVES

A design may be a mirror image, repeating about either a vertical or a horizontal center line. Only one half of such a design needs to be charted: the second half is worked as a mirror image of the first.

Vertical center

Horizontal center

Begin by working the first half exactly as charted. This may be above or below the horizontal center line, or to the left or right of the vertical center line. Then match the second half exactly in reverse.

QUARTERED REPEATS

There are three types of quartered repeats. In each case, only one quarter of the design needs to be charted.

Square quartered repeat (mirror image)

The chart (right) shows the top right quarter of a design.

Mark the top of the canvas or fabric to match the chart. Work the first quarter exactly as the chart, matching the center lines.

Work the top left quarter as a mirror image of the top right quarter.

Then work the bottom half as a mirror image of the top half.

Square quartered repeat (turning 90 degrees)

This design is also quartered, but the quarters are repeated in a different way.

Work the top (first) quarter of the design exactly as charted.

There are two ways to work the successive quarters:

If you turn the fabric or canvas through 90 degrees to work each successive quarter, the direction of the stitches will change for each quarter.

If you turn the chart (instead of the canvas/fabric) through 90 degrees for each successive quarter, the stitch direction will remain the same across the whole design.

Diagonal quartered repeat

A third type of quartered repeat is made by dividing the design diagonally. Such designs on canvas may be centered by means of diagonal miter lines instead of center lines. Baste matching miter lines on the canvas, diagonally across the canvas intersections.

Work the first quarter exactly as charted.

If you turn the fabric or canvas through 90 degrees to work each successive quarter, the direction of the stitches will change for each quarter.

If you turn the chart (instead of the canvas/fabric) through 90 degrees for each successive quarter, it is easier to keep the stitch direction the same across the whole design.

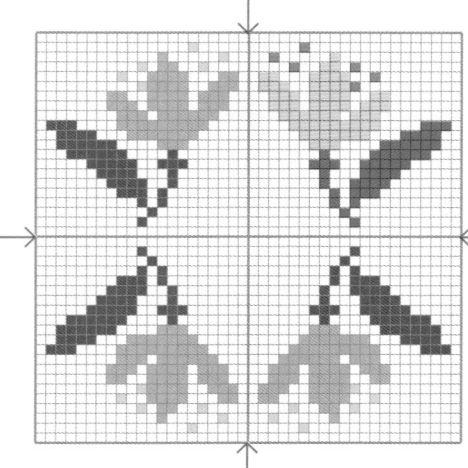

Adapting Patterns

A simple charted design may be adapted in many ways, changing the size, materials, colors, or stitches.

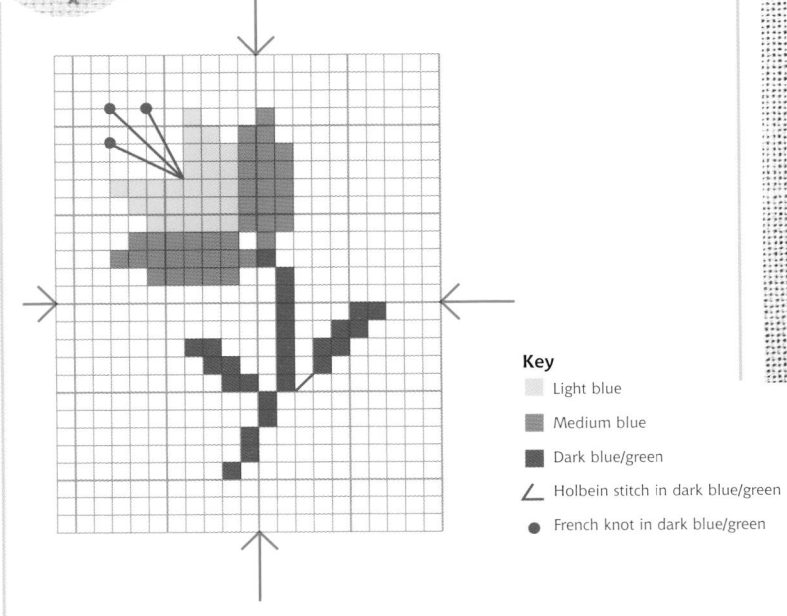

Key

■ Light blue
■ Medium blue
■ Dark blue/green
∠ Holbein stitch in dark blue/green
● French knot in dark blue/green

CHANGING THE STITCH

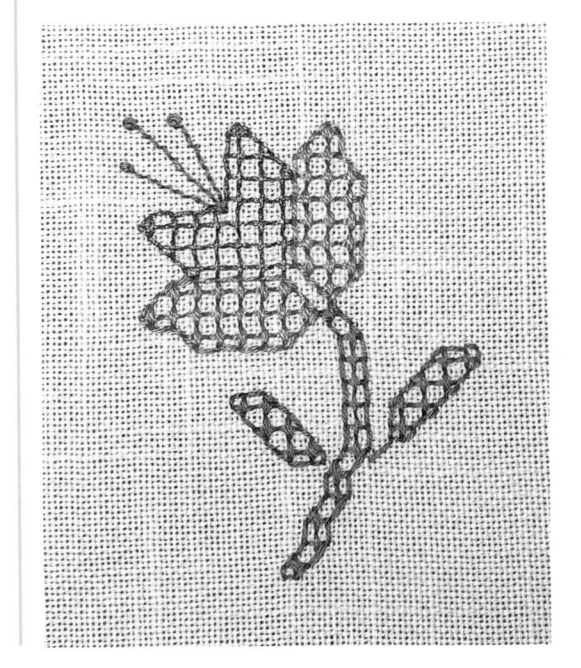

You can change the appearance of a design by using a different stitch. This flower motif was worked in upright cross stitch (page 35), with added outlines, using stranded cottons on evenweave linen.

CHANGING THE SCALE

Here the same flower motif has been worked on **1**, 22-count Aida (cross stitch with two strands of stranded cotton), **2**, 14-count Aida (cross stitch with three strands of stranded cotton, and small beads), and **3**, 10-gauge canvas (tent stitch in tapestry wool). Version **4** was worked on 14-count Aida, in Pearl cotton no. 5 stitching each cross over two squares in each direction. Version **5**, the largest, was stitched in Pearl cotton no. 5 on Binca fabric (6-count).

USING BEADS

You can also substitute beads for cross stitch. Choose beads to match the size of the squares on Aida fabric so that each bead covers one square.

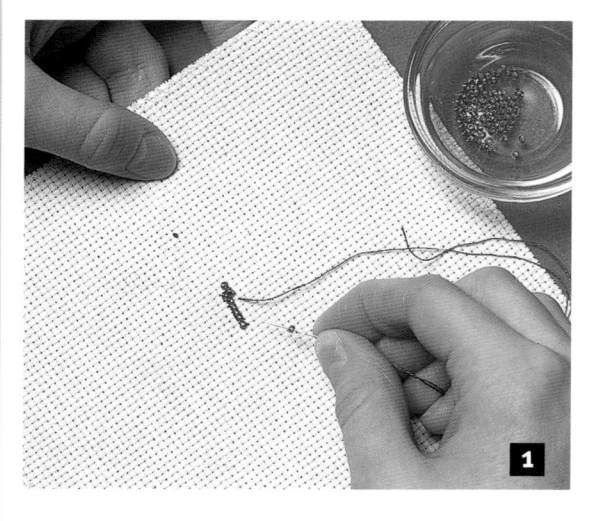

1 Choose a needle that fits easily through the beads: it may need to be a sharp needle to be small enough. Use thread to match the beads. To sew on a bead, bring the needle up at one corner of a square and thread a bead onto the needle.

2 Insert the needle at the opposite corner of the square and pull through. Beads may sometimes be sewn with a stitch along the side edge of a square. The center bead on the chart is positioned over a hole: bring the needle through the hole, thread a bead onto the needle, then take the needle down again through the same hole.

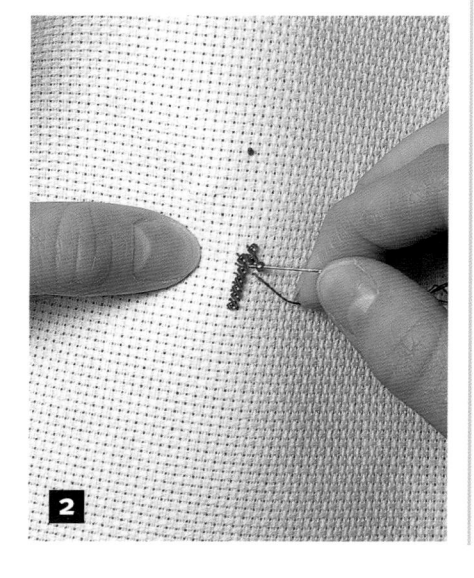

Chart

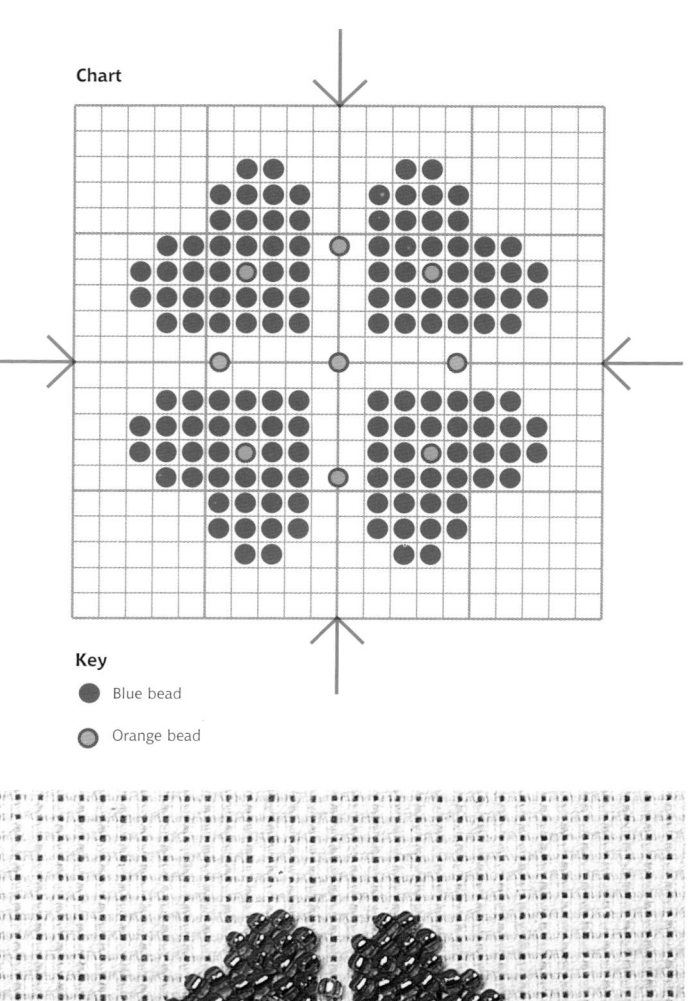

Key

● Blue bead

◉ Orange bead

USING OTHER GROUNDS

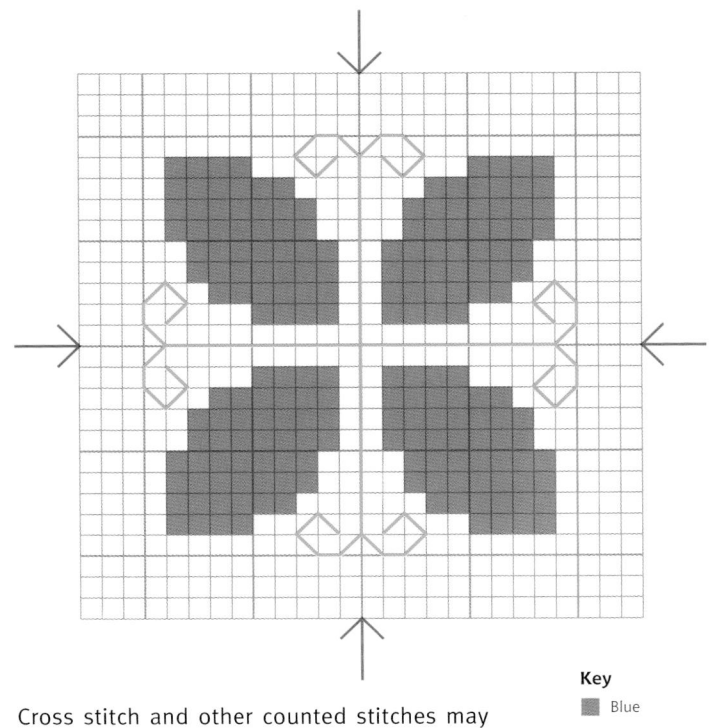

Key
- ▨ Blue
- ⌒ Holbein stitch in turquoise

Cross stitch and other counted stitches may also be worked on any fabric or material that forms a regular grid.

Wire mesh

The wire mesh shown here forms a square grid that may be stitched in exactly the same way as canvas, although it is not necessary to cover the wire completely. Bind the edges of the wire securely with masking tape (page 59). Plan the stitching carefully to avoid carrying threads across the back of empty mesh. This flower motif was worked in cross stitch and Holbein stitch using stranded cottons.

Grid patterned fabric

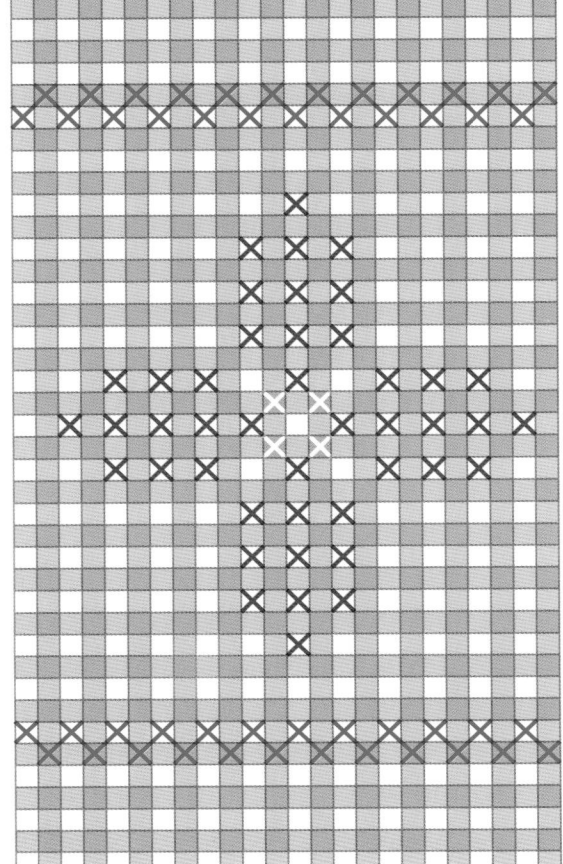

Key
- ✕ Dark cross on white square
- ⊠ Light cross on dark square
- ✕✕✕ Herringbone stitch in turquoise

Woven gingham fabric provides an interesting background for cross stitch. Such lightweight fabric is best backed with stabilizer and stretched in a hoop or frame (pages 60–61). Dark areas may be stitched by simply covering the white squares with stitches in a dark thread, and light areas stitched by covering the dark squares with white stitches. Herringbone stitch is also effective on gingham.

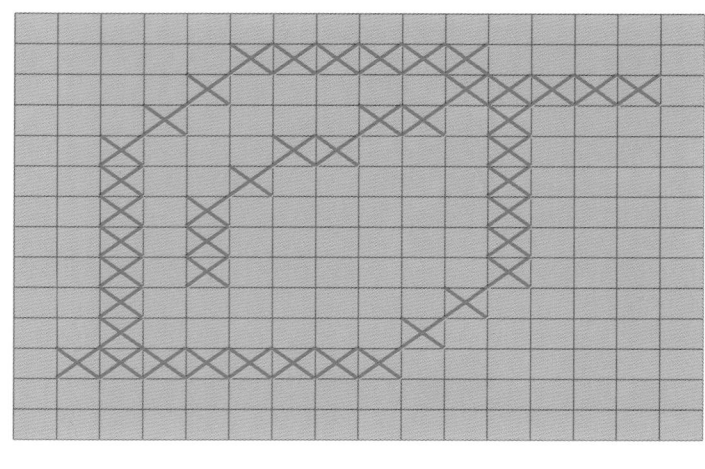

Knitting

Key

✕ Cross stitch in turquoise

Plain stockinette (stocking stitch) knitting can also be decorated with cross stitch. Such knitted stitches are normally slightly wider than they are long, so distorting the crosses. For an accurate appearance the design may be charted on a grid of rectangles to match the knitting (as page 108). Use thread slightly heavier than the knitting yarn for good coverage.

Note how the crosses are slightly distorted because the woven pattern is not quite square. This border pattern was worked in stranded cottons on gingham with approximately eight squares to the inch (25mm).

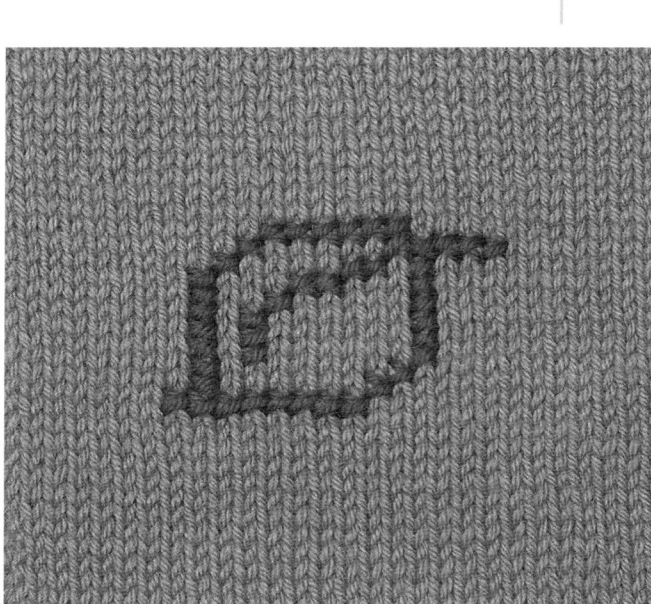

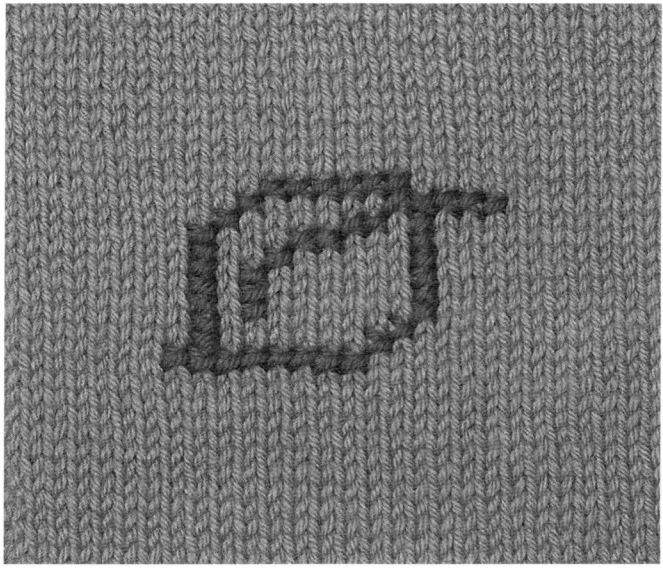

To form the cross stitches, take the needle up and down through the centers of the knitted stitches.

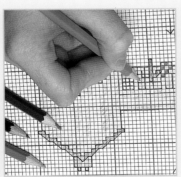

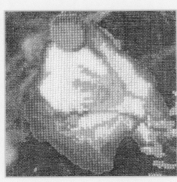

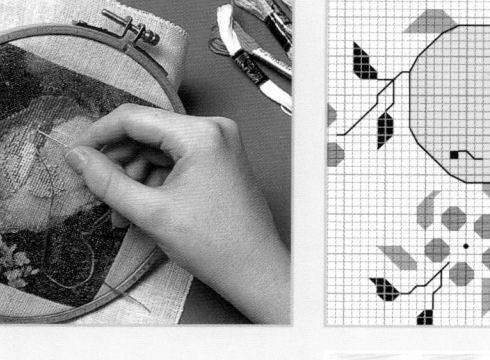
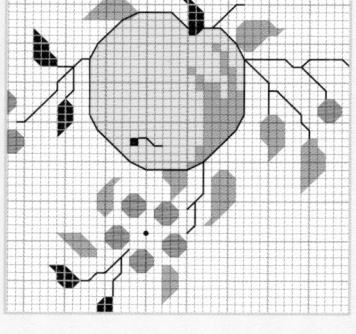

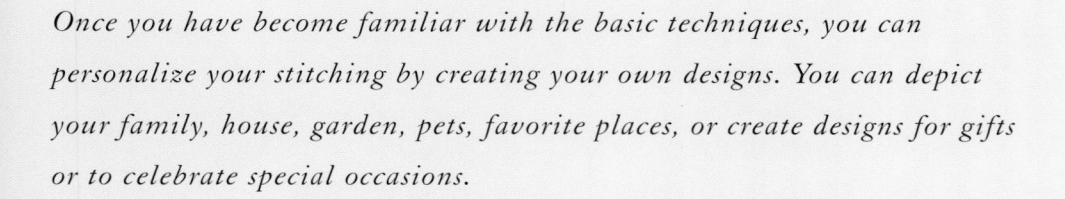

CHAPTER 4

Design Your Own

Once you have become familiar with the basic techniques, you can personalize your stitching by creating your own designs. You can depict your family, house, garden, pets, favorite places, or create designs for gifts or to celebrate special occasions.

Design Sources

Inspiration can come from many sources: photographs, drawings, paintings, collages, motifs designed for other crafts, printed fabrics, china . . .

Some images can be used exactly as they are, while others may need to be simplified or changed to make them suitable for stitching, as described under "Preparing the Image" (pages 96–97) and "Adjusting the Image" (page 98).

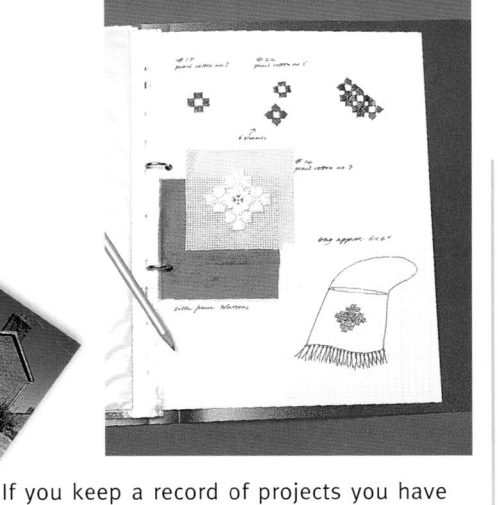

If you keep a record of projects you have completed, this information will help you to make informed choices in the future.

Keep any charts or drawings you make with their stitch samples. Note the size of each piece and the fabrics and threads you used, together with any special stitches or techniques. You can also include photographs of finished projects.

Which Method to Use?

Several different ways of working are described in this chapter, suitable for various types of design and for different counted thread techniques.

For multicolor cross stitch designs on fabric or tent stitch designs on canvas

You can use any of the methods described, either applying the design direct to the material or preparing a chart. If you can prepare an image that requires no simplifications or alterations, the color transfer or acetate grid methods are simple and easy to use, as are the direct tracing or painting methods.

For more stylized cross stitch designs (including Assisi work) and for charted blackwork

Designs are simplified and less realistic, so a chart is required. Try the tracing graph paper method, or the plain graph paper method, or use computer software.

For freestyle blackwork

Use the direct tracing method or prepare an outline transfer.

For Hardanger work

The correct positioning of stitches is crucial, so draw directly onto plain graph paper, or work on a computer.

Preparing the Image

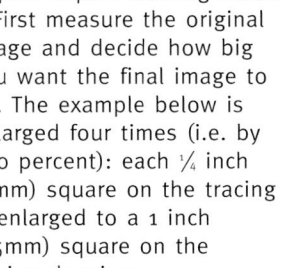

ENLARGING AND REDUCING

It is usually useful to begin by making a copy of the image to the exact size required. You can do this automatically by photocopying or by using a computer with a scanner, or manually by "squaring up" a drawing.

For most types of counted thread embroidery, curves and sloping outlines must be interpreted as a series of steps. The larger the image, the easier it will be to stitch these steps evenly.

By photocopying or scanning

Changes in the size of an image are often expressed as a percentage of the original size.

If the original image measures 4 inches (100mm) square, a 50 percent reduction will halve the measurement in each direction, making an image 2 inches (50mm) square. A 200 percent enlargement will double the measurement in each direction, making an image 8 inches (200mm) square. You can specify any percentage you need: a 175 percent enlargement, for example, would make the image 7 inches (175mm) square.

If you greatly enlarge an image the outline will become fuzzy and indistinct, but you can easily draw over it to make it sharper.

By squaring up

The manual method does not require expert drawing skills.

First measure the original image and decide how big you want the final image to be. The example below is enlarged four times (i.e. by 400 percent): each ¼ inch (6mm) square on the tracing is enlarged to a 1 inch (25mm) square on the design drawing.

YOU WILL NEED:
tracing paper
pencil
ruler (or better, a sketching T-square)
plain paper

1 Trace the original image in pencil.

200 percent enlargement

original size

50 percent reduction

2 Draw a grid of small squares over the traced image (¼ inch [6mm] squares shown here).

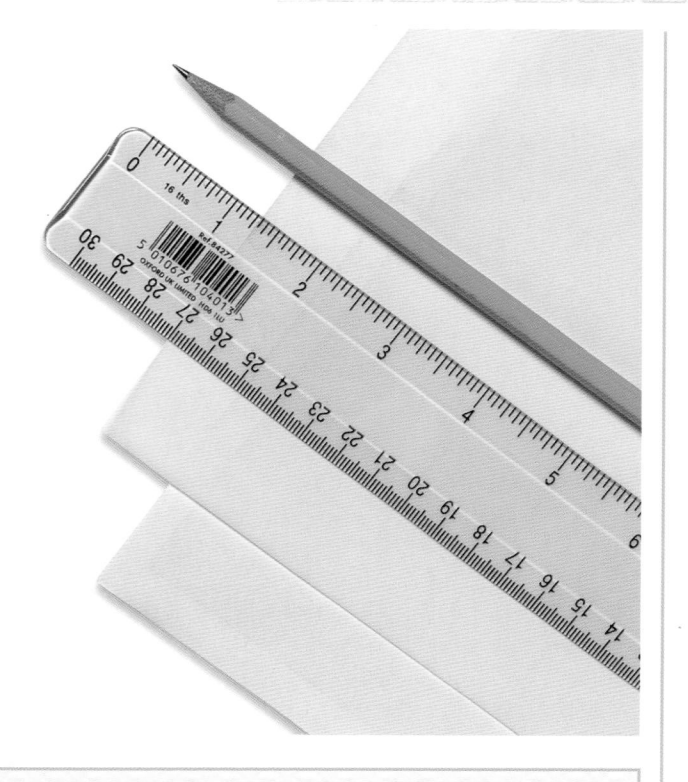

3 Draw a grid on the paper with the same number of large squares (1 inch [25mm] squares shown here). Using the grid as a reference, copy the design lines square by square.

TIPS
• If you are going to draw a chart from the image, you can copy the design directly onto graph paper.

• If the image you want to copy is on a curved surface (such as a plate), use lightweight dressmaker's interlining instead of tracing paper, held in place with tape.

Adjusting the Image

Now your image is the size you want, consider carefully whether it needs to be simplified or changed in any way.

If you want to use a photograph to make a transfer, it can be surprisingly difficult to find exactly the right picture!

If you have access to a computer with photoprocessing software, you can change the colors or the contrast and eliminate unwanted details or backgrounds, then print out the version you want.

With access to a photocopier you can change the contrast or color balance, print a copy, then cut away any parts of an image you don't want.

You can make a collage with copies of photographs, or draw in details that are missing.

CHOOSING COLORS

Always choose thread colors by daylight.

To help visualize the effect of a new color combination, make a sample card: wind a short length of each color around a small piece of card to make a solid block of colors, approximately in the same ratio as the colors appear in the design. Then consider carefully if the balance is right: too dark? too light? not enough contrast? View the colors from a distance as well as close up. When stitching, be prepared to change your mind: each time you begin a new color, work a few stitches and consider the result before continuing.

Applying Designs Direct to Fabric

Having prepared your image to the size you want, you can trace it directly onto fabric or canvas, paint it onto canvas, or make your own transfer.

1 Tape the design to the lightbox (or windowpane). Protect the design with a sheet of clear plastic, also taped in place.

2 Tape the fabric (or canvas) over the design and trace off the outlines.

YOU WILL NEED:
a lightbox
masking tape
water-soluble marker
   (for fabric) or
permanent markers
   (for canvas)

TRACING METHOD
This method may be used on either fabric or canvas. The design must be drawn or printed on a fairly thin paper: this method is not suitable for printed photographs.

On fabric, you can use a water-soluble marker so that the design lines may be removed after stitching is complete. On canvas, the stitching will normally cover the lines completely, so you can use permanent fibertip markers (in different colors if you wish).

glass or perspex

support (bricks)

light source

If you do not have a lightbox, you can tape the design and material to a sunny windowpane, or improvize with a sheet of glass or perspex supported over a table lamp.

PAINTING A CANVAS

Canvas may be painted with acrylic paints, thinned with a little water. Natural (unbleached) canvas absorbs the paint more easily. Use a lightbox in the same way as for tracing. Leave the canvas flat to dry.

MAKE YOUR OWN TRANSFERS

There are various products on the market to enable you to make your own transfers. Always follow the manufacturer's instructions.

Bear in mind that any transferred image will be in reverse (sometimes this is not important). To reverse an image, make a tracing and turn it over, or use "flip" or "mirror image" on a computer.

Transfer pens and pencils:

These are normally used to trace an outline design (for example, for freestyle blackwork, page 80) onto tracing paper, greaseproof paper, or baker's parchment. The transfer is then applied to the material by ironing the back.

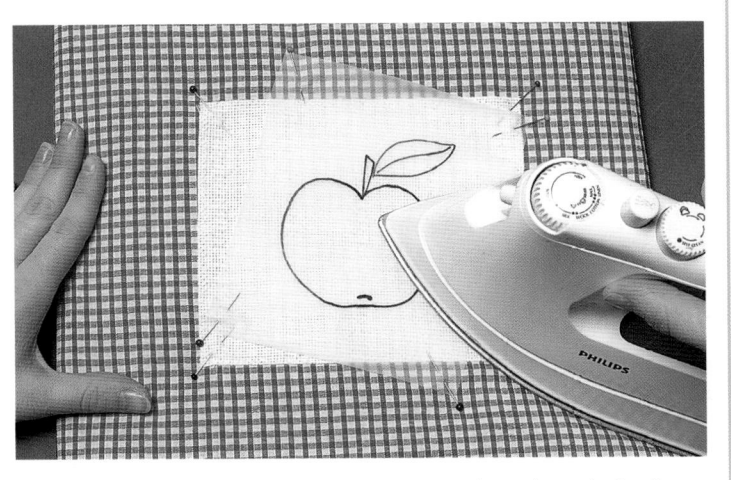

Press the fabric flat, pin it to your ironing board, and pin the transfer in position, marked side down, over it. Heat the iron as instructed and press down firmly for the time required, lifting and replacing the iron rather than sliding it across. To check whether the image has transferred, carefully lift one corner. If the transfer is moved during the ironing process the lines will blur. Most transfer lines are indelible and so must be covered by stitching.

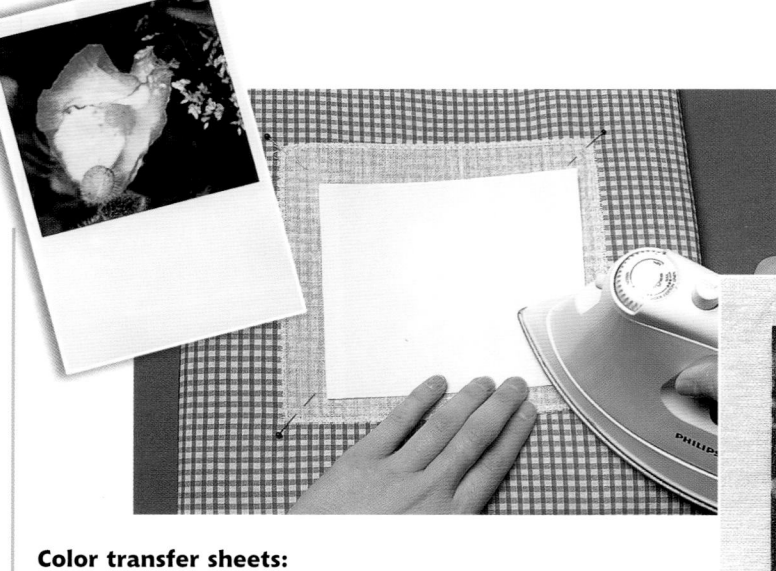

Color transfer sheets:

Special transfer sheets are available to use with color photocopiers, laser printers, or inkjet printers. The transfer is normally ironed onto the material and, after cooling, the backing is removed. Again, follow the manufacturer's instructions carefully: ironing heat and time can be crucial.

TIPS

- *For any type of transfer, avoid expensive mistakes by always making a test piece: prepare a separate piece of transfer and use a scrap of your intended fabric. You can then check that the ironing heat and time are correct for your purpose.*
- *Some fabrics will give better results if they are first washed (and dried) to remove starch or dressing.*

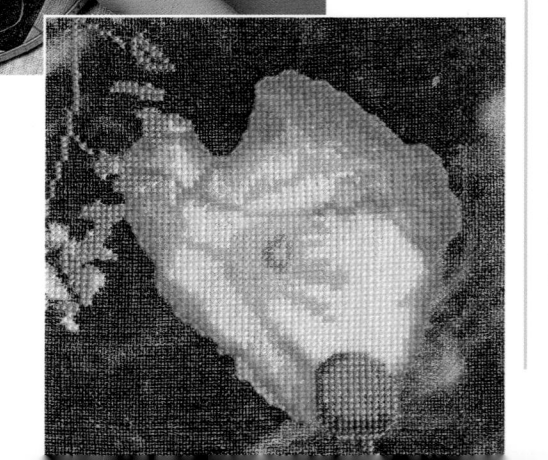

RUBBER STAMPS

A huge variety of rubber stamps are available in craft stores: flowers, birds, animals—any subject you could wish for! You can also purchase special ink pads for printing onto fabrics, or color the stamp with a thin layer of fabric paint: choose a color that will blend with the stitching. Always test first on a scrap of spare fabric.

Preparing Charts

There are several ways of preparing your own charts: to copy a realistic photographic image exactly, try the printed acetate grid method.

If you wish to simplify an image, try the tracing graph paper method.

To produce a more stylized design, or change the image considerably, use the plain graph paper method; this method is slower than techniques involving photocopiers and computers, but you may prefer it for that very reason: as you prepare the chart, you can consider how best to interpret your subject and make the decisions on paper rather than as you stitch. You can also prepare the chart larger than the finished piece, making it easier to read.

If you have access to a computer, you can choose from a wide variety of software designed to prepare cross stitch and other types of charts; a scanner will enable you to work directly from an original photograph or drawing.

ACETATE GRID METHOD

You can buy sheets of clear acetate, already printed with grids of various sizes, or you can print any size of grid you require onto plain acetate sheet, with a computer or photocopier. Different types of clear acetate sheet are sold to suit different types of printer—be sure to use the correct type.

Choose the grid size to match your fabric. Enlarge or reduce the image to the size you want (page 98).

YOU WILL NEED:
acetate grid
image
access to a photocopier

Lay the acetate grid over the image and photocopy the two together. Count the squares on the chart to find the center lines and indicate these with arrows.

Some squares may contain more than one color: interpret them as you wish as stitching proceeds.

TRACING GRAPH PAPER METHOD

Sheets of graph squares printed onto tracing paper are available with grids of various sizes to match the different counts of Aida fabric.

Choose the grid size to match your fabric.

Enlarge or reduce the image to the size you want (page 98).

YOU WILL NEED:
tracing graph paper
image
sharp pencil
colored pencils or pens
masking tape
smooth, flat working surface (a sheet of card is ideal)

2 Color the squares with colored pencils: draw only lightly, so the grid squares are easy to see. If the squares are not too small you can use felt tip pens in light colors.

The colors need not be exact, they are just an indication of the colors of threads to use. Sometimes it is useful to highlight the difference between two close shades by coloring them quite differently, so they are easy to read.

Count the squares on your chart to find the center point and indicate this with arrows.

1 Tape the image to a flat surface, and tape the tracing graph paper in position over it. Use a sharp pencil to lightly outline the design. At this stage you can adjust the steps for curves and sloping lines, add or omit details, and indicate any part stitches or outlines.

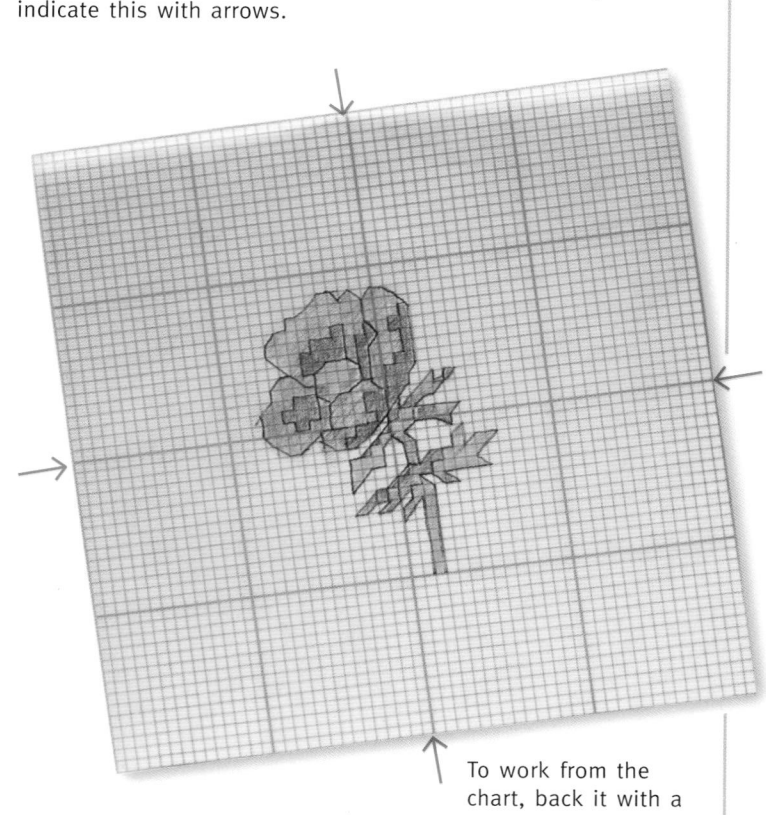

To work from the chart, back it with a sheet of white paper.

YOU WILL NEED:

graph paper (10 squares to 1 inch [25mm] is a useful size)

image

tracing paper

hard and soft pencils

colored pencils

fine fiber tip pen (black or dark color)

eraser

masking tape

smooth, flat working surface (a sheet of card is ideal)

PLAIN GRAPH PAPER METHOD

Decide what size your image needs to be on the graph paper. This will only be the same as the size of the finished piece if the grid size on the graph paper matches the size of the stitches on your fabric. For example, a picture measuring 6 x 3 inches (150 x 75mm) on 14-count Aida fabric (14 squares to the inch [25 mm]) will cover 84 x 42 squares of fabric.

So on graph paper with 10 squares to the inch (25mm), the chart for the picture will measure approximately 8½ x 4¼ inches (215 x 105mm). This is the size your image needs to be for this method of charting.

Enlarge or reduce your image to the size it will be on the chart (pages 96–97).

2 Turn the tracing over and use the soft pencil to scribble over the wrong side of all the traced lines.

3 Tape the graph paper to the work surface. Turn the tracing over again and place it right side up at the center of the graph paper, matching any horizontal and vertical lines as accurately as you can. If your image is distorted (as photographs often are) or sketchy, match an important horizontal or vertical line at the center of the image. Hold the tracing in place with more masking tape. Use the hard pencil to draw over the design outlines, so transferring them to the graph paper.

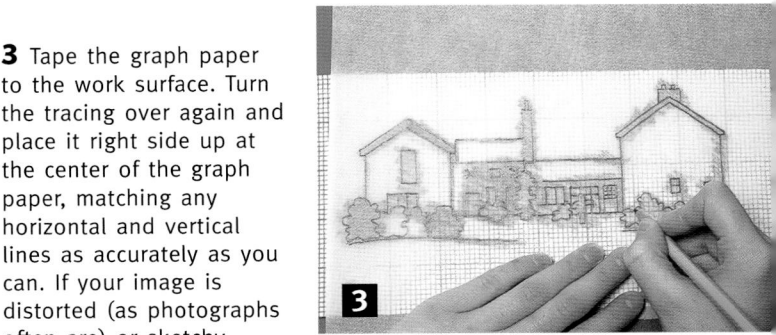

1 Tape the image to a smooth, flat surface. Tape the tracing paper over the image and use the hard pencil to trace off the outlines of the design, drawing round the outside of each part.

4 Remove the tracing and use the hard pencil to redraw all the lines along the nearest grid line. Simplify, making curves into straight lines or steps. Turn slanting lines into a series of even steps. Indicate any outline stitches (page 69) and part stitches (page 69). As you draw, think how best to interpret different elements such as foliage and brickwork.

5 When you are happy with the squared-off outlines, draw over them again with a fine fiber tip pen, then erase all the pencil marks.

Color the different areas lightly with colored pencils, so you can still see the grid lines. The colors don't have to be exact, they just need to indicate to you what color threads to use. Sometimes it is best to highlight a color difference (for example, between subtle shades of green) by coloring with quite different shades, so they are easy to read.

6 Count the squares on your chart to find the center point and indicate this with arrows.

7 Interpret the colors on your chart as you wish: a photograph is useful, even if taken from quite a different viewpoint. In this picture the old brickwork was stitched in blended shades of terracotta and golden brown, and two close shades of gray were used together for the slate roof. Dark brownish gray was used to outline most of the buildings, with black outlines for the doors and the roofline on the right. French knots were added to some of the bushes and climbing plants. The swallows were worked with French knots and small straight stitches.

COMPUTER SOFTWARE TIPS

Different computer programs work in slightly different ways, so follow the guidelines supplied, and don't forget the "Help" button!

As a guide, follow this general working procedure:

1 Choose the colors you need to work with from the huge palette available. These colors can then be kept on-screen so you just click on them to use them.

2 Decide how many chart squares you require in each direction for your image to be the size you want on the fabric/canvas you intend to use. This bears no relation to the size of the image on-screen: the smaller your intended design, the larger you can view it on-screen, making it easy to use the mouse accurately. For large images, you can use the zoom button to view all or part of the image at any size.

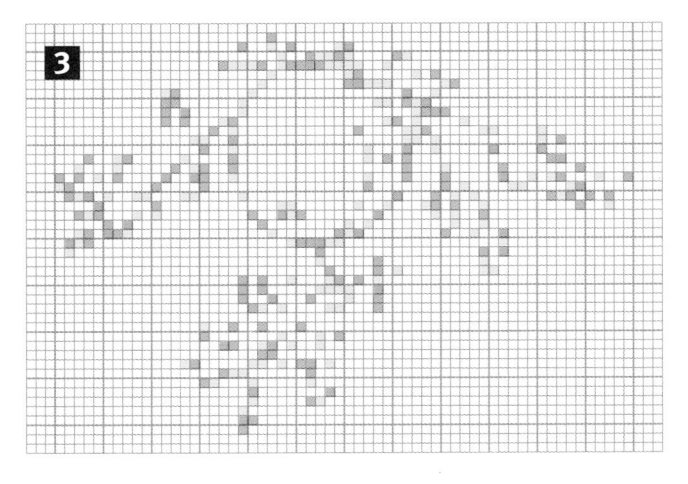

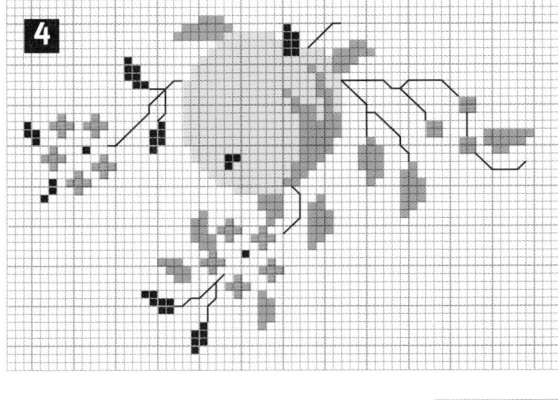

3 If you have a scanner, scan in the image at a suitable size, when it will probably not look anything like what you are expecting. Otherwise, you can use the mouse to roughly sketch in the design outlines: fill the chart squares with a contrasting color rather than one of your intended colors: then it's easy to delete the sketchy shapes at a later stage.

4 Then use the correct colors to block in the shapes. You can add outlines in color or as different line styles.

Key

- ▢ Yellow
- ▨ Green
- ▤ Red
- ■ Black
- • Black French knot
- ⌐ Black straight stitch

5 Add any part stitches or details such as French knots. Use the delete facility to remove all traces of the original scan or sketch. (This is easy if your original sketch is in a contrasting color).

On this chart, some of the straight stitches pass at an angle across two chart squares, to smooth the outline of the fruit. These may be stitched as one long stitch, or as two stitches (inserting the needle halfway along the side of a square).

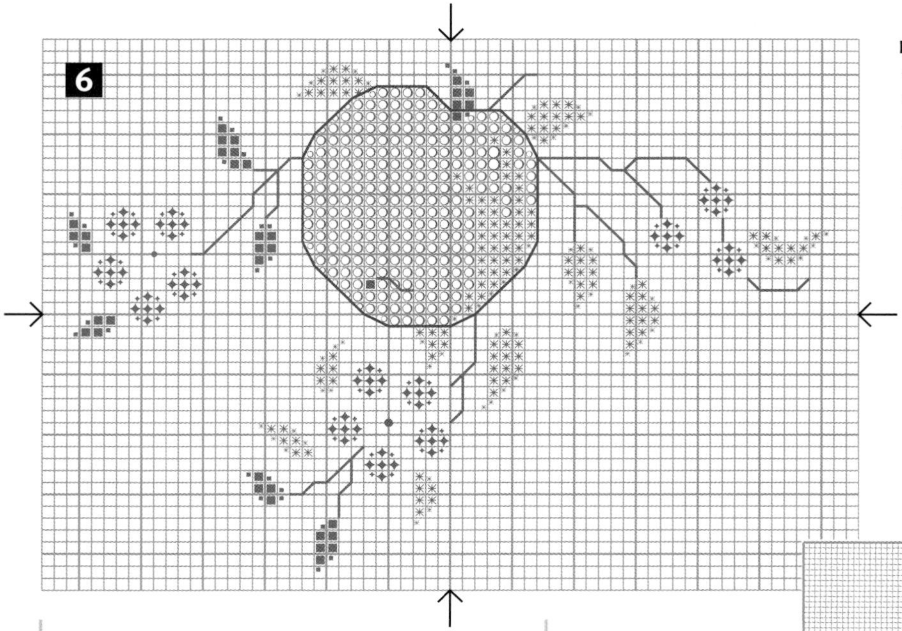

6

Key
○ Yellow
✳ Green
✦ Red
■ Black
● Black French knot
⌐ Black straight stitch

TIPS
- *If your first chart doesn't look quite right, don't delete it or change it: copy it on-screen, then rework the copy.*
- *Save all the different versions, either on the same page or separately. That way you can return to any previous version to copy and rework it.*

Key
▫ Yellow
▪ Green
▪ Red
■ Black
● Black French knot
⌐ Black straight stitch

6 You can then print out the chart in color, or as black and white symbols. You may need to change some of the colors to make them easier to read. Choose symbols that are easily distinguishable—black dots for black, for example, or empty circles for white—any combination that makes your chart clear. Large charts may be printed over several pages and then taped together. Print a key to your colors or symbols.

7

7 Cross stitch design programs normally include select, copy, paste, flip, and rotate facilities: you can use these buttons to create repeating patterns of various types, as on pages 85–87. Explore the other facilities in your program: these may include autocentering, lettering, and printing a facsimile of a finished embroidery.

Charts on Non-square Grids

Some fabrics, such as stockinette knitting (see page 91), have a regular grid that is not made up of squares, but of rectangles. Your design must be charted on a matching grid.

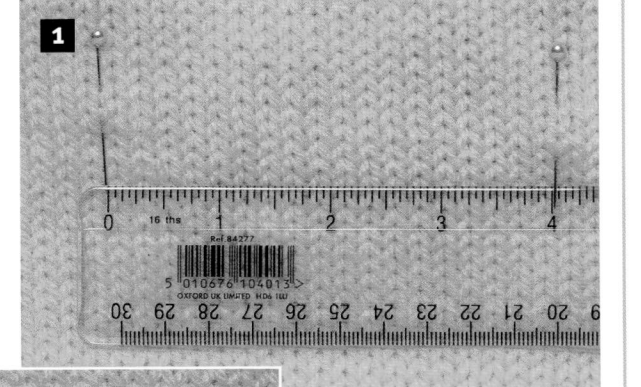

1 First measure the gauge of the knitting or other fabric: count the number of holes (stitches) in 4 inches (100mm) across the width, and the number of holes (rows) in 4 inches (100mm) along the length.

2 Draw a matching grid by hand, measuring carefully, or use a computer drawing program.

This grid is suitable for stockinette knitting with a gauge of 18 stitches and 24 rows to 4 inches (100mm), or any gauge with a similar ratio of stitches to rows.

The embroidered cat is shown on page 137.

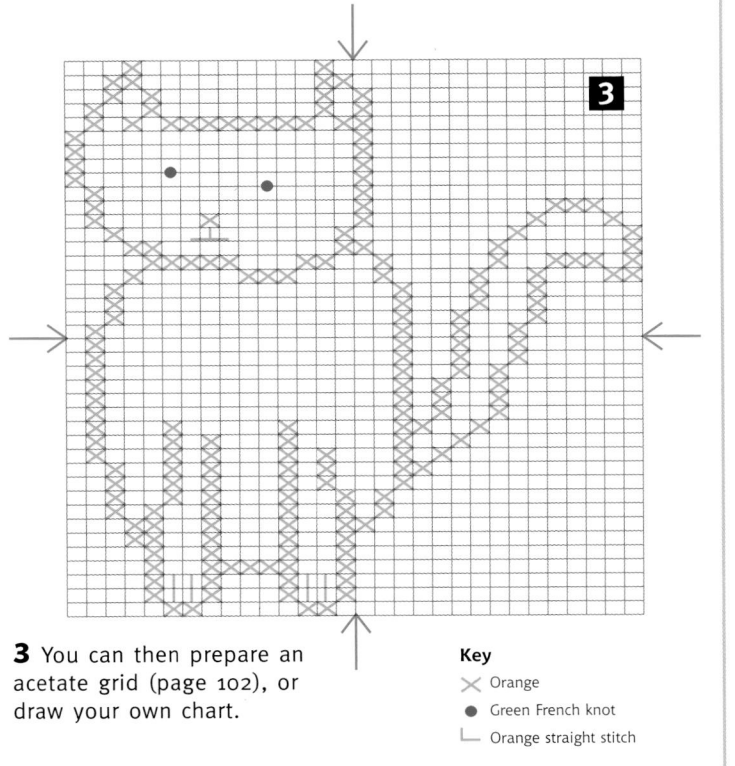

3 You can then prepare an acetate grid (page 102), or draw your own chart.

Key
✕ Orange
● Green French knot
└ Orange straight stitch

Charts for Hardanger Work

Begin by working in pencil on graph paper, or work on a computer: in a cross stitch design program, you can draw symbols for the different stitches (Kloster blocks, bars and fillings), then copy and paste them where they are required.

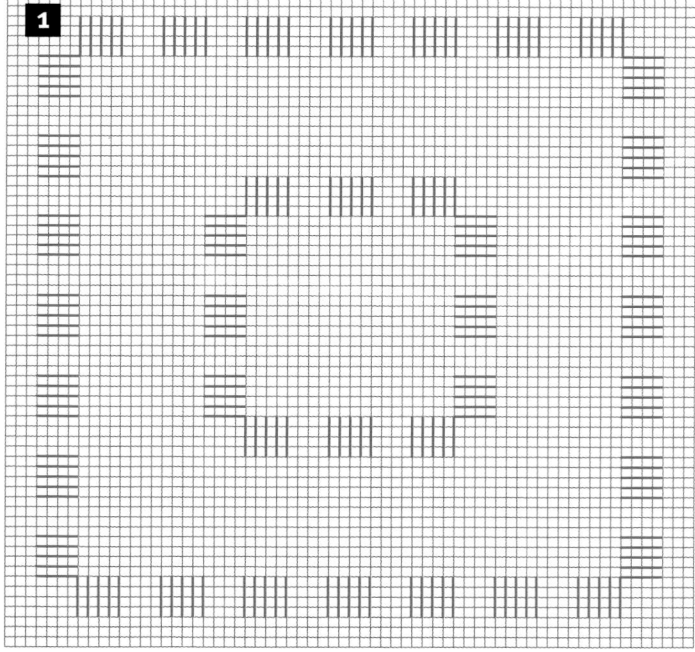

1 Establish the main areas of the design, outlined with Kloster blocks. Where threads will be cut, the direction of the Kloster blocks is important.

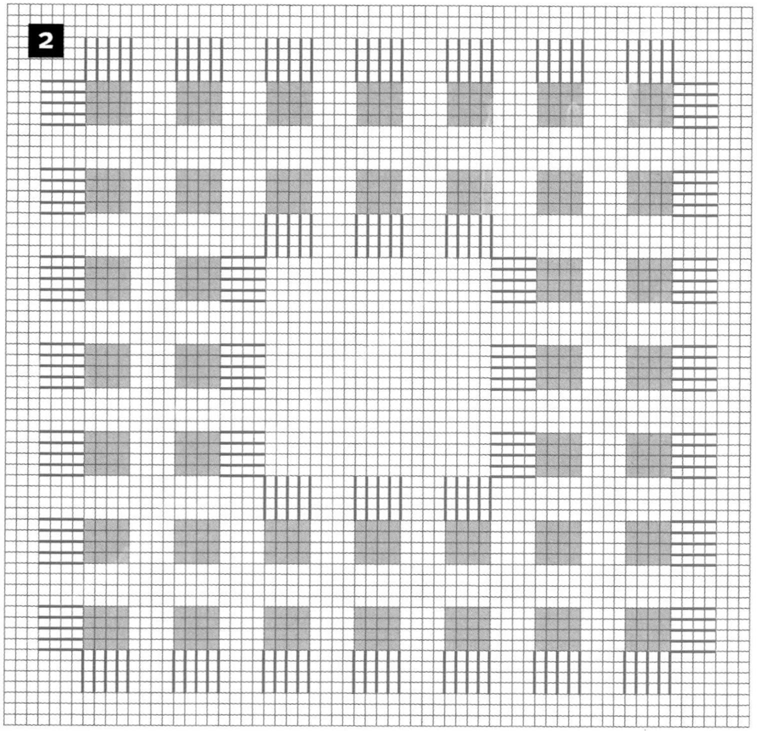

2 Indicate where the spaces will be when the threads have been cut and withdrawn.

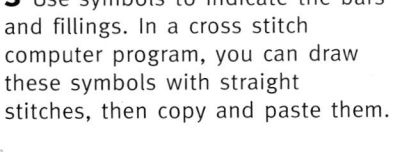

3 Use symbols to indicate the bars and fillings. In a cross stitch computer program, you can draw these symbols with straight stitches, then copy and paste them.

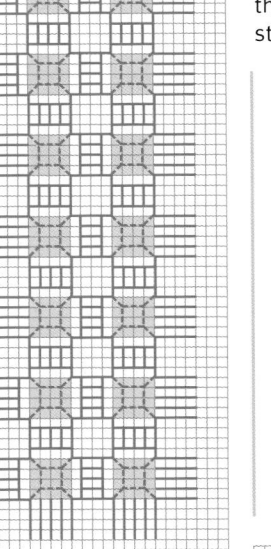

Key

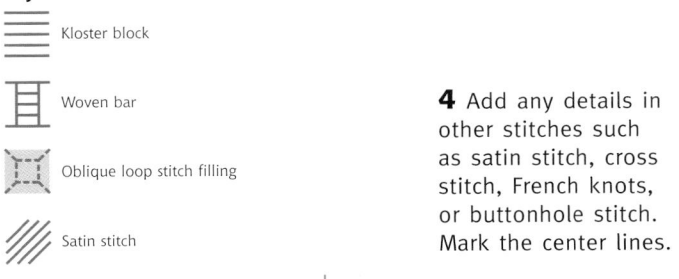

≡≡≡ Kloster block

⊞ Woven bar

▣ Oblique loop stitch filling

⫽⫽ Satin stitch

4 Add any details in other stitches such as satin stitch, cross stitch, French knots, or buttonhole stitch. Mark the center lines.

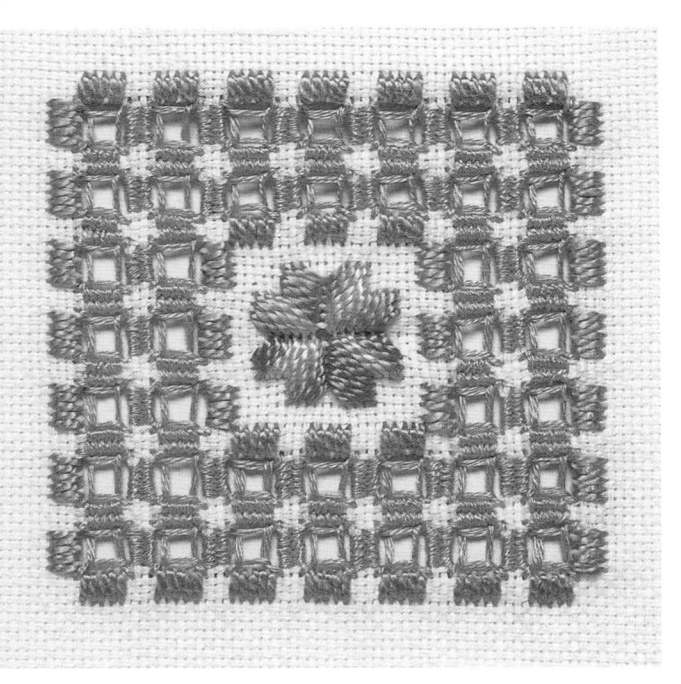

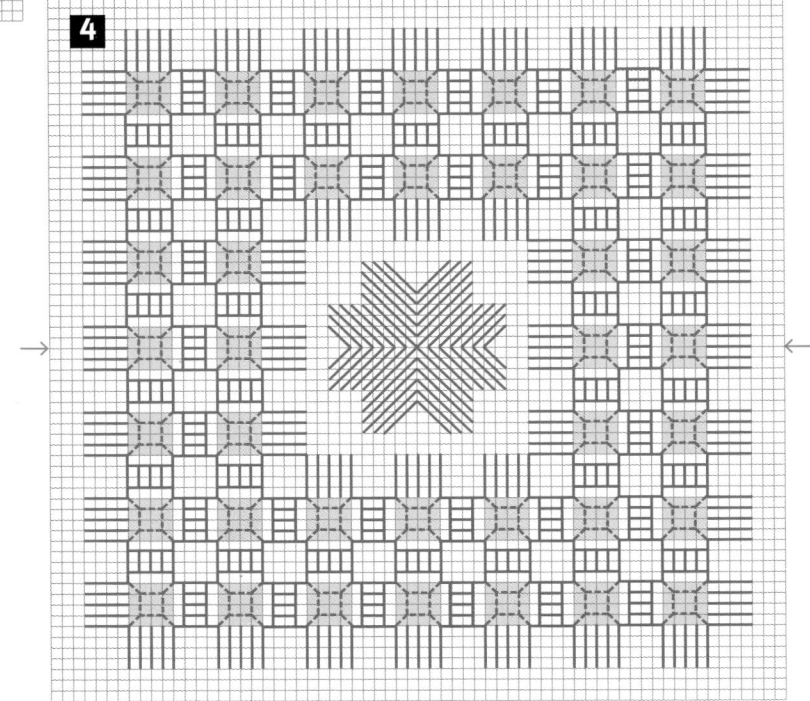

Charting Repeats, Borders, and Corners

The various types of pattern repeats are described on pages 85–87. If you are working on a computer you can quickly copy, paste, flip, or rotate images to help you decide on the arrangement you want. If you are working on graph paper, try the techniques below.

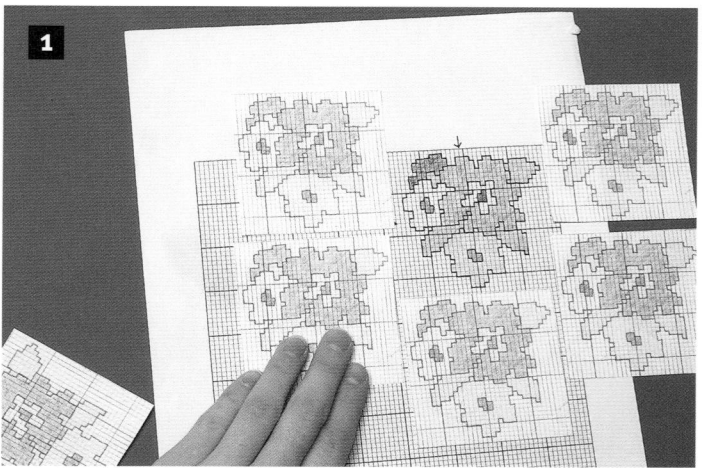

1 To visualize how an image or chart will look when repeated, photocopy it several times and arrange the copies as required.

2 To view an image in reverse, use a small mirror.

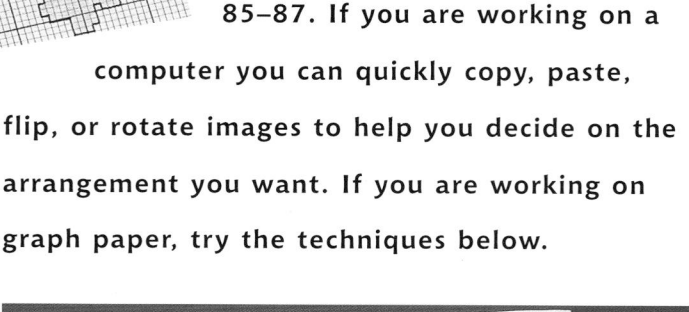

3 You can also use a mirror to design the corners of a border.

4 Two mirrors taped together can be used to design a quartered repeat.

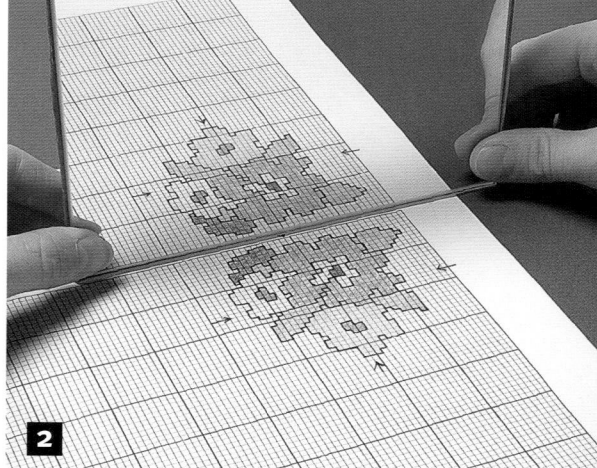

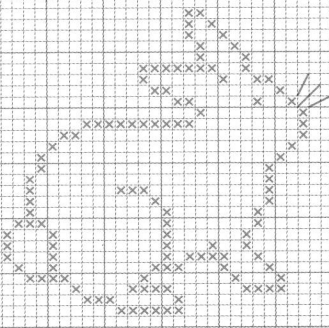

SEWING GUIDELINES

For a neat finish to your work, follow these guidelines when sewing any project.

1 Pre-wash any fabric that is liable to shrink. Press all fabrics flat and square before cutting out.

2 For straight edges, cut Aida fabric and canvas along straight lines of holes. Other fabrics (incuding evenweave) should be cut straight with the fabric grain.

3 To prevent fraying, all edges that will not be hemmed should be oversewn or machined with zigzag stitch.

4 Straight seams should be sewn along lines of holes or straight with the fabric grain. Pin and tack them before stitching, positioning the tacking close to the seam line but not exactly on it—that way the tacking is easy to remove.

5 To turn a double hem, fold and press ¼ inch (6mm) to the wrong side. Then fold again by a further ½ inch (12.5mm), press, pin in place, and tack. Use matching sewing thread to hemstitch by hand, or machine stitch close to the fold through all layers.

Showing Off

The projects in this section show you how to use your embroidery for decorative articles such as pictures and hangings, or more practical items like cushions and table linen. You can make special gifts and greetings cards, or personalize ready-made items such as towels or garments. Some of the designs include charts, while others use motifs charted elsewhere in this book. You can adapt any of these projects by using your own choice of motif, threads, and/or fabrics, to make a finished piece that is unique to you.

CHAPTER 5

Make your own Greetings Cards

A homemade greetings card adds a personal touch to any special occasion. You can buy aperture cards in a wide range of colors, shapes, and sizes, or simply fix a fringed panel to plain colored card.

2 Decide how deep the fringe will be on each side. Loosen the threads with a pin and pull them out one by one.

3 Make a fringe on all four sides. Press flat.

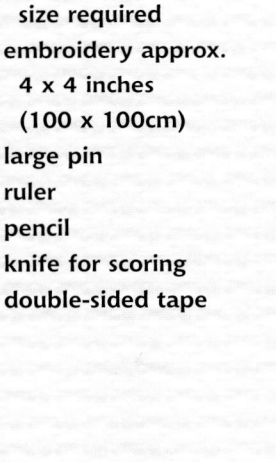

FRINGED PANEL CARD

YOU WILL NEED:
1 sheet of card cut to
   size required
embroidery approx.
   4 x 4 inches
   (100 x 100cm)
large pin
ruler
pencil
knife for scoring
double-sided tape

1 Press the embroidery and trim the edges to the final size (including fringe) required, along a straight line of holes.

4 On the wrong side of the card, mark the center of each long side. Use the ruler and the blunt edge of a knife to score between the two marks.

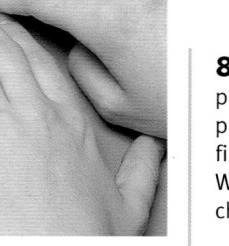

5 The card may then be folded neatly in half.

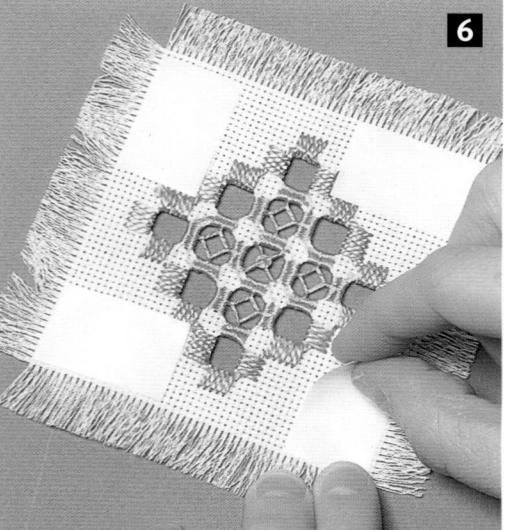

6 Fix pieces of double-sided tape to the back of the embroidery, just inside the fringed edges. Leave the backing paper on the tape.

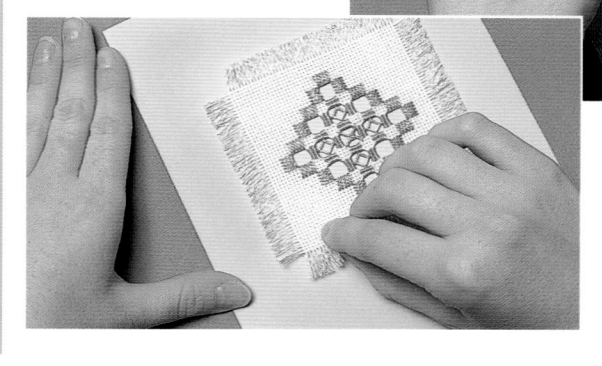

8 Remove the backing paper from the tape and press the embroidery firmly in place. We used the motif charted on page 82.

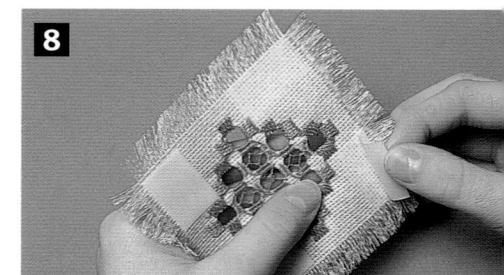

▶ This card with a Hardanger motif will suit any occasion.

7 Position the embroidery as required and mark the corners lightly in pencil.

NOTE
• *To fray the edges of the embroidery as shown, there must be at least ½ inch (12.5mm) of unstitched fabric all around the embroidered motif.*

APERTURE CARD

YOU WILL NEED:
aperture card to suit
  embroidery
double-sided tape
lightweight batting to fit
  card aperture
fabric marker

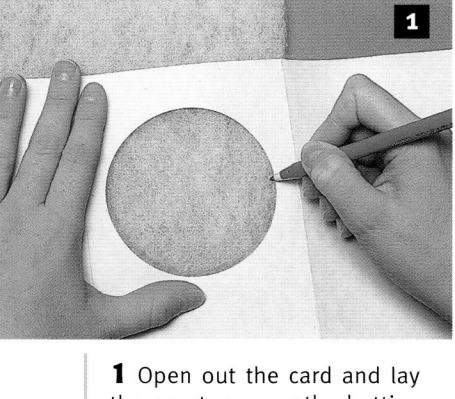

1 Open out the card and lay the aperture over the batting. Draw round the inside of the aperture (without marking the card).

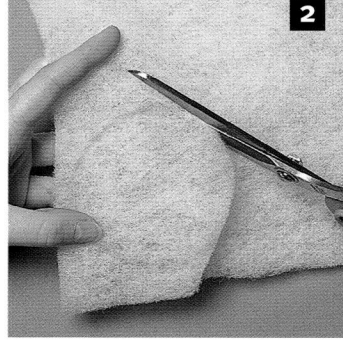

2 Cut out the batting just inside the marked line.

3 Close the card and fix a length of double-sided tape at the center of the aperture. Remove the backing paper from the tape.

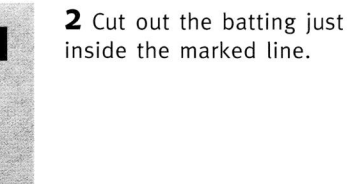

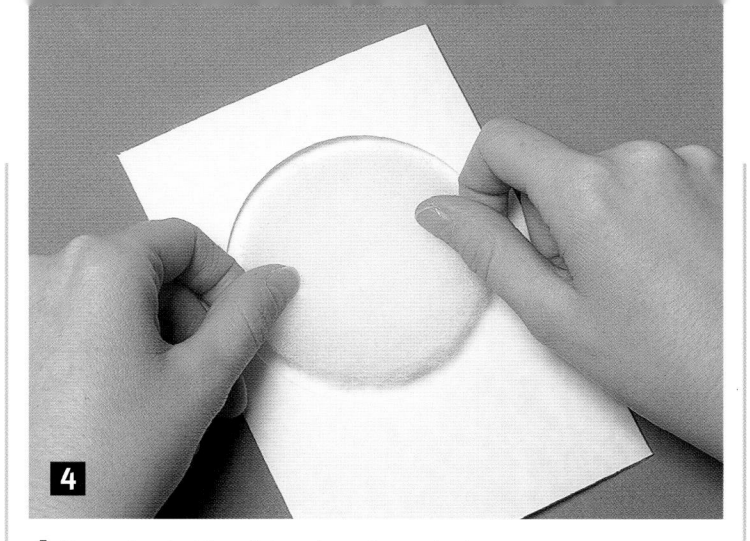

4 Press the batting into place through the aperture.

5 On the wrong side of the card, fix lengths of double-sided tape all around the aperture. You can cut pieces lengthwise to make them narrower if necessary. Remove the backing paper from the tape.

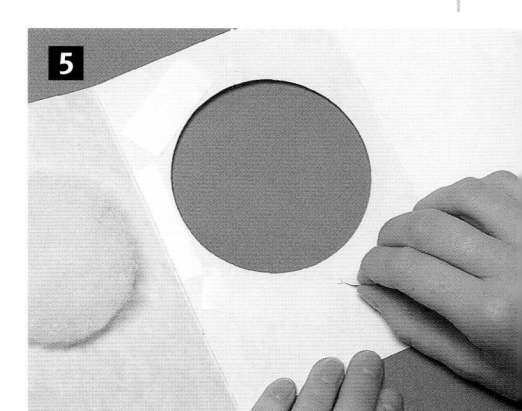

5 Position the aperture over the embroidery and press the mount in place.

7 Turn the card over and fix more double-sided tape all round the back of the aperture panel, close to the edges.

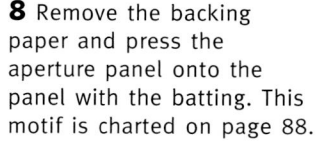

8 Remove the backing paper and press the aperture panel onto the panel with the batting. This motif is charted on page 88.

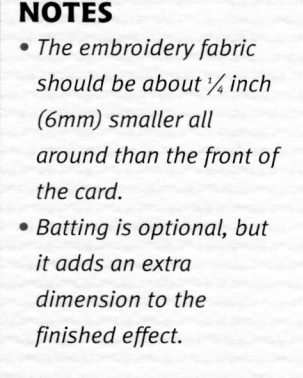

NOTES
• The embroidery fabric should be about ¼ inch (6mm) smaller all around than the front of the card.

• Batting is optional, but it adds an extra dimension to the finished effect.

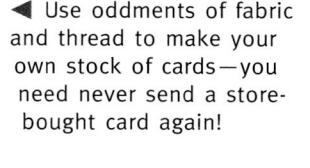

◀ Use oddments of fabric and thread to make your own stock of cards—you need never send a store-bought card again!

Mat and Frame a Picture

When framing embroidery under glass it is advisable to use a cardboard window mat, so that the glass does not actually touch the embroidered surface. Choose the mat color and shape to suit your embroidery.

The fabric should be at least 1 inch (25mm) larger all around than the backing board of the frame so that it may be stretched over it and laced at the back to keep the work flat.

YOU WILL NEED:
suitable frame with
  glass, backing board
  and window mat
sharp needle
strong thread

1 Lay the embroidery right side down on a flat surface. Place the backing board at the center.

Fold two opposite sides of fabric over the edges of the board. Thread the needle from the spool (without cutting the thread) and lace the two edges together as shown, pulling the thread through from the spool as required.

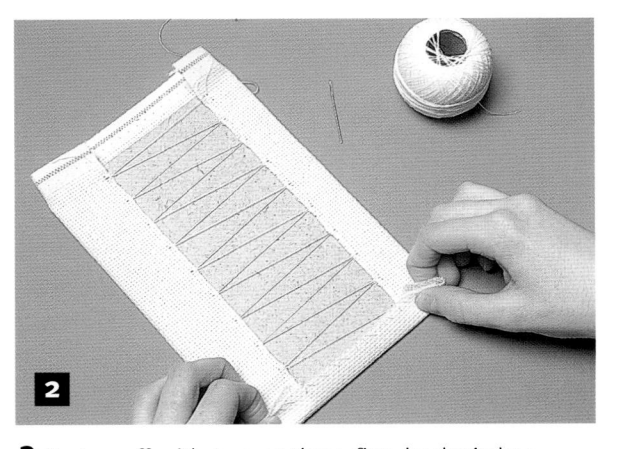

2 Fasten off with two or three firm backstitches. Cut the thread at the spool end leaving a long tail.

Fold in the other two sides, making neat square corners, as flat as possible. Lace these two sides in the same way.

4 Place the frame right side down on a flat surface. Clean the inside of the glass and put it in the frame. Then put in the window mat and the embroidery. If the frame is deep enough, you can add another layer of card or board at the back to hide the lacing. Fold down the tags to hold all the layers in place (or use panel pins inserted sideways into the frame).

3 Turn the work over and check the position: adjust the lacing to place the embroidery at the center (check with the window mount), then fasten off the long tails of thread securely.

▶ Stitch a picture of a friend's house for a very special gift.

Make a Hanging

Any embroidered panel on fabric or canvas can be lined and hung by loops from a pole. If the work is on suitable fabric, you can fringe the lower edge, adding knots or beads as a decorative finish.

YOU WILL NEED:

embroidery with at least
4 inches (100mm)
extra fabric at lower
edge, for fringing
lining fabric, same size
as embroidery
braid or ribbon for loops
(approx. 4 inches
[100mm] per loop)
sewing thread to match
embroidery fabric
pole such as ¾ inch
(18mm) wooden
dowel rod, length to
match unfinished
width of embroidery
cord approx. 6 inches
(150mm) longer than
pole
tapestry needle
sharp needle
beads with large holes

NOTES
• *For a large or heavy hanging, use thicker dowel rod and correspondingly more and longer loops.*
• *Check to see if lining fabric shows through embroidery; if necessary, use lining to match embroidery fabric, or back embroidery with a layer of interlining.*

Key

▨ Pink cross stitch
• Pink French knot
╱ Black Holbein stitch

Chart for embroidery

Our hanging was worked from this chart: you can substitute the initials you require from the alphabet on page 48. We used 10 x 15 inch (250 x 375mm) of 10-count white Aida fabric, with pink Pearl cotton no. 5 for the cross stitch and French knots, and black coton à broder for the Holbein stitch. Follow the guidelines for Assisi work on page 74–75.

1 Cut the embroidery to size along straight rows of holes, allowing ½ inch (12.5mm) for seams on top and side edges, and at least 4 inches (100mm) for fringe on lower edge. Mark the top edge of the fringe with a line of basting.

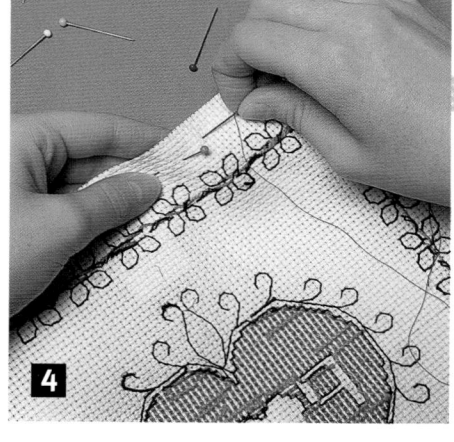

2 Cut the lining fabric to the same size, minus 3½ inches (88mm) at lower edge: the lining will be turned inside for ½ inch (12.5mm) at the lower edge, to match the top of the fringe. (For a hanging without a fringe, cut the lining to the same size as the embroidery.)

3 Cut three 4 inch (100mm) lengths of braid or ribbon, or number required. Double each piece into a loop, then pin and baste loops to right side of lining, evenly spaced along top edge, avoiding seam allowance at each side.

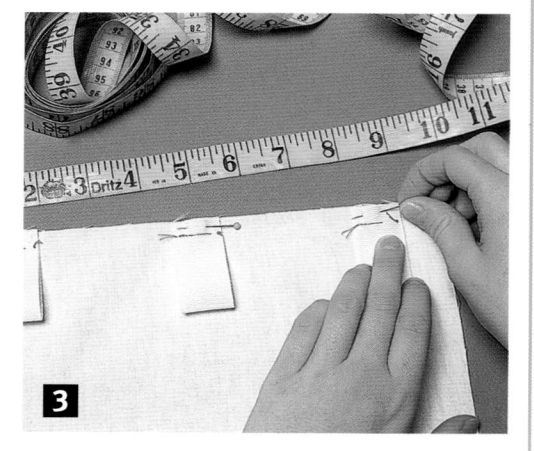

4 Place embroidery and lining, right sides together, with loops inside, matching top and side edges. Pin and baste top and side edges.

5 Use matching sewing thread to machine or backstitch these three sides, working from the embroidered side so you can stitch along straight rows of holes.

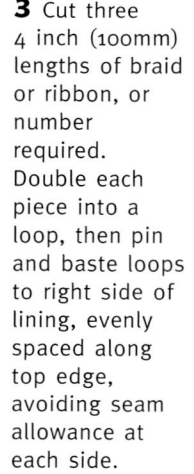

6 Clip across the top corners close to the stitching.

7 Press ½ inch (12.5mm) of lining to wrong side along lower edge, so fold matches basted fringe line. (For a hanging without a fringe, press both seam allowances to wrong side.)

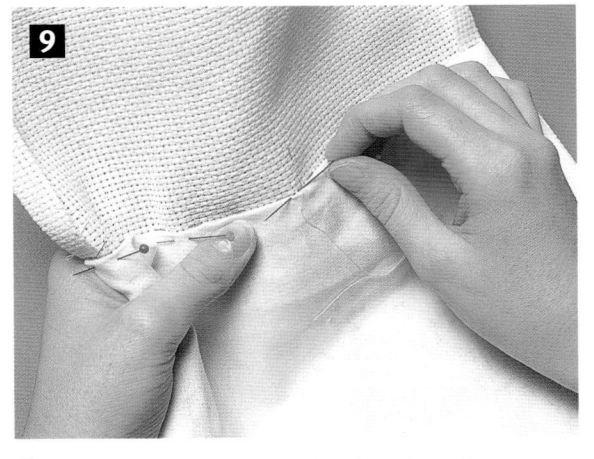

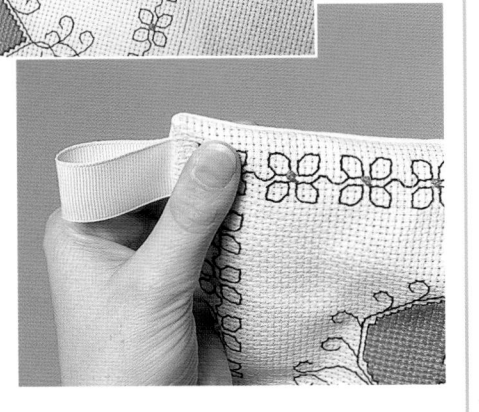

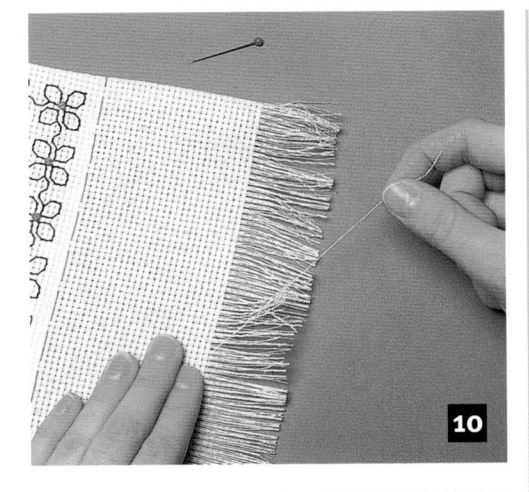

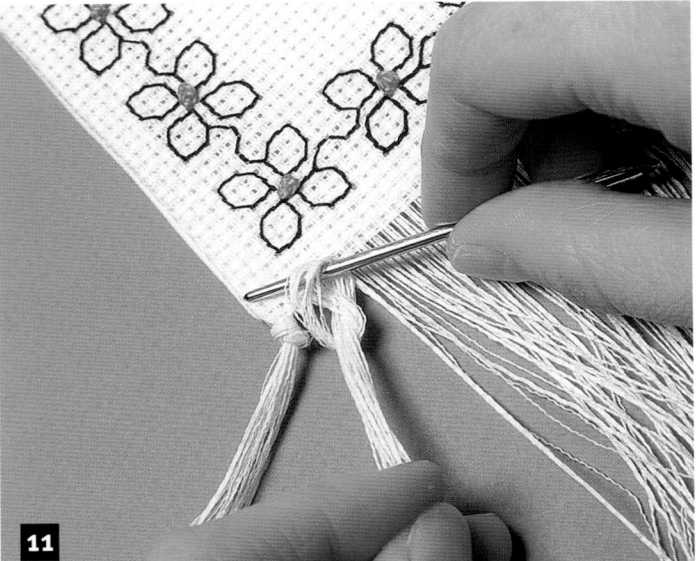

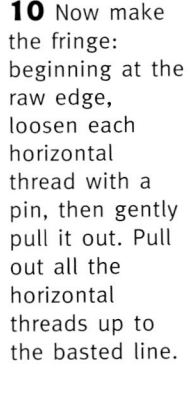

8 Turn right side out. Push out the corners with a blunt point such as a knitting needle. Press.

9 Pin lower edge of lining in place just above basted fringe line, then slipstitch by hand. (For a hanging without a fringe, pin both lower edges together and slipstitch in same way.) Press again.

10 Now make the fringe: beginning at the raw edge, loosen each horizontal thread with a pin, then gently pull it out. Pull out all the horizontal threads up to the basted line.

11 Divide the fringe into equal bundles. Knot each bundle with an overhand knot, easing the knot into place with a large tapestry needle.

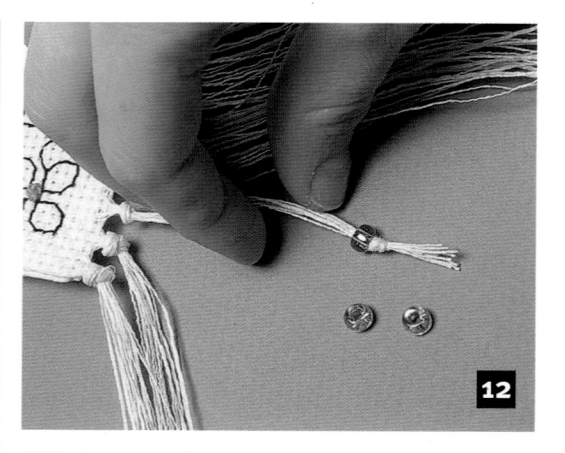

12 If you wish, thread a bead onto each bundle and tie another knot near the bottom of the fringe.

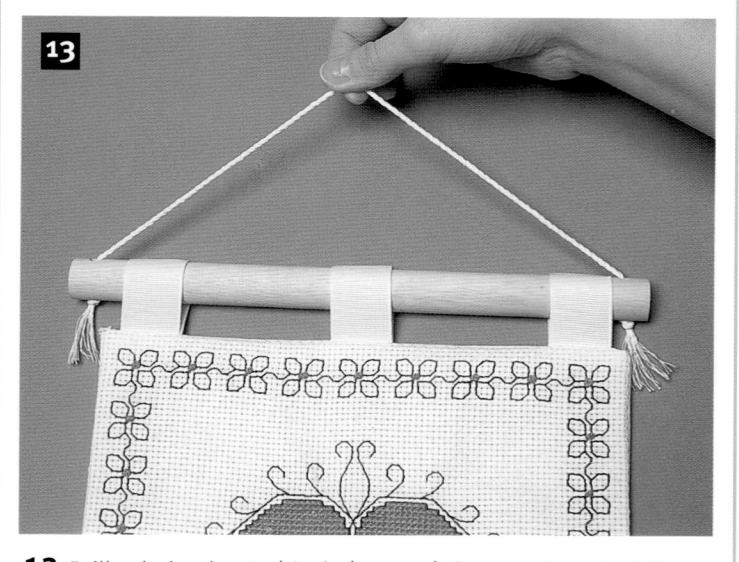

13 Drill a hole about ½ inch (12.5mm) from each end of the pole, to fit the cord. Thread the pole through the loops, then thread the cord ends through the holes and finish each end with a knot. You can add beads to the cord ends or fray them to form small tassels. Hang the finished panel by the cord and if necessary trim the ends of the fringe level.

▲ Stitch our hanging with your choice of initials (from the chart on page 46), for a wedding or anniversary gift.

Make a Pillow Cover

A pillow cover is a great way to show off your work, provided the embroidery is durable enough to withstand the wear and tear, and may be washed or drycleaned.

This simple pillow has an overlapping back, so no zipper or other fastening is required.

A small embroidered panel on fabric or canvas may be mounted on a larger piece of fabric, as shown here. You can arrange the panel in any way you like.

YOU WILL NEED (FOR A PILLOW 15 x 15 inches [380mm]):

embroidered panel,
plain fabric 16 x 40 inches (400 x 100mm),
sewing threads to match fabrics,
Sharp needle,
Tape measure or ruler.

NOTES
• For a pillow of a different size, you will need fabric measuring:
height of pillow plus 1 inch (25mm) x twice width of pillow plus 8 inches (200mm). This size allows ½ inch (12.5mm) for seams and an overlap of approx. 6 inches (150mm) at center back.
• Choose a weight of fabric to suit the embroidery. For embroidery on canvas a heavyweight furnishing fabric is advisable.

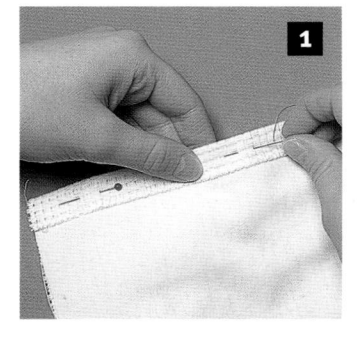

For embroidery on fabric
1 Turn the raw edges of the embroidery under by about ½ inch (12.5mm) all around and press. If the pillow fabric is a strongly contrasting color, you may need to back with plain fabric: cut this to the same size as the panel and baste it in place.

2 To find the center of the fabric, fold it in half in one direction and press the fold lightly. Repeat in the other direction and where the two folds cross marks the center front. If your embroidery has center lines, you can line these up with the folds, or position your embroidery as desired. Pin and baste the panel in place.

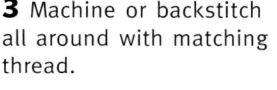

3 Machine or backstitch all around with matching thread.

4 Add a decorative border if you wish (herringbone stitch [page 32] is used here).

For embroidery on canvas
Cut the panel about ¼ inch (6mm) outside the stitched area and paint the edges with anti-fray solution. Leave to dry. Pin and baste the piece in place, then work decorative stitching all around (such as the buttonhole stitch used here), working through both layers and covering the raw edges completely. Use a sharp crewel needle and position the stitches evenly through the canvas mesh. Alternatively, you can cover the raw edges with lengths of ribbon or braid.

To make up the pillow
1 First turn and stitch a small hem to the wrong side along each short edge of the fabric.

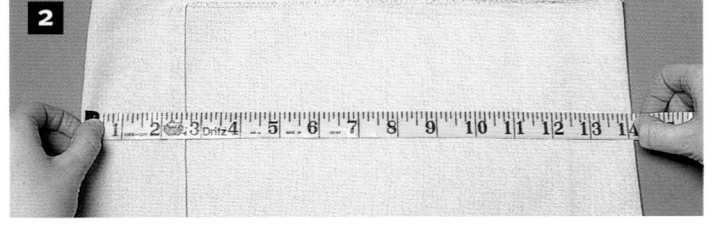

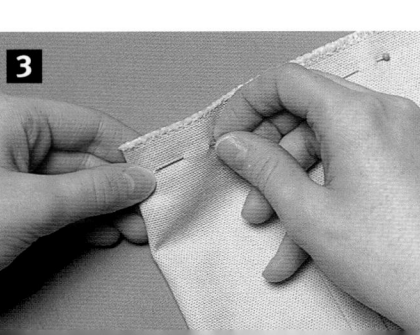

2 Lay the fabric right side up on a flat surface. Fold in the hemmed edges by the same amount at each side, overlapping them to make the width 15 inches (38mm) (or width required).

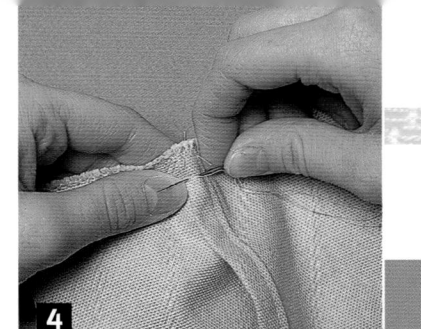

3 Pin the top and bottom edges together through all layers. The seam allowance is ½ inch (12.5mm).

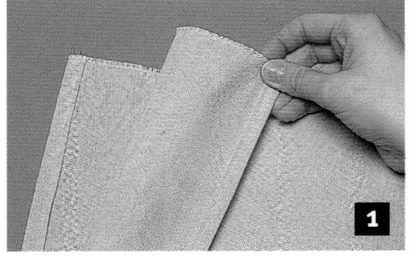

4 Machine or backstitch the top and bottom seams.

5 Clip the corners.

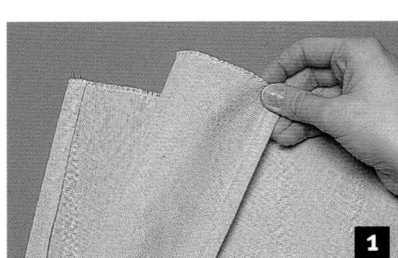

6 Turn right side out. Push out the corners with a blunt-tipped knitting needle or similar. Press and insert pillow pad.

▲ The tent stitch panel was worked from the painted canvas design on page 100.
The cross stitch design was adapted from the chart on page 88 and worked in Pearl cotton no. 5 on 6-count Binca fabric.

Make a Pincushion

A small piece of embroidery can be made into a pincushion—a great gift for a sewing friend.

YOU WILL NEED:
embroidery approx.
5 x 5 inches (125 x
125mm)—this
includes a seam
allowance of ½ inch
(12.5mm) all around
backing fabric same
size
24 inches (600mm)
cord or braid
filling such as toy
stuffing or kapok
sewing thread to
match fabric
sharp needle

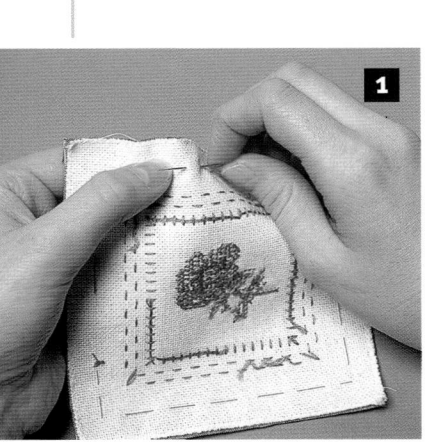

1 Cut backing fabric to same size as embroidery. Place the embroidery and the backing fabric with right sides together, pin and baste around the edges with a seam allowance of ½ inch (12.5mm).

2 Machine or backstitch, leaving a 3 inch (75mm) gap at the center of one side.

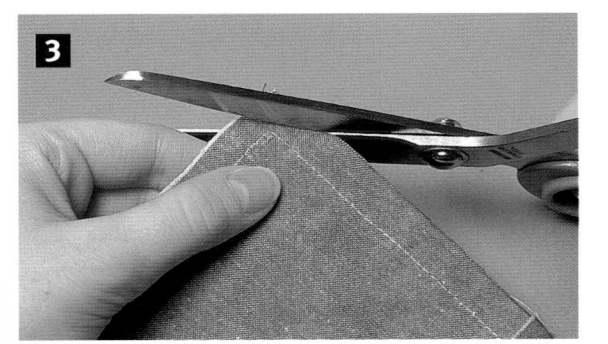

3 Remove the basting. Clip across the corners close to the stitching.

4 Press the seam allowances to the wrong side along each edge of the opening, making sharp folds.

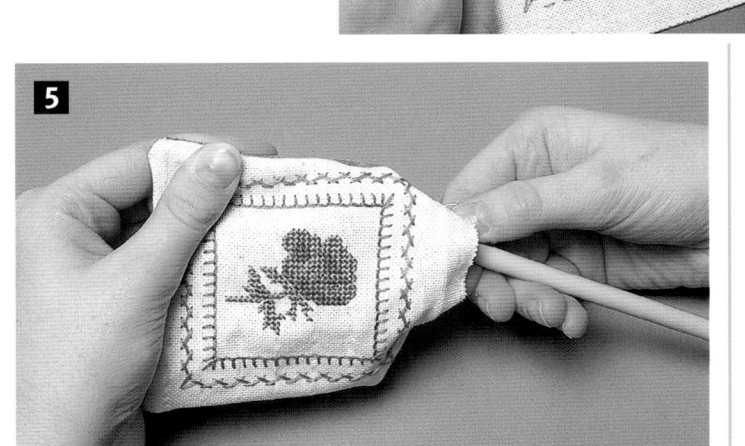

5 Turn right side out. Use a blunt point (such as a large knitting needle) to push out the corners.

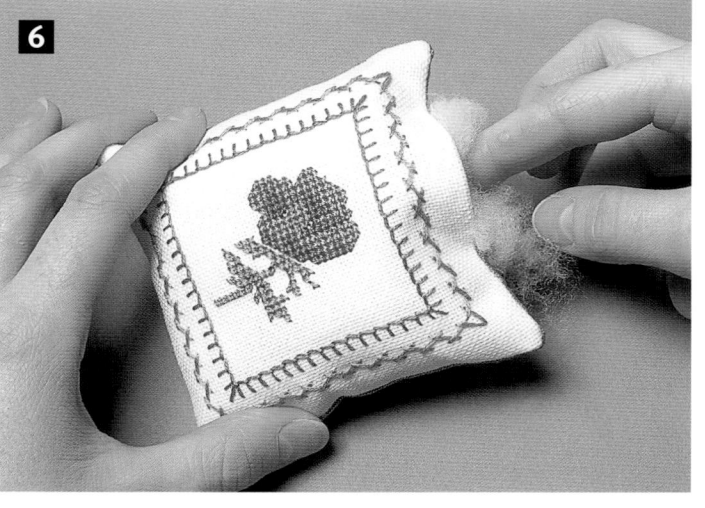

6 Insert the filling: a pincushion should be stuffed quite firmly.

8 Form a loop knot at the center of the cord and pin it at one corner. Then pin the ends of the cord around the sides to cover the seam, meeting at the opposite corner to the loop. Stitch the cord in place by hand.

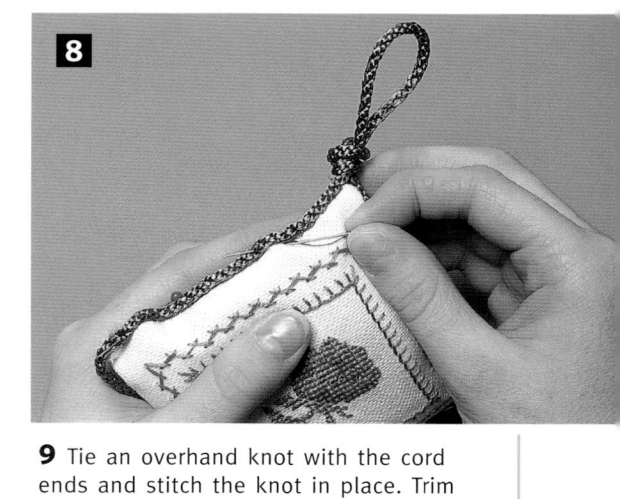

9 Tie an overhand knot with the cord ends and stitch the knot in place. Trim the ends to about 1½ inches (37.5mm) and fray them to form a tassel.

7 Slipstitch the opening with matching thread.

▶ The design on this pincushion was worked from the chart on page 103, adding a border of herringbone stitch (page 32) and blanket stitch (page 53).

Frame a Mirror

Plastic canvas is useful for projects such as this mirror frame: the cut edges require no turned hems, and the canvas will keep its shape without support.

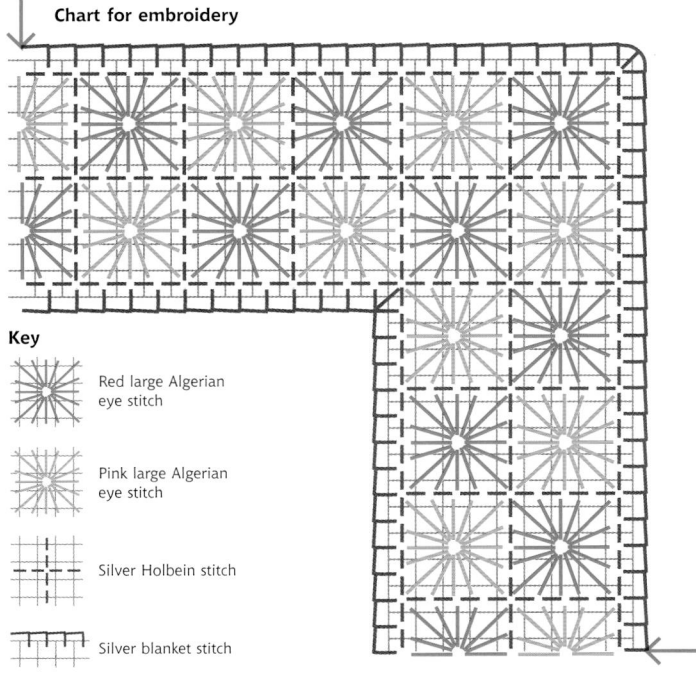

Chart for embroidery

Key

	Red large Algerian eye stitch
	Pink large Algerian eye stitch
	Silver Holbein stitch
	Silver blanket stitch

NOTES

• The plastic canvas is approx. ⅜ inch (10mm) larger all around than the mirror tile. If you are charting your own design, or using canvas of a different gauge, count the required number of holes/bars carefully. On outer edges, the number of bars will always be one more than that of the holes. If you need to adjust the size, make the canvas larger rather than smaller.

• The felt is approx. ¼ inch (6mm) larger all around than the mirror tile.

YOU WILL NEED (TO FIT A 6 x 6 inch [150 x 150mm] MIRROR TILE):

7-gauge plastic canvas 6¾ x 6¾ inches (170 x 170mm)
yarns for embroidery
tapestry needle
6 inch (150mm) braid
felt backing 6½ x 6½ inches (160 x 160mm)
sewing thread to match felt
sharp needle
felt tip pen
large and small scissors

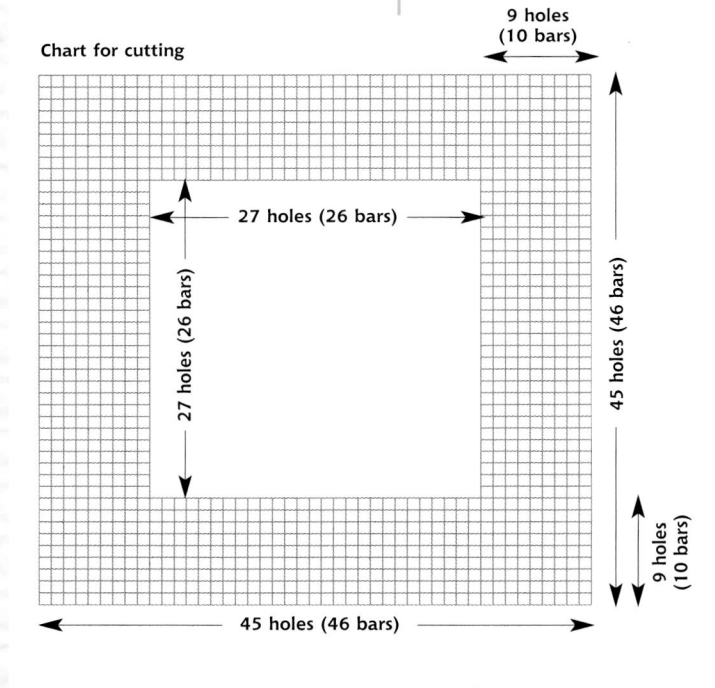

Chart for cutting

9 holes (10 bars)

27 holes (26 bars)

27 holes (26 bars)

45 holes (46 bars)

9 holes (10 bars)

45 holes (46 bars)

Work this design as a quartered repeat (page 87), keeping the stitch direction constant throughout. Large Algerian eye stitch is worked in the same way as Algerian eye stitch (page 52), but over a square of four bars (or threads) in each direction, with 16 stitches passing through the center hole.

Our frame was worked on 7-gauge plastic canvas, using tapestry wool in red and pink, with silver lurex knitting yarn used single for the Holbein stitch and double for the blanket stitch.

Work the large Algerian eye stitches in red and pink, then the Holbein stitch (page 31) in silver lurex. Lastly work the blanket stitch edgings (page 53) using the silver lurex double.

1 Counting the holes and bars carefully, mark out the required shape on the plastic canvas using a felt tip pen, following the chart for cutting.

Cut out the plastic canvas with large scissors, cutting along rows of holes.

2 Use small scissors to trim off all the little "nubs," leaving smooth edges.

3 Work following the chart for embroidery.

Fold the braid in half to make a loop for hanging and sew it to the back of the frame at the center of the top edge.

4 Pin the felt to the back of the frame, just inside the blanket stitch edging. Use matching sewing thread to slipstitch the two side edges and the lower edge, leaving the top edge open.

5 Insert the mirror tile. You can slipstitch the top edge if you wish.

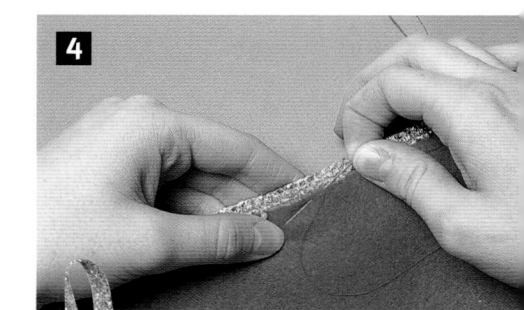

▲ Stitch our mirror frame in your own choice of colors.

TIP *You can also use this frame for a photograph. Mount the photograph on a 6 x 6 inch (150 x 150mm) piece of firm cardboard and protect it with a sheet of clear acetate.*

Make a Box

Plastic canvas can also be used to make three-dimensional objects, such as our snowflake box.

YOU WILL NEED:

7-gauge plastic canvas
10 x 12 inches (250 x 300mm)

yarns in two colors

tapestry needle

large and small scissors

felt tip pen

felt and fabric glue for lining

Our box was worked on 7-gauge plastic canvas and measures 3½ x 3½ x 2½ inches (85 x 85 x 60mm). We used lilac double knitting wool for the main color and silver lurex 4-ply yarn for the contrast, using this double for the cross stitch and joining stitches, and single for the backstitch. The felt lining is optional. For a smaller box, you could work the same design on 10-count plastic canvas with suitable yarns. You could also use the outlines of our pieces to design a box with another motif: notice how the base is one square smaller than the lid.

← 23 holes (24 bars) →

23 holes (24 bars)

LID TOP: make 1

7 holes (8 bars)

LID SIDE: make 4

16 holes (17 bars)

BASE SIDE: make 4

21 holes (22 bars)

BASE: make 1

← 21 holes (22 bars) →

Key

■ Lilac
▨ Silver
⌐ Silver backstitch
⌐ Cutting line

You could also use the outlines of our pieces to design a box with another motif: notice how the base is one square smaller than the lid.

Count the squares and bars very carefully. Each square on the chart represents one cross stitch worked on the canvas. The number of bars will always be one more than the number of holes for the cross stitch to be surrounded by a solid edge. Mark out the pieces on the canvas with a felt tip pen, cut them out and trim the edges, as steps 1 and 2, page 129.

1 Work all the cross stitch and backstitch on all the pieces. To line the box, lay the base and the four base side pieces on the felt and draw around them.

TIP *You may prefer to work the cross stitch first, then cut out the pieces, but a small piece of plastic canvas is easier to hold.*

2 Cut out the felt just inside the marked lines, so the felt pieces are about one bar smaller all around than the canvas pieces.

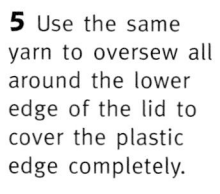

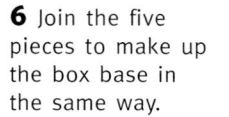

5 Use the same yarn to oversew all around the lower edge of the lid to cover the plastic edge completely.

6 Join the five pieces to make up the box base in the same way.

3 Apply a line of glue all around the edge of each piece of felt and fix to wrong side of embroidered canvas. Leave to dry. (If you prefer, the felt may be slipstitched in place to the back of the embroidery.) You can line the lid pieces in the same way if you wish.

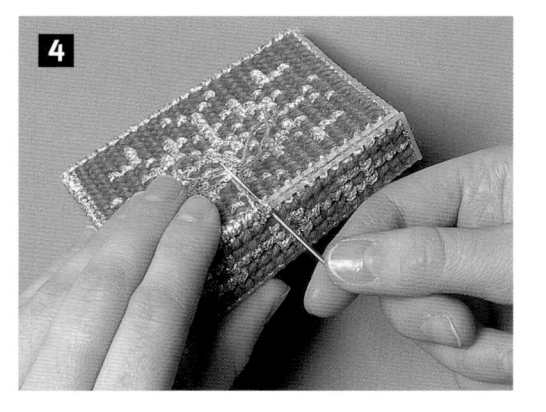

4 To join the pieces, use contrasting yarn: begin at one corner of the lid top. Hold one lid-side piece in place, matching the holes along the edges, and oversew twice through each pair of holes, along to the next corner. The plastic edge should be covered by the stitches. Then pick up the next lid side piece and join the short side edges down to the corner. Fasten off the yarn. Join in new yarn at the corner of the lid top to sew the second side to the lid. Continue in this way until the lid is complete.

◄ Fill the box with candy or pot-pourri, or use it to present a special gift.

Frame a Photo

Perforated paper, like plastic canvas, can be cut to shape without finishing the edges, as they will not fray. It can also be painted, as here: use acrylic paint and make sure it is completely dry before beginning to stitch.

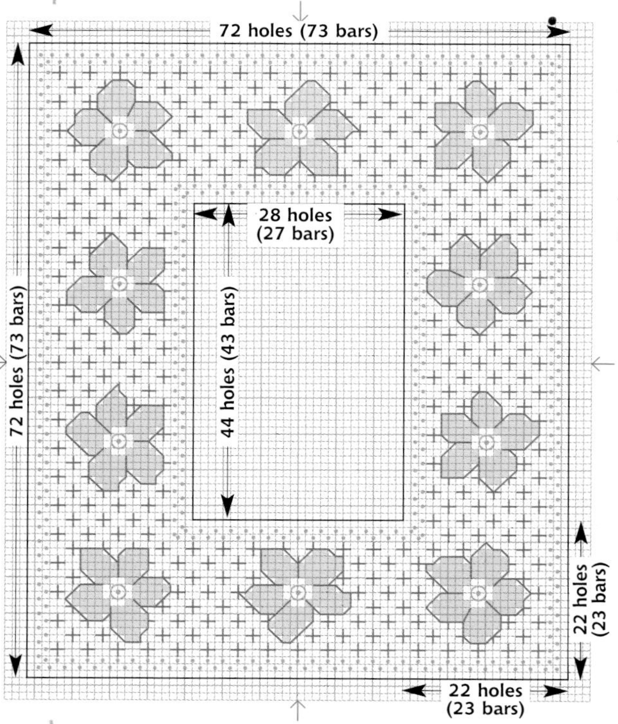

72 holes (73 bars)

28 holes (27 bars)

44 holes (43 bars)

72 holes (73 bars)

22 holes (23 bars)

22 holes (23 bars)

Key

- ▦ Cream cross stitch
- + Bronze upright cross stitch
- ⌐ Bronze Holbein stitch
- · Bead
- ⌐ Cutting line
- ⊙ Bead and sequin

This frame is worked on 14-count perforated paper, and measures 6¼ x 5 inches (155 x 125mm), with an aperture to suit a photo of 3¼ x 2 inches (80 x 50mm). We used cream paper, painted with gold craft paint; cream viscose and bronze metallic threads, with small bronze beads and gold sequins.

YOU WILL NEED:

14-count perforated paper
threads for embroidery
approx. 400 small beads
10 sequins
sewing thread to blend with paper
small tapestry needle
plain card in a toning color
6 inches (150mm) cord or braid
clear acetate sheet at least ¼ inch (6mm) larger all around than photograph
large and small scissors
masking tape
pencil
metal ruler
craft knife
craft glue or double-sided tape

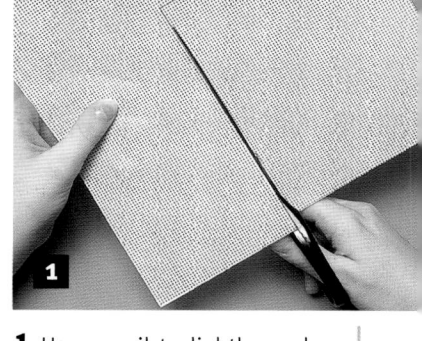

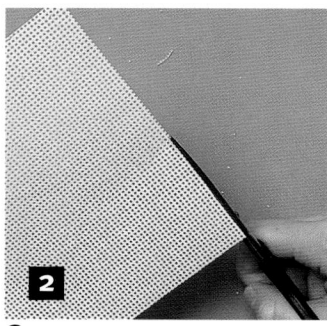

1 Use pencil to lightly mark out the cutting lines on the perforated paper (along rows of holes) following the chart, counting carefully.

Cut out along the marked pencil lines. Use large scissors to cut along the rows of holes.

2 Then use small scissors to trim off all the little "nubs," in the same way as for plastic canvas (page 129).

3 Mark the center lines with basting in the usual way. Work the embroidery. Work the cross stitch in cream viscose thread, using strands equivalent to three strands of stranded cotton. Work the Holbein stitch outlines in fine bronze metallic thread, using strands equivalent to one strand of stranded cotton. Use the same thread to work the background pattern in upright cross stitch, then use sewing thread to sew on all the beads. Note that each bead is sewn along the straight side of a square, not diagonally across, except at the outside corners.

To attach the sequins, bring the needle up through the required hole in the paper, thread on a sequin and a small bead, then insert the needle back through the sequin and the same hole in the paper. The bead will hold the sequin in place.

4 Fold the cord or braid in half and sew it to the wrong side, at center top.

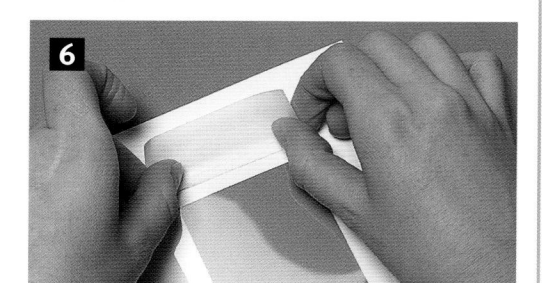

5 Cut a piece of plain card the same size as the embroidery, but with the window ⅛ inch (3mm) larger all around.

6 Fix the acetate over the window with masking tape, on the wrong side of the card.

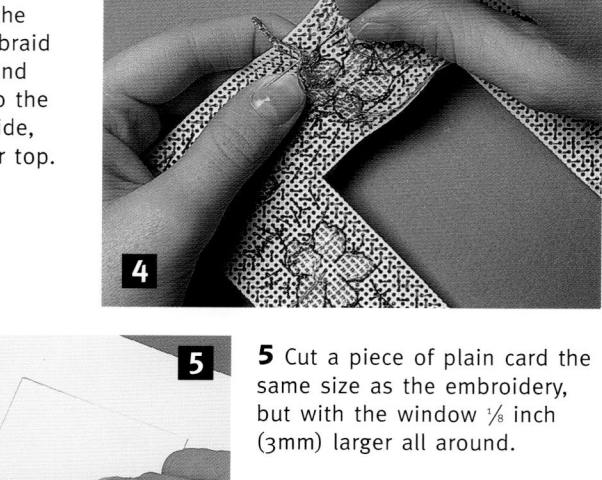

7 Use masking tape to mount the photograph behind the window.

8 Use glue or double-sided tape to fix the embroidery to the card. If desired, another piece of card may be fixed to the back to strengthen the frame and protect the photograph.

◄ Our threads were chosen to suit a sepia photograph; for a color snap, choose your own bright colorway.

TIPS

- *Handle the paper gently when stitching, to avoid creasing: use the stab method of stitching (page 64).*
- *Do not pull stitches too tightly or the paper may tear.*
- *If you should tear the paper, don't despair! Mend it with masking tape on the wrong side and use a sharp needle to re-pierce the holes.*
- *When designing for perforated paper, avoid part cross stitches; these are impossible to stitch without tearing the paper. Also avoid stitches such as Algerian eye stitch, where many threads pass through one hole.*

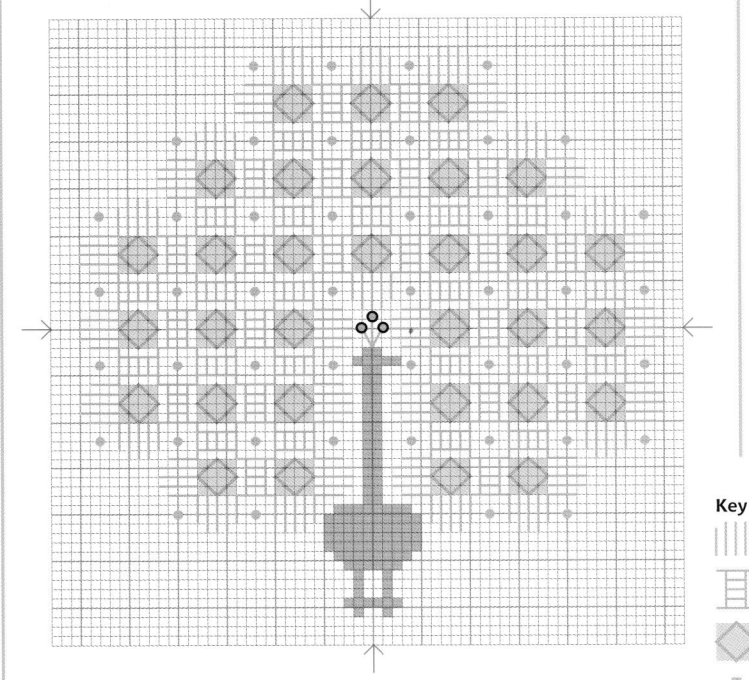

Line a Purse

Use this technique to turn any piece of fabric embroidery into a purse; we used a piece of Hardanger work, but cross stitch or blackwork would be equally suitable. Our purse measures 8 x 8 inches (200 x 200mm), but you can adapt the instructions to any size you wish.

YOU WILL NEED

- embroidery for the front, approx. 9 x 9 inches (225 x 225mm) (this includes a ½ inch [12.5mm] seam allowance all around)
- fabric for the back, same size as front
- 2 pieces of lining fabric, same size as front
- sewing threads to match fabrics
- sharp needle
- 18 inch (450mm) medium cord or braid for the handle
- 18 inch (450mm) fine cord or braid for the ties

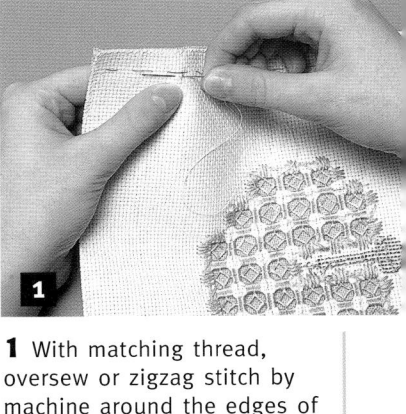

1 With matching thread, oversew or zigzag stitch by machine around the edges of all the pieces to prevent fraying. Place the front and back panels with right sides together. Pin and baste around three sides, leaving the top edge open. Machine or backstitch these three sides, stitching from the embroidered side following straight lines of holes.

Key

|||||	Pale blue adapted Kloster block
☰	Pale blue woven bar
◈	Pale blue straight loopstitch filling
▪	Gold cross stitch
↓	Gold straight stitches
◉	Gold French knot
•	Gold bead

Our peacock is worked on 14-count white Aida fabric, using Pearl cotton no. 2 for the Kloster blocks, with matching stranded cotton for the bars and fillings, and gold viscose thread for the cross stitch and French knots; the beads are light gold. See pages 82–84 for instructions on working Hardanger embroidery.

Note the varied stitch length used for the Kloster blocks, giving a less geometric outline than normal.

TIP *For a good color match, we braided our cords from the Pearl cotton used for the embroidery. For the handle we braided nine strands in bundles of three, and for the ties, three single strands. The ends to be attached to the lining were stitched firmly across to secure all the thread ends, then painted with fabric glue and left to dry before cutting to length. The unattached ends of the ties were knotted and trimmed to form small tassels.*

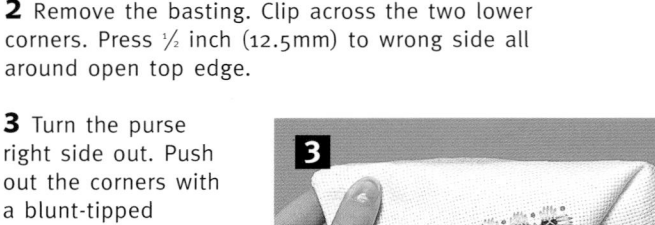

2 Remove the basting. Clip across the two lower corners. Press ½ inch (12.5mm) to wrong side all around open top edge.

3 Turn the purse right side out. Push out the corners with a blunt-tipped knitting needle or similar, in the same way as on page 126. Press the seams.

4 Place the two lining pieces with right sides together. Pin, baste, and stitch them in the same way. Press the side seams open at the top edge, then press ½ inch (12.5mm) to wrong side all round top edge.

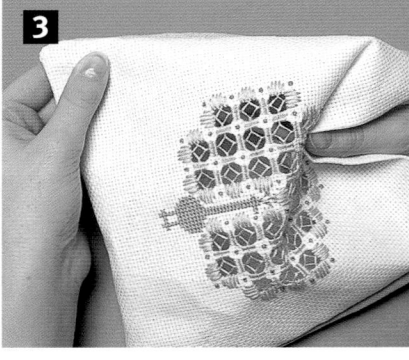

5 Stitch the two ends of the handle to the lining at the top of the side seams.

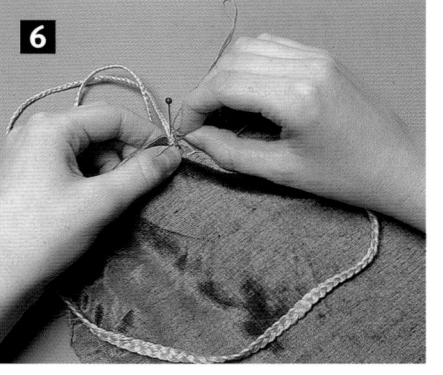

6 Cut the tie cord in half and stitch one length at the center top of each side of the lining.

7 Leave the lining inside-out. Slip the lining inside the outer purse, matching the side seams. Pin and baste the layers together around the top opening, then slipstitch the lining to the outer purse, using thread to match the lining.

▶ Make a purse for a special occasion, using any embroidered panel you choose.

Quick Makes

Simple ideas for gifts or for your home. Evenweave fabric is perfect for table linen, and you can choose any motif to decorate it, or try out a design of your own. You can personalize ready-made articles such as our towel, baby vest, and sweater, or use the same techniques on T-shirts, bathrobes, bed linen, kitchen accessories... whatever you fancy!

TIP *For ready-made items such as garments, pillowslips, or bags, plan your embroidery in an accessible position.*

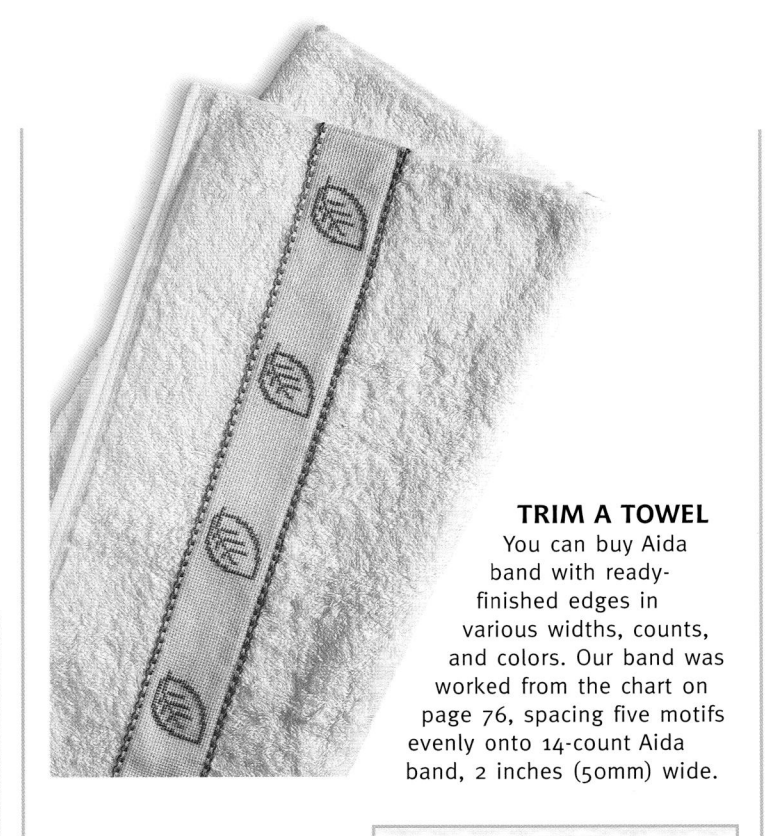

TRIM A TOWEL
You can buy Aida band with ready-finished edges in various widths, counts, and colors. Our band was worked from the chart on page 76, spacing five motifs evenly onto 14-count Aida band, 2 inches (50mm) wide.

COORDINATE A NAPKIN
Our napkin was embroidered with the motif charted on page 106. We used 28-count linen evenweave, working the cross stitch over two threads in each direction, and stranded cottons to match the colors of the plate.

TIPS
- *Allow 1 inch (25mm) for a double hem all around the fabric, and place motifs accordingly.*
- *To work in a hoop or frame, you may prefer to work the motifs before cutting out the fabric.*
- *Work the embroidery first, then turn a double hem all around the piece.*

TIPS
- *Cut the band to the length required, allowing ½ inch (12.5mm) at each end for turning under. Mark the center lines of each motif, spacing the pattern repeat evenly as on page 85.*
- *To work in a hoop, baste waste fabric to either side of the band.*
- *When complete, stitch the band in place by hand or machine, turning the raw edges under at each end.*

DECORATE A VEST

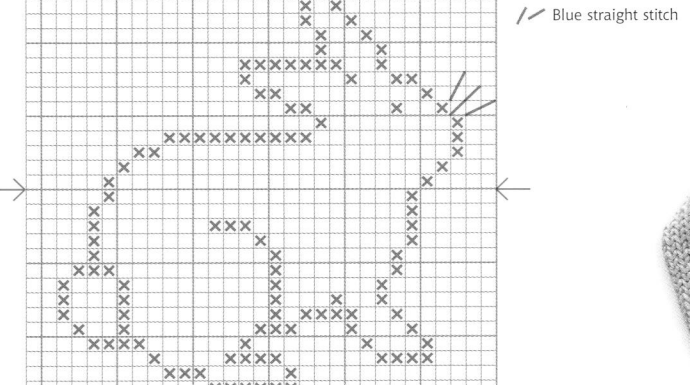

Key

× Blue cross stitch

/ Blue straight stitch

We used the waste canvas technique from page 77, working the embroidery with stranded cotton.

TIPS

• *When working on stretchy fabric such as T-shirt material, baste the waste canvas firmly. It is not advisable to use a hoop, but you can back the area with self-adhesive embroidery stabilizer to make a firmer surface for stitching.*

• *Choose thread such as stranded cotton that will withstand repeated laundering.*

PERSONALIZE A SWEATER

This handknitted sweater was embroidered with the cat design from the chart on page 108, following the guidelines for embroidery on knitting on page 91. You can decorate a purchased sweater in the same way.

Original child's drawing

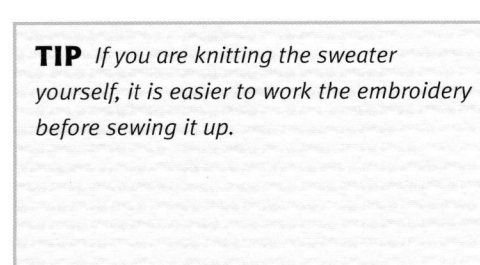

TIP *If you are knitting the sweater yourself, it is easier to work the embroidery before sewing it up.*

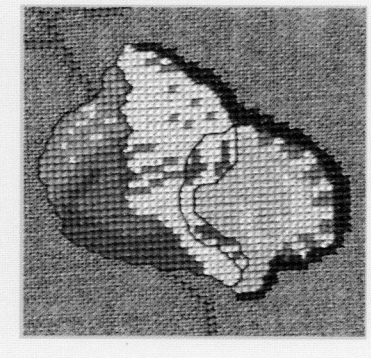

Gallery

Cross stitch and other counted thread stitches are so versatile, they can be used in a wide variety of ways. Today we can choose from a wide variety of wonderful threads, fabrics, and other materials and use them in any way we choose, limited only by our imagination.

CHAPTER 6

Gallery

Some techniques such as blackwork

lend themselves to formal, stylized

designs. Other techniques, such as

multicolored cross stitch or tent stitch, may be

used to represent a subject with almost

photographic accuracy. More decorative designs

find a balance between the interest of the

subject and the intricacy of the stitches.

TRADITIONAL MOTIFS WITH A TWIST

Birds, animals, flowers, hearts, and stars have always been favorite subjects for embroiderers, re-interpreted across the world, in every century, according to the style and fashions of the time. Stitchers today enjoy taking these motifs and making their own versions, as a musician might improvize on a traditional tune.

◄ TREE OF LIFE PILLOW
Jolly Red
16 x 16 in (400 x 400mm)
Tent stitch using tapestry wools on 10-gauge canvas
A favorite embroidery subject since the seventeenth century, the Tree of Life is interpreted here with an unmistakably modern twist.

▲ INDIAN ELEPHANT PILLOW
Jolly Red
15 x 15 in (375 x 375mm)
Tent stitch using tapestry wools on 10-gauge canvas
The elephant has been widely represented in embroidery in every technique imaginable. Here he is accompanied by a border of motifs derived from other elements of Indian embroidery, translated into tent stitch.

▲ BLACKWORK STARBURST
Leon Conrad
4¼ x 4¼ in (105 x 105mm)
Back stitch, running stitch, and Holbein stitch using silk threads on 32-count evenweave linen
This quartered design, inspired by the stylized foliage of sixteenth-century blackwork, is accentuated with tiny beads.

► HEART SAMPLER
The Bold Sheep
4½ x 5¼in
(110 x 132mm)
Cross stitch using stranded cottons on 14-count Aida fabric
Another traditional motif, repeated in a simple straight arrangement, with different patterns used to fill the heart shapes.

▲ GINYA GUSI (GIRLS AND GEESE)
Leon Conrad
11 x 18 in (280 x 455mm)
Cross stitch and backstitch using stranded cottons or silk threads on 28-count evenweave linen
Stylized Ukranian folk motifs of peasant girls, birds, and flowers are repeated in bands of traditional cross stitch.

▲ **QUEEN OF HEARTS PILLOW**
Jolly Red
12 x 12 in (300 x 300mm)
Tent stitch using tapestry wools
on 10-gauge canvas
Vibrant, modern colors update
this design based on traditional
heart motifs, decorated with sprigs
and flowers.

▲ ◄ **ANTIQUE QUILT,**
COUNTRY QUILT
Charlotte's Web Needlework
5⅞ x 5⅞ in (147 x 147mm)
Cross stitch using stranded cottons
on 14-count Aida fabric
These two designs are based on
traditional patchwork quilt patterns.
The bold geometry of the shapes
adapts well to cross stitch.

▼ **TASTE OF THE ORIENT PILLOW**
Coats Crafts
20 x 20 in (500 x 500mm)
Cross stitch, double cross stitch, back stitch,
star stitch, French knots, and straight stitch
using stranded cottons on Irish linen
Blackwork elephants are surrounded by filigree
arches, and highlighted by metallic threads.

▲ **REVERSIBLE BLACKWORK SAMPLER**
Leon Conrad
7⅛ x 3 in (178 x 75mm)
Reversible cross stitch and Holbein stitch
using silk threads on 22-count Hardanger
fabric
Geometric patterns are cleverly worked making
a hanging that is identical on both sides.

SCENES AND TOWNSCAPES

Complex outdoor subjects present a special challenge—
the treatment may be representational or stylized, but
the designer always has to decide how much detail to
put in, and what to leave out.

**▲ ▶ VENICE DOME, PIT
HEAD, WINDMILL
Michael Powell**
8 x 8 in (200 x 200mm)
*Cross stitch and backstitch
using stranded cottons on
14-count Aida fabric*
The freely-drawn outlines, and
rich colors lend a magical,
story-book quality to these
cross stitch townscapes.

▶ SHOOTING STAR PILLOW
Jolly Red
6 x 9 in (152 x 227mm)
*Tent stitch using tapestry yarns on
10-gauge canvas*
The embroidered panel of sleepy houses
beneath a sky blazing with stars is enhanced
by the plain dark background of the pillow.

▼ STARRY NIGHT
Bothy Threads
10¼ x 12½ in (256 x 312mm)
Cross stitch using stranded threads on 14-count Aida fabric
Another sky full of swirling stars, adapted from the
well-known painting by Vincent van Gogh.

▲ PATCHWORK VILLAGE
Jolly Red
13 x 13 in (325 x 325mm)
*Tent stitch using tapestry wools on 10-gauge
canvas*
A restricted color palette of reds, pinks, and
golden browns is used to "hold together" the
overall variety of different little houses.

ANIMALS

Living creatures may be stitched in a realistic, life-like style, or they may be adapted in many decorative ways. An animal such as a cat or a zebra is so well-known to us that a design may be almost completely abstract, but we will still recognize and respond to the subject.

▲ POLAR BEARS
Joanne Louise Sanderson
1¾ x 3½ in (44 x 88mm)
Cross stitch and backstitch using stranded cottons on 14-count Aida fabric
A careful use of outline stitches and subtle shading animates these bears, and the unstitched blue fabric provides a suitably chilly background.

▲ ▶ RENAISSANCE CAT PILLOW, PATCHWORK CAT PILLOW
Jolly Red
16 x 16 in
(400 x 400mm)
Tent stitch using tapestry wools on 10-gauge canvas
Needlepoint (tent stitch) on canvas is robust and hardwearing, making it ideal for household articles such as pillows. The Patchwork Cat uses motifs derived from patterned patchwork fabrics, while the motifs on the Renaissance Cat were inspired by the Cluny tapestries.

◀ MARCH HARES PILLOW, SPECKLED HENS PILLOW
Jolly Red
16 x 16 in
(400 x 400mm)
Tent stitch using tapestry wools on 10-gauge canvas
Subtly faded colors complement these country themes. Notice the wide borders used to focus the design at the center of each pillow.

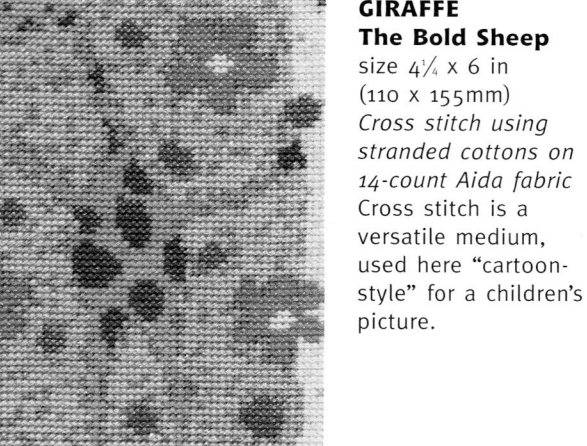

◄ GEORGE THE GIRAFFE
The Bold Sheep
size 4¼ x 6 in
(110 x 155mm)
Cross stitch using stranded cottons on 14-count Aida fabric
Cross stitch is a versatile medium, used here "cartoon-style" for a children's picture.

◄ ▲ NOAH'S ARK
Bothy Threads
4¾ x 4¾ in (120 x 120mm)
Cross stitch using stranded cottons and small beads on 14-count Aida fabric
Beads and special buttons are added to simple cross stitch to tell the story of Noah's Ark.

◄ KINGFISHER
Joanne Louise Sanderson
2¾ x 3 in (70 x 75mm)
Cross stitch, backstitch, and French knots using stranded cottons on 14-count Aida fabric
Tones of blue and orange are speckled together in this naturalistic treatment, bringing the bird to life.

NATURAL FORMS

Decorative subjects taken from nature such as flowers, leaves, and shells have always been popular with embroiderers, presenting the challenge of representing flowing, organic shapes with precise individual stitches.

◀ **ASSISI POPPIES**
Daphne Ashby
9 x 5 in (225 x 125mm)
Cross stitch and Holbein stitch using stranded cottons and beads on 14-count Aida fabric
The traditional technique of Assisi work is used here for a naturalistic floral design, with the petals and leaves left unstitched (except for the yellow stamens) on a background of solid stitching.

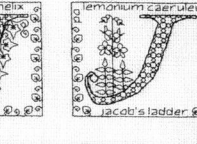
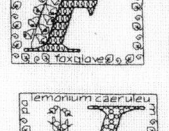
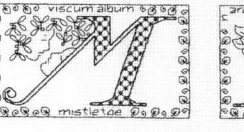
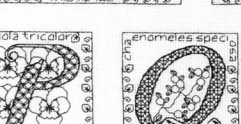
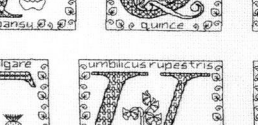

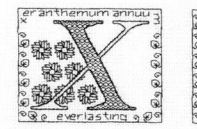

◀ **FLORAL ALPHABET**
Claire Crompton
14¼ x 22 in (360 x 560mm)
Blackwork using stranded cottons on 14-count Aida fabric
Each letter is filled with a different blackwork pattern and decorated with an appropriate flower or plant, with a border of tiny leaves incorporating the plant name in Latin and the common English name.

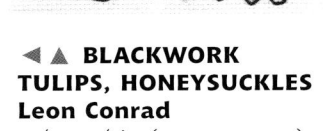

◀▲ **BLACKWORK TULIPS, HONEYSUCKLES**
Leon Conrad
3⅞ x 3⅞ in (100 x 100mm)
Blackwork using Pearl cotton and metallic threads with glass beads and crystals on 18-count Aida fabric
These quartered blackwork designs are worked with black thread outlines and metallic thread for all the filling stitches, then decorated with sprinkled crystals, each sewn down with a tiny bead.

► CARIBBEAN SHELLS
Charlotte's Web Needlework

10⅛ x 13 in (253 x 325mm)
Cross stitch, backstitch, and fractional stitches using stranded cottons on 32-count Aida fabric
Simple stitches, used with a restricted palette of colors to express the variety and wonder of the natural world.

▼ IRIS
Claire Crompton

8 x 17¾ in (200 x 445mm)
Blackwork using stranded threads on 14-count Aida fabric
The blackwork fillings used for the leaves and petals read as different tones. Notice how the border varies, including several insects as well as more traditional motifs.

▲ ► RHODODENDRON, SEA PINK
Charlotte's Web Needlework

7½ x 9 in (188 x 225mm)
Cross stitch, backstitch, and fractional stitches using stranded cottons on 32-count Aida fabric
Botanical subjects are popular in cross stitch and may be represented with great accuracy. Here, the lightness of the treatment is not strictly realistic, but imitates the effect of watercolors by Charles Rennie Mackintosh.

INNOVATIONS

Some embroiderers are inspired by the possibilities of certain stitches or techniques, others by the challenge of a particular subject. If you have a bright idea, work a small experimental piece to see how your idea translates into stitches, before commencing a larger work.

▲ BLACKTHORN AND JAPONICA
Charlotte's Web Needlework

10¼ x 15 in (257 x 375mm)
Cross stitch, backstitch, and fractional stitches using stranded threads on 32-count Aida fabric
Taken from the work of Charles Rennie Mackintosh, limited colors and delicate stitching express the grace of natural forms, balancing outlined areas with solid areas for a light, airy feel.

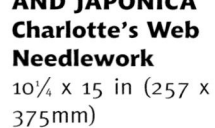

▲ MOON DAISY
Betty Barnden

8¼ x 12¼ in (210 x 310mm)
Hardanger stitches, satin stitch, Holbein stitch, single chain stitch, and cross stitch using Pearl cotton, stranded cottons and stranded viscose threads on 20-count evenweave fabric
The flower centers are worked in Hardanger stitches, with the petals added using a variety of other counted stitches. The cross stitch background is worked with a shaded thread.

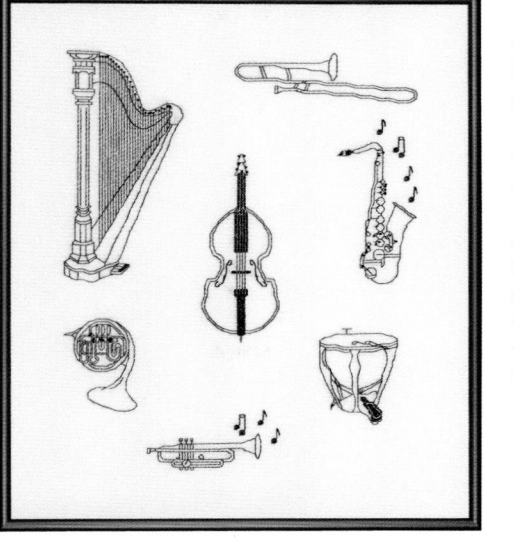

◄ THE RIGHT NOTE
Charlotte's Web Needlework

9½ x 11½ in (238 x 288mm)
Cross stitch, backstitch, and fractional stitches using stranded threads on 32-count Aida fabric
Simple black outline stitches are used to draw the interesting shapes of the musical instruments in great detail.

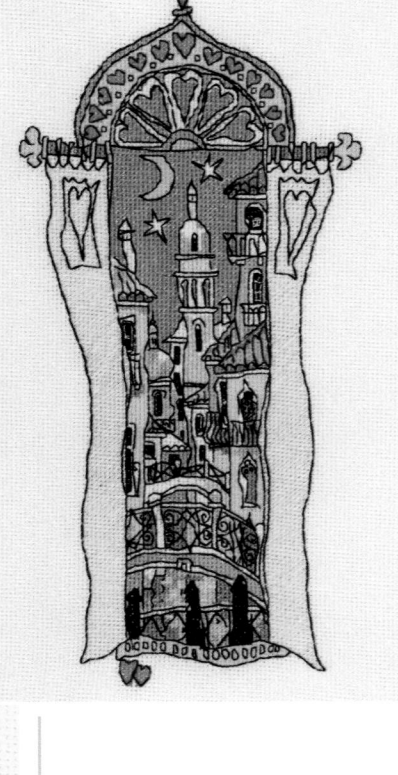

◄ VENICE WINDOWS
Michael Powell

6 x 12 in (150 x 300mm)
*Cross stitch and backstitch
using stranded cottons on
14-count Aida fabric*
Michael Powell works from
his own paintings and
drawings, using cross stitch
and backstitch to express
his particular style of boldly
fluid lines and rich, glowing
colors.

▼ LINEN BAG WITH ADDED PATCH
Claire Crompton

panel 4½ x 4½ in
(113 x 113mm)
*Cross stitch, long stitches,
beads and punched metal
using stranded cottons on
14-count Aida*
Punched metal shapes are
held in place by long stitches
worked around them, on a
background of cross stitch
squares, with small beads
for the center
square and border
lines of bugle
beads and
small beads.

Care of Embroidery

Whether your embroidery is framed for display, or used for a practical item such as a pillow, with a little care you can keep the colors fresh and the fabric or canvas in good condition, so your work will last for many years.

DISPLAYING YOUR WORK
Avoid placing any embroidery, framed or unframed, in bright sunlight, which will eventually cause the colors to fade. Dusty and damp conditions should also be avoided.

STORAGE
Should you wish to store your work for any length of time, it is best to protect it between layers of acid-free tissue paper, then keep it flat in a dark place.

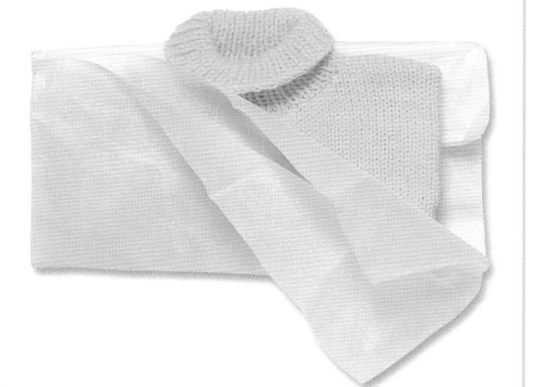

For large pieces, obtain a cardboard tube (the wider the better) and cover it with acid-free tissue, then roll the work right side out over the tube and wrap with more tissue.

If you cannot avoid folding embroidery, use acid-free tissue between the folds. From time to time, open out the work and rearrange it in different folds. Always protect the storage area against moths.

VACUUM-CLEANING EMBROIDERY
Embroidery on canvas may be cleaned with a vacuum cleaner. Use an upholstery tool and fix a piece of muslin over the nozzle with a rubber band to reduce the suction.

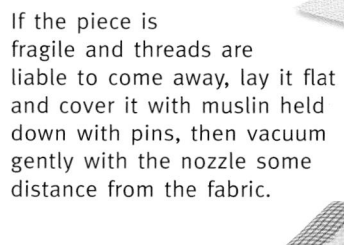

If the piece is fragile and threads are liable to come away, lay it flat and cover it with muslin held down with pins, then vacuum gently with the nozzle some distance from the fabric.

DRY-CLEANING EMBROIDERY
Most types of fabric and canvas work may be dry-cleaned. If possible, it is always a good idea to test first on a sample piece of identical material.

WASHING EMBROIDERY

If possible, first remove any lining or backing fabric; this may be washed separately before reassembly. This is particularly recommended for work on canvas, which will probably require reblocking. For canvas work made to a particular size or shape (such as a chair seat) it is a good idea to prepare a paper template, so that you can reblock the piece to the same size after washing.

Then check for colorfastness. If you do not have a suitable sample piece to test, dampen a piece of absorbent cotton and press it on the wrong side of the work, in an inconspicuous corner. If any traces of color come off on the absorbent cotton, do not wash the work. Make sure you test all the colors in the piece.

YOU WILL NEED:

a flat-bottomed bowl, large enough to allow the work to lie flat (a shower tray is ideal)

warm water

mild soap or an embroidery shampoo (never use detergent)

sponge

towel

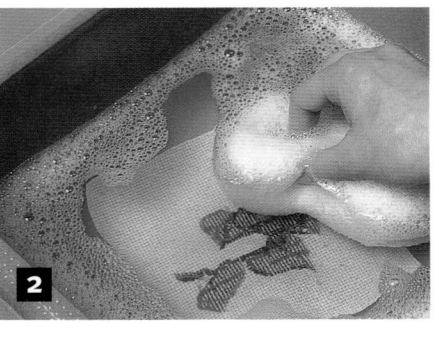

2 Gently lower the embroidery into the bowl, wrong side up. Press the back gently all over with the sponge. Never rub or squeeze the work; keep it flat without any folds or creases.

If necessary, repeat the wash with more warm water and soap or shampoo. When changing the water, avoid dragging the work: do not lift it out of the water, but pour the water away, leaving the work flat in the bowl.

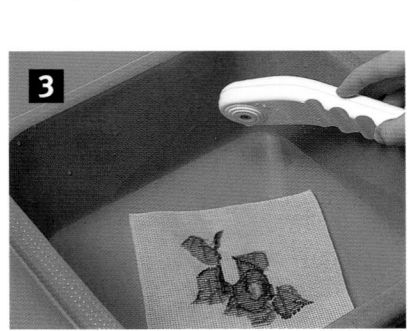

3 When the work is clean, rinse away all traces of soap with several changes of cool water. A shower head may be used for this, but make sure the water jet is not too fierce.

4 Lay the work right side up on a towel, on a flat surface. Use a dry sponge to gently blot the work, removing excess moisture.

The canvas work may now be reblocked in the same way as on page 67, using a paper template if required.

Leave the work flat until it is completely dry.

1 Pour 2 or 3 inches (50–75mm) of warm water (never use hot water) into the bowl. Add a little soap or shampoo and dissolve it thoroughly.

Glossary

AIDA BAND finished bands of Aida fabric, available by the meter (yard) in a range of widths and colors

AIDA FABRIC evenly woven fabric with regular holes, forming a grid of squares

ASSISI WORK a type of cross stitch with a solidly stitched background, the motif left unstitched

AWAY WASTE KNOT a method of starting to stitch

BASTING (TACKING) temporary stitching, usually worked as large running stitch, used to hold fabrics in place until final stitching is complete, and to mark center lines

BATTING a sheet of synthetic or natural wadding, sold for quilting

BINCA FABRIC evenly woven fabric, similar to Aida but with larger squares

BLACKWORK a type of counted thread embroidery featuring repeating patterns of small straight stitches, traditionally worked in black thread on white linen

BLENDING FILAMENT a very fine thread intended to be used in combination with other threads

BLOCKING BOARD a padded board for blocking

BLOCKING damping and stretching finished work to fix its shape

BRICK ARRANGEMENT a type of repeating pattern, the motifs arranged like bricks in a wall

CANVAS an open, woven mesh, usually firm and stiff, with a regular number of threads (and therefore holes) to the inch (25mm) in each direction

CANVAS WORK embroidery worked on canvas, with stitches placed regularly by counting the threads

CENTER LINES lines marked on a chart to indicate the center of the design, and the corresponding lines tacked (basted) onto fabric to mark the center point

CHENILLE NEEDLE a medium to large needle with a large eye and a sharp point

COLOR FASTNESS the ability of threads and fabrics to withstand washing without color running or fading

COTON À BRODER a fine, twisted, matte thread

COTTON a natural thread or fabric made from fibers of the cotton plant

COUCHING attaching a thread or cord (the "laid thread") to the fabric surface by stitching it in place with a second, finer thread (the "tying" or "couching" thread)

COUNT the number of holes (or threads) to the inch (25mm) of an evenweave or Aida fabric

COUNTED THREAD EMBROIDERY any type of embroidery where stitches are accurately placed by counting the threads or squares of the fabric

EMBROIDERY HOOP a round frame with two overlapping rings, used to stretch fabric while stitching to avoid distortion

EVENWEAVE FABRIC is woven with the same number of threads to the inch in each direction

FABRIC GRAIN the straight lines of the threads from which the fabric is woven

FILLING a small pattern repeated to fill an area, as in blackwork, or a stitched motif used to fill a space in Hardanger work; also, material (fiber) used to stuff an article such as a cushion or pillow

FLOSS a stranded silk thread

FRACTIONAL STITCHES see part stitches

GAUGE the number of holes (or threads) to the inch (25mm) of a canvas

HALF-DROP ARRANGEMENT a type of repeating pattern

HARDANGER FABRIC a type of firmly-woven Aida fabric, normally 22 or 24-count

HARDANGER WORK a type of counted thread openwork embroidery featuring threads cut and drawn in geometric patterns, originating in the Hardanger district of Norway

INTERLINING non-woven fabric (various weights and colors available) used to strengthen a finished article,

or to prevent a lining color from showing through

KLOSTER BLOCK a block of satin stitches (normally 5) used in Hardanger work to secure edges where threads will be cut

LINEN a natural thread or fabric made from fibers of the flax plant

LUREX a metallic thread used to make yarn or fabric

MUSLIN a lightweight, open-weave cotton fabric

OPENWORK any type of embroidery producing holes in the surface of the fabric (e.g. Hardanger work)

PART (OR PARTIAL) STITCHES such as three-quarter and quarter cross stitch form incomplete units to neaten the edge of a stitched area

PEARL COTTON a firmly twisted, glossy thread

PERFORATED PAPER strong paper perforated with a grid of small holes, available in different counts and colors

PERSIAN WOOL a stranded wool yarn

PICOT a small knot or loop made with the needle

PLASTIC CANVAS a molded plastic mesh

PRESSING CLOTH a clean white cloth used to protect work while ironing it

QUARTERED REPEAT a type of repeating pattern where only one quarter is charted

SAMPLER a piece of fabric worked with examples of different stitch and patterns, kept as a record

SHEARS large scissors with a flat lower edge, designed for cutting fabric

SILK a natural thread or fabric made from the unraveled cocoons of silkworms

SKEIN thread or yarn supplied in a loose coil or hank

SLATE FRAME a rectangular frame with two adjustable rollers, used for stretching large pieces of fabric or canvas to avoid distortion while stitching

STABILIZER FABRIC (normally non-woven) used to back embroidery, to prevent distortion while stitching

STRANDED COTTON normally six fine strands, loosely wound in a skein

TAPESTRY NEEDLE a medium to large needle with a large eye and a blunt tip

TAPESTRY WOOL a smooth, non-stranded wool yarn

TEMPLATE paper or card cut to the exact shape and size required for a fabric piece

VISCOSE a man-made fiber derived from cellulose, used for high-gloss threads

WASTE CANVAS is designed to pull apart when wet, and is used to apply counted thread designs to plain fabric

WOOL a natural yarn or fabric made from the shorn wool of sheep

Suppliers

FOR DETAILS OF LOCAL AND MAIL-ORDER STOCKISTS IN THE USA PLEASE CONTACT:

COATS AND CLARK
(for threads, yarns, fabrics, canvas)
Two Lake Pointe Plaza
4135 South Stream Boulevard
Charlotte, NC 28217
tel: 1-704-329-5800
www.coatsandclark.com

DAYLIGHT COMPANY LLC
(for daylight bulbs)
116 King Court Industrial Park
PO Box 422, New Holland
PA 17557-0422
tel: 1-866-329-0422
www.daylightcompany.com

THE DMC CORPORATION
(for threads, yarns, fabrics, canvas)
10 Port Kearny
South Kearny, NJ 07032
tel: 1-201-589-0606
www.dmc.com

GAY BOWLES SALES, INC.
(for Mill Hill beads, perforated paper)
P.O.Box 1060
Janesville, WI 53547
tel: 1-608-754-9466
www.millhill.com

FROM THE HEART
(for books, fabrics, and accessories)
5386 Kemps River Dr.
Virginia Beach, VA 23464
tel: 1-757-523-0177
www.fromtheheart-needlework.com

THE FUZZY PENGUIN
(for threads, fabrics, and accessories)
3922 60th St.
Sacramento, CA 95820
Toll Free: 1-888-739-1190
tel: 1-916-457-9077
www.thefuzzypenguin.com

JANLYNN
(for kits and charts)
34 Front Street
PO Box 51848
Indian Orchard
MA 01151-5848
tel: 1-800-445-5565
www.janlynn.com

JUST NEEDLIN'
(for threads, yarns, fabrics, and accessories)
611 NE. Woods Chapel Rd.
Lee's Summit, MO 64064
tel: 1-800-646-5102
www.justneedlin.com

KREINIK MANUFACTURING CO. INC.
(for metallic and silk threads)
3106 Lord Baltimore Drive,
Suite 101
Baltimore, MD 21244
tel: 1-800-537-2166
e-mail: kreinik@kreinik.com
www.kreinik.com

LAZERTRAN LLC (USA)
(for photo-transfer papers)
650 8th Avenue
New Hyde Park
New York 11040
tel: 1-800-245-7547
e-mail: lazertran@msn.com
www.lazertran.com

MADEIRA USA LTD.
(for threads, accessories)
30 Bayside Ct. PO Box 6068
Laconia, NH 03246
tel: 1-800-225-3001
www.madierausa.com

THE SILVER NEEDLE LTD
(for fabrics and other accessories)
6068 S. Sheridan
Tulsa, OK 74145
tel: 1-888-543-7004
www.thesilverneedle.com

TRISTAN BROOKS DESIGNS
(for silk threads, accessories)
182 Green Glade Road
Memphis, TN 38120-2218
tel: 1-901-767-8414
www.TristanBrooks.com

YANKEE CROSS STITCH
(for charts and accessories)
29 Lafayette Road
North Hampton.
NH 03862-2436
tel: 603-964-9434
www.yankeecrossstitch.com

USEFUL WEBSITE:
try www.i-craft.com for craft stores in the USA, listed by zip code

FOR DETAILS OF LOCAL STOCKISTS IN THE UK PLEASE CONTACT:

THE BOLD SHEEP
(counted cross stitch and needlepoint kits)
PO Box 15, Preston, PR29FG
tel:+44 (0)1772 655393
www.theboldsheep.co.uk

BOTHY THREADS
(thematic kits based around artistic themes)
19 The Avenue, Newmarket
Suffolk, CB8 9AA
tel: +44 (0)1638 665149

CHARLOTTE'S WEB NEEDLEWORK
(needlepoint kits and charts)
PO Box 771, Harrow
Middlesex, HA2 7WE
tel: +44 (0)20 8869 9410
www.charlotteswebneedlework.com

COATS CRAFTS UK
(for threads, yarns, fabrics, canvas, stabilizers, kits)
Darlington, DL11 1YQ
tel: +44 (0)1325 394 237
www.coatscrafts.co.uk

DMC CREATIVE WORLD LTD.
(for threads, yarns, fabrics, canvas, beads)
Pullman Road
Wigston, LE18 2DY
tel: +44 (0)116 281 1040
www.dmc.com

JOLLY RED
(designers, manufacturers, and stitchers of stitching kits)
FREEPOST, Langport
Somerset, TA10 0BR
tel: +44 (0)1458 250088
e-mail: info@jollyred.co.uk
www.jollyred.co.uk

LEON CONRAD DESIGNS
(supplier of embroidery and needlework materials and kits based on historic needlework techniques. Specializes in blackwork embroidery)
20 Courtenay Street
London, SE11 5PQ
tel: +44 (0)20 7582 8213
e-mail: info@lcdesigns.org
www.lcdesigns.org

MADEIRA THREADS UK LTD.
(for threads, accessories)
Thirsk Industrial Park
York Road, Thirsk, YO7 3BX
tel: +44 (0)1845 524 880
www. madeira.co.uk

MICHAEL POWELL CROSS STITCH ART
(for kits and charts)
6 Vere Street, Roath
Cardiff, CF24 4DS
tel: +44 (0)2920 496000
www.michaelpowellcross-stitch-art.com

PEARSALLS EMBROIDERY SILKS
(for silk threads)
Tancred Street
Taunton, TA1 1RY
tel: +44 (0)1823 274700
www.pearsallsembroidery.com

FREUDENBURG NONWOVENS LP
(for wadding, stabilizers)
Vilene Retail
Lowfields Business Park
Elland, HX5 9DX
tel: +44 (0)1422 327 900

LAZERTRAN LTD. (UK)
(for photo-transfer papers)
8 Alban Square, Aberaeron
Ceredigion, SA46 0AD
tel: +44 (0)1545 571 149
e-mail: mic@lazertran.com
www.lazertran.com

THE DAYLIGHT COMPANY
(for daylight bulbs)
89-91 Scrubs Lane
London, NW10 6QU
tel. +44 (0)20 8964 1200
www.daylightcompany.co.uk

TEXTILE HERITAGE COLLECTION
(colorful counted cross stitch kits)
5 India Buildings
Victoria Street
Edinburgh, EH1 2EX
tel: +44 (0)131 220 2730
www.textileheritage.com

USEFUL MAIL-ORDER ADDRESSES IN THE UK:

THE CRAFT COLLECTION
(for threads, yarns, fabrics, canvas)
Terry Mills
Westfield Road, Horbury
Wakefield, WF4 6HD
tel: +44 (0)1924 811 905
sales@craftcollection.co.u

FRAMECRAFT MINIATURES
(for glass beads, perforated paper)
Lichfield Road, Brownhills
Walsall, WS8 6LH
tel: +44 (0)1543 360 842
www.framecraft.com

BARNYARNS
(for threads, sewing accessories)
Brickyard Road
Boroughbridge, YO 51 9NS
tel: +44 (0)1423 326 423
www.barnyarns.com

FOR DETAILS OF LOCAL STOCKISTS IN AUSTRALIA PLEASE CONTACT:

THREADS & MORE
(threads, fabrics, kits)
2/141 Boundary Road
Bardon
Queensland 4065
tel: +61 7 3367 0864
www.threadsandmore.com.au

LYNS FINE NEEDLEWORK
(patterns, threads, fabrics)
2/9 Seven Hills Road
Baulkham Hills
Sydney, NSW
tel: +61 2 9686 2325
www.lynsfineneedlework.com.au

Index

Credits

The author would like to thank the following companies who supplied threads, fabrics, and materials for this book:

Coats Crafts UK, DMC Creative World Ltd., Lazertran UK

Jan Eaton and Marina Blank for the loan of embroideries from their collections.

Quarto would like to thank the following for lending their work to be reproduced in this book:

(Key: b=Bottom, t=Top, c=Center, l=Left, r=Right)

The Bold Sheep 141br, 147tl; **Bothy Threads** 12tr, 145br, 147tr, 147c; **Charlotte's Web Needlework** 12tl, 26bl, 142tr, 142bc, 149tc, 149lc, 149bc, 150bc, 150tc, 150tr; **Claire Crompton** 148bl, 149br, 151br; **Coats Crafts UK** 42bl, 44br, 78b, 143r; **Daphne Ashby** 148tr; **Jan Eaton** 8tr, 9tr, 10tc, 10rc; **Joanne Louise Sanderson** 146tr, 147bl; **Jolly Red** 140bl, 140cr, 142tl, 145l, 145tr, 146lc, 146c, 146b; **Leon Conrad** 141l, 141tr, 143l, 148c, 148cr; **Michael Powell** 144l, 144tr, 144br, 151l, 151tr; **Textile Heritage Collection™** 27br

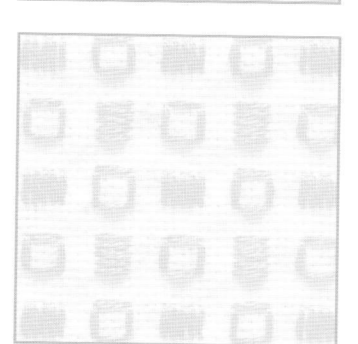